# Terrorism
## and the Media

For the inimitable (not capable of being intimidated)
Susannah Batia Felicity Paletz

# Terrorism
## and the Media

Edited by

David L. Paletz
Alex P. Schmid

SAGE PUBLICATIONS
*International Educational and Professional Publisher*
Newbury Park   London   New Delhi

*For information address:*

SAGE Publications, Inc.
2455 Teller Road
Newbury Park, California 91320

SAGE Publications Ltd.
6 Bonhill Street
London EC2A 4PU
United Kingdom

SAGE Publications India Pvt. Ltd.
M-32 Market
Greater Kailash I
New Delhi 110 048 India

Printed in the United States of America

**Library of Congress Cataloging-in-Publication Data**

Main entry under title:
Terrorism and the media / edited by David L. Paletz, Alex P. Schmid.
     p.  cm.
    Includes bibliographical references and index.
    ISBN 0-8039-4482-9.  — 0-8039-4483-7 (pbk.)
    1. Terrorism and mass media.  2. Terrorism in mass media.
I. Paletz, David L., 1934-  II. Schmid, Alex Peter.
P96.T47T48  1992
303.6'25—dc20                       92-3738


     93  94  10  9  8  7  6  5  4  3  2

Sage Production Editor: Diane S. Foster

# Contents

# Acknowledgments

This volume originated at a congress with the theme "Towards a European Response to Terrorism: National Experiences and Lessons for the Europe of 1992," organized by the Association des Etats Generaux des Etudiants de l'Europe (AEGEE) and the Center for the Study of Social Conflicts (COMT) and held March 16-17, 1989, in Leiden (the Netherlands). Schmid had invited Mark Blaisse and David Paletz to participate. Blaisse had just published a book in Dutch on his search for Abu Nidal. His chapter herein is based on that work; we thank the Arbeiderspers for permission to use it.

Had Paletz not been appointed a Fulbright Scholar at the University of Leiden, where he met Alex Schmid, this book might never have been conceived. Thanks are thus due to the Council on the International Exchange of Scholars and its director, Cassandra Pyle. Appreciation also goes to Professors Jan van Cuilenburg and Marten Brouwer, and Jan de Ridder and Karin Mulie-Velgersdijk, of the Communications Institute of the University of Amsterdam, for providing Paletz with facilities and support during his stay in the Netherlands.

Thanks also go to Professor Tapio Varis, the communication workshop director of the International Peace Research Association, who gave the contributors to this volume a chance to meet and discuss their work in early June 1990 and at a meeting of the Association in July 1990 in Groningen (in the Netherlands).

At Duke University, the Trent Foundation, the Center for International Studies, and the Research Council all contributed essential financial support.

John Ayanian and Peter Fozzard accompanied Paletz on his initial research foray into media coverage of terrorism when they were undergraduates at Duke. They shared credit on the two published articles that resulted, and their influence is in this book. Mark Bildner, first among equals, Carolyn Karr, and Ben Sharp, Duke undergraduates at the time, helped cut the literature down to size.

We thank Birthe Croes, Joke van Engelenburg, Lillian Fennell, Kim Holder, Phia Koppers, and Angela van der Poel for their secretarial and editorial assistance. We acknowledge also the 20 editors (who, for obvious reasons, cannot be identified here) who answered the lengthy questionnaire on which Schmid's chapter is based, and the media administrators who provided the information for the Paletz and Tawney chapter.

C. Danielle Vinson and Marie Louise Penchoen, indispensable and a pleasure to work with, deserve credit for helping bring the manuscript to publication. We also give thanks to and for Ann West our editor and Diane (pronounced "De-ann") Foster our cherished production editor at Sage.

Gabriel from Prague and Hetty and Harry from Hove provided love and delights. Judith Onlney, who proposed a cover design, diverts and is diverting. The book is dedicated to Susannah.

David L. Paletz
Alex P. Schmid

# 1

# Introduction

David L. Paletz

C. Danielle Vinson

Terrorism comes in many forms. To mention just the most prominent, there are state terrorism, waged against inhabitants of a state; state-sponsored terrorism, against the people of other states; and insurgent terrorism. Our focus in this volume is on insurgent terrorism, "social-revolutionary, separatist and single issue terrorism aiming at the top of society" (Schmid & De Graaf, 1982, p. 1). The "violence is mainly perpetrated for its effects on others [rather] than the immediate victims" (p. 2).

Insurgent terrorism may not be as deadly as state terrorism, nor its victims as numerous. It has, however, achieved far more visibility and provoked an extensive, often passionate and polemical, literature. Yet, until now, no single volume has existed containing the range of significant perspectives on the relation between insurgent terrorism and the media. So here they are, as best we and our contributors can find and present them: the views and reactions of the terrorists themselves, of broadcast organizations, of journalists, of editors, of reporters, of the public(s), and of the victims. To put these perspectives in context, we precede them with a chapter that surveys and categorizes the research literature. And because so much of that literature is progovernment, this book's chapter on governments' perspectives (Chapter 5) takes a different approach.

Before proceeding further, we would note that the word *terrorism*, particularly when used to describe the actions of insurgents, has profoundly negative connotations. A more neutral term is preferable, but unavailable. Some of our contributors modify *terrorism* with the word *insurgent*; others leave it to stand alone.

The book begins with Paletz and Boiney's critical assessment of the terrorism literature. They divide it into four categories, based on the perspectives or approaches of researchers. First, researchers have addressed the issue of terrorists' strategies and tactics, but there is little empirical work in this area, and the terrorists' perspective is neglected. The second category of research deals with indictments of the media—usually as proterrorist, but also occasionally as antiterrorist. While the indictments can be valid in some respects, they often are not based on systematic research. Material in the third category moves a step beyond the media indicters to suggest ways the media can provide "better" (depending upon one's perspective) terrorism coverage. Finally, there is research that actually examines media coverage of terrorism. Because Paletz and Boiney criticize the literature for numerous shortcomings, they conclude with suggestions for future research.

The terrorists come next. Relying primarily on their memoirs, Gerrits presents the insurgent terrorists' perspective in Chapter 3. He discusses how terrorists seek publicity to bring about their psychological goals and how they use violence to produce various psychological effects—demoralizing their enemies, demonstrating their movement's strength, gaining public sympathy, and creating fear and chaos.

To succeed in these goals, terrorists must publicize their actions. Publicity can be gained in many ways. For example, terrorists can try to raise the news value of their actions, choose times and places for actions that will attract attention, release statements or give interviews directly to the press, claim responsibility for actions, spread the group's own literature, and use symbols or choose particular targets to publicize a particular issue. Gerrits also discusses other public relations strategies of terrorists, such as self-published papers and political meetings.

Irvin continues our focus on terrorists' perspectives in Chapter 4. On the basis of interviews with insurgents from Northern Ireland, Spain, and the PLO, and from their press releases and documents, she shows that insurgents do not believe that media attention is always good for their causes. In fact, they claim that the media often employ propaganda offensives against insurgents' struggles.

Irvin explains that because insurgents recognize the potential damage to their public image that media coverage can inflict, the ways in which insurgent organizations attempt to use the media vary with the stages of their development and the audiences they are trying to reach. While violence can attract media coverage in a movement's early stages, organizations later try to downplay their links to militant groups when they are more concerned with political strategies. Irvin thus argues for a more dynamic assessment of the media-terrorism connection than is found in the conventional literature.

Nowhere is the media and terrorism literature more conventional than in its presentation of governments' perspectives. In Chapter 5, Hocking offers a different approach. Using Australia and Great Britain as her examples, she describes government counterterrorism guidelines that attempt to deal with terrorism incidents, particularly the supposed symbiotic relationship between terrorism and the media. Instead of relying on outright censorship, these measures emphasize media "cooperation" and voluntary restraint. Although these counterterrorism guidelines were originally intended to be used only in response to terrorist incidents, Hocking argues that their application has gradually expanded to some internal policing and civil action.

Hocking places this increased usage of counterterrorism procedures in the context of counterinsurgency theory. This enables her to frame counterterrorism strategies as a military doctrine that emphasizes relationships of dominance and control over information. According to Hocking, this approach to counterterrorism has led to the establishment, in effect, of relatively similar guidelines in many liberal democracies. Based on Bonanate's (1979) argument that terrorism is an effect of a blocked political structure, Hocking concludes that these government counterterrorism procedures do not solve the root cause of terrorism, and, in fact, they may create conditions that breed terrorism.

This brings us to the media's own perspectives on their relation to terrorism. In Chapter 6, Paletz and Tawney describe five levels of guidance for media coverage of terrorism based on responses to questionnaires they sent to broadcasting corporations around the world. From the first level, which is a complete lack of guidelines, to higher levels of progressively more detailed rules, the authors provide explanations and examples of each.

Paletz and Tawney identify several themes evident in their data: the need for broadcasters to maintain credibility, the belief that terrorism is newsworthy mixed with a desire for prudent coverage, and care not to legitimate terrorists or endanger hostages. The authors credit these themes with minimizing government pressure on and criticism of terrorism coverage—or minimizing the willingness of broadcasting administrators candidly and publicly to discuss with researchers such government reactions.

Editors make key decisions about media coverage of terrorism, so their views matter. Using answers to a survey he conducted with 20 editors from around the world, Schmid discusses editors' perceptions in Chapter 7. He finds that most editors believe that terrorists use violence to gain media access. And while most editors agree that the media have a responsibility to combat terrorism, they do not seem to recognize their complicity with terrorists' goals through their continued coverage of terrorism. However, editors do acknowledge a variety of effects of media coverage of terrorism.

Schmid also examines the numerous pressures that editors face—from the public, government officials, terrorists, and media values—in deciding how terrorism should be covered. He observes that editors must be aware that reporting an event changes that event, that the prominence given to terrorism incidents might increase public fear and the potential for contagion, and that media coverage of terrorism could endanger lives.

The book then moves from editors to reporters with Blaisse's personal memoir in Chapter 8. Blaisse acknowledges that reporters sometimes submit to the terrorists' rules to obtain information and interviews, and often the stories that result can appear to be tools of the terrorists. However, he also points out that this does not necessarily make the reporters accomplices to terrorism. According to Blaisse, sometimes the only way to obtain information is to agree to the terrorist's terms. The resultant stories, in spite of the government's claims, are not always favorable to the terrorists.

Because some governments see reporters as tools used by terrorists, government censorship and control over the media can be a problem for reporters even in democratic countries. In his conclusion, Blaisse argues that this censorship is unnecessary and unwarranted. He strongly advocates freedom for reporters covering terrorism, citing the people's need to be informed and the role of the press as an obstacle to government excesses.

This raises the issue of the effects of media coverage of terrorism on public opinion. After delineating three types of publics—terrorists' constituencies, terrorists' enemies, and bystanders—Hewitt, in Chapter 9, uses public opinion polls to explain the public's perceptions. He discusses the use of terrorism as a means of attracting public attention, and he finds that generally public concern about terrorism is directed toward the violence and does not translate into political results. Distinguishing between nationalist and revolutionary terrorism, Hewitt describes how levels of public support for terrorist groups vary according to the type of terrorism involved.

Hewitt attempts to draw a connection between the public's perception of terrorism and media coverage of terrorism events. His discussion reveals that the media reflect and reinforce public attitudes, and their influence on public opinion depends on the type of public and its prior knowledge of the terrorist group.

Last, but hardly least, are the victims of terrorism and their families. As Crelinsten shows in Chapter 10, they are far more than simple pawns of terrorists and government. After explaining the functions of terrorist victimization, Crelinsten describes the interaction of terrorists, government officials, the media, and victims. He claims that media coverage of victimization is part of terrorists' strategy of political communication and, as such, coverage has several impacts on government.

Most of Crelinsten's discussion centers on the nexus of victims and their families and the media and government. He presents two sides to the relationship. The first is what he calls "double victimization," in which the media contribute to the crisis through invasions of privacy and harassment of victims' families or the victims themselves. But the other side of this relationship is one in which victims and their families seek relations with the media to gain information and to pressure government officials to act to obtain freedom for hostages. He illustrates this with a discussion of the hostage family network and its attempts to keep the Western hostages in Lebanon in the consciousness and consciences of government and public.

## References

Bonanate, L. (1979). Some unanticipated consequences of terrorism. *Journal of Peace Research, 16,* 197-213.

Schmid, A. P., & De Graaf, J. F. A. (1982). *Violence as communication: Insurgent terrorism and the Western news media.* Beverly Hills, CA: Sage.

# 2

# Researchers' Perspectives

David L. Paletz

John Boiney

In this chapter, we try systematically to categorize and survey the academic literature on terrorism and the media. By *academic*, we mean the writings of scholars, or at least researchers, most of whom teach at universities or are associated with putatively nonpartisan research institutions.

One question dominates this literature: Does media coverage aid and encourage or obstruct and deter terrorism in general and terrorist causes in particular? Beyond their answers to this question, the various books, articles, and other works cited can be characterized by how they address the question, their implicit assumptions and ideological perspectives, whether they present and/or analyze original data, and the prescriptions, if any, they include.

This bibliographic review and assessment is based on the above factors. Each of the representative or paradigmatic examples we cite and discuss falls predominantly into one of four categories: terrorists' strategies and tactics, indictments of the media, prescriptions, and studies of media coverage and content. These categories are explained and subcategories established as the review proceeds. With all our categories, it is possible to distinguish between works that focus directly on the subject and those that contain tangential observations.

Since this essay tends to be a critical chronicling of the literature's inadequacies, we conclude with a brief discussion of desirable future research. (See Barnhurst, 1991, for a related but different approach and review.)

## Terrorists' Strategies and Tactics

We begin with the terrorists' side. Unfortunately, there is little in the literature from those to whom so much is attributed. The contributions to this category are usually not by terrorists, but by researchers who seek, more or less dispassionately, to identify terrorists' perspectives, to understand why and how they use or attempt to use the media.

Laqueur's (1977) book is a definitive, albeit unsympathetic, study of the origins, philosophy, and patterns of terrorism. He makes the point, reiterated many times since by others, that terrorists target free societies because the media are correspondingly free and will tend to cover violent events: "The success of a terrorist operation depends almost entirely on the amount of publicity it receives" (p. 109).

Leeman (1986) and Weimann (1987) attempt to develop analytical frameworks for understanding terrorism as communication. Leeman argues that terrorism often takes the form of epideictic rhetoric. Such rhetoric is not merely ceremonial or decorative; instead, it "certifies the correctness of one's value hierarchy" (p. 34). Leeman's analysis suggests that the essence of terrorism may lie in the values it supports and challenges, and that the media should be more aware of the values implicit in their terrorism stories. Weimann classifies the terrorist act as a new kind of media event, a "coercion." He offers this perspective, alongside other types of events—contests, conquests, and coronations—as a way of understanding the content of terrorist appeals, the function of the media, and the impact of events and coverage on audiences.

Picard (1986) has suggested a behavioral analysis of terrorist groups, the better to understand their motivation, their tactics, and how they measure success. Indeed, there are almost as many objectives ascribed to terrorists in the literature as there are terrorists. Among those listed are obtaining publicity about their existence and purposes; achieving legitimacy, status conferral, or at least a boost in morale; eliminating opponents; getting their desires on the agendas of policymakers and the public; obtaining obedience from the public; achieving a contagion effect in which other individuals or groups join the violence; coercing bargaining from policymakers; provoking oppressive measures from the authorities; undermining the authority of the state; and having their grievances settled (if possible) (Crenshaw, 1990; Schmid & De Graaf, 1982, pp. 53-54; Stohl, 1983, pp. 3-5; Wardlaw, 1982, p. 77).

## USING THE MEDIA

Seeking to advance their causes through the media, terrorists engage in press relations activities. These include statements of responsibility and of apology, manifestos, the provision of visual materials, news conferences, news releases, interviews, and even press tours. The prevalence and deployment of each technique depend on whether the group has a legal arm and is large or small; they are also related to such factors as the specific acts of terrorism, targets, location, and intended audiences (Picard, 1989). Kramer (1990) has shown how Hizballah uses "rallies and speeches, a newspaper, and a radio station" (p. 131) to justify its actions and to assert its integrity among its adherents, potential supporters, and the public.

Livingstone (1986) warns that terrorists will put increasingly inexpensive portable video technology to use. This may include sending tapes of violent acts in process to television stations. Such otherwise unobtainable prime news fodder would present television news executives with a difficult "show and be damned" dilemma. Terrorists will, writes Livingstone, find ways to get their message out, placing an extra burden on media to devise standards for dealing with those messages. Certainly, media executives face painful decisions when provided by terrorists with videos of hostages they have executed or of their captives making apparently voluntary but probably coerced statements. Besides, journalists and their employing media are not immune to terrorist violence, as Picard (1991) has briefly documented.

Some terrorist tactics are more newsworthy than others. Quester (1986) undertook a somewhat cold-blooded inquiry into differences between cruise-ship attacks and skyjackings (in the process providing a sort of miniguide for terrorists trying to decide what their next target should be). He identifies seven variables involving terrorists' use of the media, and concludes that only one, the novelty of an attack on a cruise ship, benefits the terrorists. Commenting on potential solutions to the problem ostensibly caused by media coverage, he advocates identifying "the kinds of technology and situations that make the media more exploitable by terrorists, and then trying to avoid them" (p. 370).

How successful are terrorists in realizing their myriad objectives through the media? For Dowling (1986), terrorists fail because of the distance between their acts and their audiences. Their acts become entertainment and do not inspire terror. Terrorists succeed, he argues, only if authorities react by taking action that is contrary to popular will (p. 20). In contrast, Gerbner, Gross, Signorielli, Morgan, and Jackson-Beeck (1976) suggest that depiction of violent acts may increase mass anxiety and foster the public's willingness to forgo certain liberties for the sake of security, essentially strengthening support for existing regimes and values. Thus acts that would have been contrary to popular will (i.e., repressive measures) are not challenged because of terrorist-created anxiety.

## REDOUNDING

Clearly the media can amplify terrorism. Uncommon in the literature, however, are thoughtful analyses and detailed examples of the ways that such amplification might redound on the terrorists and their alleged sponsors. Thus it takes an attorney-adviser to the State Department Office of the Legal Adviser during the Reagan administration to describe collective response initiatives against types of terrorism taken by the Summit Seven nations (United States, Canada, United Kingdom, France, the Federal Republic of Germany, Italy, and Japan) (Levitt, 1988). And we must rely on journalist Bob Woodward (1987, pp. 408-431) to recount how the national security principals in the Reagan administration decided to retaliate on Qaddafi and Libya for allegedly supporting terrorism. Vivid television coverage of the 1985 17-day, video-age hijacking of TWA Flight 847 brought home to them images of vulnerability and possibilities of humiliation redolent of those wreaked on the Carter administration by the Iran hostage crisis. Appalling television pictures of the post-Christmas carnage of terrorist attacks on the Rome and Vienna airports were further proof and incitement. The combination of personal outrage, need to protect against political vulnerability, and need for policy assertion fueled by media coverage of the terrorist actions contributed to the U.S. retaliation. It is not at all evident that the terrorists sought this particular response.

Indeed, Livingston (in press) contends that the Reagan administration contrived and exploited a terrorism scare to achieve its agenda of military adventurism abroad and intelligence investigations at home. He argues that these policies would otherwise have been difficult if not impossible to pursue, and that the perspective was legitimated, the process facilitated, by the U.S. media.

SUMMARY

There is little empirical research presenting terrorists' points of view. Analyses of events from the perspective of terrorist goals is almost as uncommon. Access to terrorists and candid answers from them may be difficult to obtain, but research on the links between terrorism and media will be incomplete until these data can be gathered and discussed. The chapters by Robin Gerrits and Cynthia Irvin in this book show that such research is possible and can be illuminating.

## Indictments of the Media

In the literature on terrorism, many works indict the media without offering much more than exhortations or nominal solutions to the problems identified. There are two diametrically opposed camps: those that indict the media as proterrorist and those that indict the media as antiterrorist.

### MEDIA INDICTED AS PROTERRORIST

The vast majority of the indictment literature argues that the media willingly and unwillingly encourage terrorism and/or obstruct attempts to fight it. (Also see Schmid & De Graaf, 1982, pp. 137-142, for a discussion of ways the media might provide motivation for the commission of violent acts.) The media are indicted on two fronts. First, they are accused of facilitating many if not all of the terrorists' objectives listed previously. Second, their presence at and reporting of particular incidents of terrorism are blamed for damaging effects. According to these arguments, the media's presence can prolong incidents, hinder police operations, provide terrorists with tactical and strategic information, place in jeopardy the lives of hostages and police, and put inappropriate pressure on authorities to resolve incidents, to settle with terrorists or meet their demands. The media can also become participants in rather than mere observers of the events (Wardlaw, 1982, p. 77).

These assertions and attacks commonly appear in edited books emanating from conferences and symposia. The participants gather, often with a common viewpoint, and proceed to deplore and denounce the media. Original data systematically marshaled to support these arguments are rare. Anecdotes are abundant and recycled. Constructive suggestions for addressing the assumed problems are infrequent. At best, the authors offer insights, ruminations, conjecture, humanistic concern, and a sermon or two. At worst, the results are rhetorical exercises, redundant clamoring. In most instances, their essential purpose seems to be to convince media practitioners, several of whose members participate in the gatherings, that something must be done about terrorism coverage. As H. H. A. Cooper (1977), then staff director of the U.S. National Advisory Committee, Task Force on Disorders and Terrorism, put it, "If the media can truly see itself as a part of the problem it is well on the way to becoming an important part of the solution" (p. 154).

A relatively respectable example of this genre emerged from a conference funded by the U.S. Law Enforcement Assistance Administration. It includes four sections titled "The Nature of the Problem," "The Law Enforcement Perspective," "A View From the Fourth Estate," and "Recommendations for Covering Terrorism," plus an appendix titled "Media Guideline Documents" (Miller, 1982).

One of the most influential indictments of the media's coverage of terrorism emerged from a conference held in Tel Aviv aimed at devising ways to combat terrorism. Based on a limited review and extension of communication theory, Nossek (1985) concludes that media coverage leads to repetition of acts and encourages terrorist supporters. Thus "the best way to avoid the impact of the mass media is to prevent the occurrences of terrorist attacks" (p. 91).

Other examples abound. Cooper (1977) writes that the media can make of the terrorist "a Saint or a Frankenstein's monster" (p. 154). For Catton (1978), "Freedom to report terrorist activities is tantamount to freedom to reinforce them" (p. 715). And Redlick (1979) somewhat tentatively concludes that the "transnational flow of information may provide dissidents with the inspirational and material spark that will cause them to resort to terrorism" (pp. 84-85).

Some media indicters are more specific about the problems they see and more systematic in documenting them. Miller (1980) voices an oft-repeated concern that media attempts to cover an ongoing terrorist action obstruct law enforcement attempts to handle the problem. Bassiouni (1983) suggests that coverage may dull the public's sense of opprobrium. Alexander (1977) does include a cautionary note in his account of Palestinian attempts to broaden recognition of their cause and enhance their legitimacy via the media: "It is debatable whether the present and possible future successes of the P.L.O. can be attributed to communications alone" (p. 192).

In sum, antiterrorist media indictments are united by the shared assumption that almost any coverage of a terrorist act benefits the terrorists (agreeing with the Hollywood ethos that any publicity is good publicity). They are also marked by a reliance on the same incidents and on anecdotal information. The indictments are repetitive instead of aggregative. And they keep coming: *Terrorism and the Media*, edited by Alexander and Latter (1990), is yet another book based on a conference (held in January 1988) whose contributors are primarily government and broadcasting figures and academics identified by their antiterrorism, critical of the media, positions.

The primary effect of all these conferences, symposia, and books is to sound the alarm constantly in the West and elsewhere that something must be done about terrorism and media coverage of terrorist acts. "The discussion about media coverage of terrorism has focused on how much should be reported. . . . That is the wrong question. What should be asked instead is, how can media coverage contribute to the fight against terrorism?" writes Clawson (1990, p. 241). The battle, according to Netanyahu (1986), is between "the forces of civilization and the forces of barbarism." This category of media indictments leaves no doubt which force the media are with.

### MEDIA INDICTED AS ANTITERRORIST

A very few works charge the media with being part of a hegemonic force pushing Western views and political power. The media are accused of having conspired, although not necessarily consciously, with public and private leaders to constrain mass understanding of the phenomenon of terrorism. Edward Herman (1982) is the most forceful proponent of this view. His latest book details the elements of what he and coauthor Gerry O'Sullivan label "the 'terrorism' industry": government officials and bodies, think tanks and analysts, and private security firms that have a vested interest in defining terrorism in terms of particular insurgent movements and exaggerating their threat to Western people. Media reliance on "industry" sources results in "structured and massive bias" (Herman & O'Sullivan, 1989, p. 203) and dissemination of the "industry's" perspective.

Herman and O'Sullivan alert their readers to alternative understandings of violent behavior by both insurgents and states. Their central point, that Western powers have essentially defined "terrorism" so that it serves their own interests, illuminates a central characteristic of the literature: that how terrorism is defined determines attitudes toward insurgent groups, state behavior, and legitimacy, and that these attitudes determine the definition of terrorism.

Two books consider the related issue of how the media shape Western views of the Middle East. Neither Said (1981) nor Chafets (1985) is immediately concerned with terrorism. Nonetheless, writing from an Arab and an Israeli perspective, respectively, they concur with the argument that journalists rely on Western sources, particularly those with a great deal at stake in the political and economic struggles, and that the result is biased reporting on Middle Eastern countries. Chafets acknowledges that gaining access to Arab nations can be difficult, thus forcing journalists to fall back on accessible sources. Still, he notes, journalists are too easily content to take what they can get, without asking what news they are not getting.

In contrast to the "media encourage terrorism" camp, whose members are often foundation supported and who tend to gather together in organized conferences to express alarm, those who portray the media as hostile to insurgent movements are relatively independent and isolated. That the two sides argue mirror interpretations of the media's influence on terrorism is indicative of their analyses and data. Neither side is particularly systematic about gathering data on media coverage and relating it to terrorist activity or public attitudes. Herman and O'Sullivan are the most rigorous, but focusing on media and terrorism is not their main aim. Each side has an agenda to pursue, a clarion to sound. Each side is probably correct in certain ways and for certain incidents. But neither significantly advances systematic research on media coverage of terrorism.

## Prescriptions

Contributors to this category of the literature usually agree with the antiterrorist media indicters, but go beyond them by suggesting various ways of combating what they see as the problem of coverage that facilitates terrorists' objectives. For the more thoughtful observers, this means trying to reconcile the public's right to know, the safety of hostages, the public's need for effective law enforcement responses, respect for the privacy of victims, and the need to deter future acts of terrorism (Bassiouni, 1982; see also Schmid & De Graaf, 1982, p. 172, for a useful summary of many of the arguments for and against censorship). Most limit their recommendations to actions the media can take or that can be imposed on the media, such as training and education of journalists, cooperation between media personnel and the authorities, informal controls, guidelines, codes of ethics, and legislation and legal sanctions. Only a few suggest that forces other than the media should share in the burden of rectification.

Jaehnig (1978) discusses the libertarian base upon which press freedom is built. He concludes that base "in large part lacks a moral code," was set before the rapid technological change seen in recent years, and is thus incongruent with the problems caused by terrorism. Controls on media coverage may therefore be necessary. Bassiouni (1982) lists four areas of regulation: government-imposed prior restraints, content regulation, time-manner-place regulations, and access restrictions. Indeed, guidelines for coverage have long been proposed (see Czerniejewski, 1977, for a set; also see Gallimore, 1991, for a preliminary study of media codes and compliance with voluntary guidelines in some of the U.S. media).

### VOLUNTARY COOPERATION

Almost all those who address the question of solutions are careful to pay obeisance to the dangers of government controls on the media. Instead, self-regulation or voluntary cooperation is urged. Scanlon (1989) notes cases where cooperation has taken place between media and law enforcement. Paust (1978) recommends efforts to foster "media awareness" rather than control. Conferees contributing to the symposium that yielded Miller's (1982) volume agree, for the most part, that self-regulation is a good idea, although some, such as Jaehnig, endorse the possibility of stricter controls; others, mainly journalists such as Hoge (1982), oppose any limits on coverage.

Proposals that could be labeled "voluntary cooperation" nonetheless do impinge on press freedom. Frey (1987) for example, advocates "thinning" the information made public concerning a terrorist act. Authorities should, he argues, try to confuse the issue of responsibility for a violent act, thereby denying the terrorists the reward they seek. Hacker (1976) encourages voluntary cooperation to delay publication, omission of names and photos, and the banning of ongoing reporting of "the drama" (p. 248). Methvin (1984) goes to past precedent by invoking the model many journalists in the U.S. South followed when covering the Ku Klux Klan during the 1930s and thereafter: He says there was "no semblance of balance or objective cover-age . . . when . . . dealing with the Klan and others of that ilk" (p. 18).

Terell and Ross (1988, pp. 49-50; see also 1991) offer a set of guidelines for reporting about terrorists and their activities. These stem from their concern that many of the voluntary guidelines adopted for coverage "threaten the freedom of the news media to act as objective observers of terrorist episodes" (p. 33). Among their recommendations: Report terrorist demands and their significance concisely, focus on contextual factors, surrender information to law enforcement authority only upon request and never covertly, always remember that lives are at stake, seek additional information and report it moderately, avoid speculation, remember that terrorists are also human beings, and oppose censorship and any attempts to impose sanctions against journalists who reject guidelines, including these (pp. 49-50).

### FORMAL CONTROLS

Some writers propose formalized controls on expression. These may appear to be relatively innocuous, such as Kupperman and Trent's (1979) advocacy of formal guidelines for coverage, something often mentioned in symposia. Others are less clear. Hacker and Scanlon hint that strong tactics may be required. Without advocating censorship, Hacker (1976) does suggest that, in particular emergency situations, "certain rights have to be curtailed temporarily in order to safeguard other, more important rights" (p. 248). Scanlon (1989) is vaguer, writing that "solutions must be extraordinary" and that "some scholars think that if the media do not act, governments will," and "some journalists agree with this approach" (p. 130).

Several authors have suggested the creation of an institution to monitor media coverage. This idea may have originated with the proposal by Schmid and De Graaf (1982) of an elected media council to decide "what news is good for us to learn, with due respect for minorities such as hostages" (p. 174). The composition of that body, how it would make its decisions, and with what effects are obviously important considerations. Clutterbuck (1983) proposes an Institute for the Mass Media; journalists would register as members of the institute and would have to follow its code or be barred from practicing their trade.

### OTHER PROPOSALS

The few contributions to this category move beyond the focus on media responsibility to consider the notion that other participants in the process could contribute to solving the perceived problems. Some suggest that law enforcement agencies or the military should change some aspects of their behavior. Hooper (1982) carefully notes the misperceptions that the military and the media have of each other, as well as the demands placed upon them.

He suggests that the military develop better training for its members regarding propaganda, public relations, and media skills. Murphy (1982) similarly explains how the law enforcement structure in the United States can create problems for dealing with terrorism and the media, and suggests possible solutions.

What is to be done? Some authors look to public opinion but find little guidance. Typical is Alexander's (1984) overview of attempts to derive solutions to the alleged problem of media coverage of terrorist events. Alexander observes that the public is divided on the issue of what should be done, if anything, about media reporting of terrorist actions (p. 143). DeBoer's (1979) review of polls in a number of countries reached similar conclusions. However, these polls come only from countries considered victims of insurgent terrorism; none, for instance, was conducted in Iran or among Palestinians. Moreover, on the question of solutions, people interviewed were given a false dichotomy: The choice was between saying that terrorism is overemphasized and saying that the public should be made aware of it.

## Coverage

We now turn to research that describes, analyzes, and categorizes coverage, sometimes by generating original data. Our purpose is to determine the extent to which the coverage facilitates or hinders terrorists' objectives.

The literature inevitably contains some discussion of the likely reasons for the supposed prominence of terrorism. Johnpoll (1977), for example, identifies five criteria he claims the media use to decide whether or not an event is newsworthy: timeliness, uniqueness, whether the event could be seen as "adventure," entertainment value, and whether or not the event affects the lives of those being informed. These criteria are impressionistic, and Johnpoll's brief piece does not document their deployment by systematic content analysis of actual news stories. Nonetheless, variations on these themes are scattered throughout much of the media indictment literature.

Support for the argument that terrorism is inherently newsworthy comes from Allen and Piland (1976), who surveyed newspaper editors to determine under what conditions they would cover an unsuccessful assassination attempt. The editors indicated that "the news value of unsuccessful attempts outweighs consideration of potential contagious effect of coverage" (p. 98).

It is not surprising, then, that Atwater (n.d.), in a brief study of network evening news coverage of the TWA hostage crisis of 1985, described it as "dramatic, reactive, and extensive."

Terrorism may be newsworthy, but media coverage is not representative of its prevalence and incidence by "actor, tactic, region, and victimization" (Crelinsten, 1989a, p. 168; see also Delli Carpini & Williams, 1984, 1987; Jenkins, 1981; Kelly & Mitchell, 1981). The focus is on international terrorism. The regional emphasis is on the Middle East (the Palestinians, not internecine conflict among Arab groups) and Western Europe. Hijacking and hostage taking are the tactics featured. Underreported and underrepresented are domestic terrorism, state terrorism and its victims, and insurgent terrorism in Latin America, the Far East, and Africa. Bombings, the most common tactic, are the least covered. Delli Carpini and Williams (1984) found that coverage on the U.S. television networks bore little relationship to actual patterns of occurrence when compared over time with a comprehensive data base of international terrorism events. Martin (1985), based on a content analysis of international press coverage of 45 separate terrorist events, found a lack of widespread coverage. Across five newspapers—the *Washington Post*, the *London Times, Frankfurter Allgemeine Zeitung*, the *Jerusalem Post*, and the *Egyptian Gazette*—only 78 items were recorded, rather than the 225 possible if every newspaper had covered every story. Martin suggests that this lack of coverage may be denying terrorists the publicity they seek. Of course, even the lower number shows that terrorism attracts media coverage. Aside from spectacular incidents, however, much of the coverage consists of brief capsules not prominently placed.

CASE STUDIES

Studies that attempt to characterize systematically the form and content of media coverage are inevitably, if not always explicitly, concerned with media influence on terrorism and the consequences of that influence. They variously conclude, or provide evidence in support of the different conclusions, that media coverage aids the terrorist cause, that it does not, and that it reinforces Western governments by working against terrorists and terrorism. The studies vary widely in originality, methodological reliability, and validity of findings. Space limitations prevent us from considering these factors in our discussion here (for a collection of some empirical studies reprinted mainly from the journal *Political Communication and Persuasion*, see Alali & Eke, 1991).

*Supports Terrorism*

The strongest evidence for media support of terrorism comes from studies of contagion both within and between states. Tan (1988) has compared coverage in the *Irish Times*, the *London Times*, and the *New York Times* of the terrorist violence carried out by the Irish Republican Army (IRA), and concludes: "The mere quantity of newspaper coverage sufficiently predicts the subsequent volume as well as scale of such terrorist violence. This relationship holds for both those newspapers that are especially critical of the violence and those especially apathetic about this violence" (p. 24).

Contagion also takes place between states. Applying sophisticated methodological techniques to the Rand Corporation's chronology of international terrorism and coverage on U.S. television networks and nine newspapers from various countries, Brosius and Weimann (1991) conclude that the "media, especially the U.S. television networks . . . contribute to the trends revealed by terrorist activity" (p. 72). Midlarsky, Crenshaw, and Yoshida (1980) suggest that the spread of terrorist violence from Latin America to Western Europe over two periods, 1968-1971 and 1973-1974, may be due in part to mass media technology and coverage. However, based on their probability modeling of the contagion of terrorist violence, they conclude that the spread of violence varies with a country's diplomatic status. Violence tends to spread from the larger, more visible, and respected units to the smaller, less visible, less respected ones. The authors also find, crucially, that not all acts of violence are equally contagious: bombings, kidnappings, and hijackings are somewhat more contagious than assassinations and raids. Their evidence thus suggests that lumping all terrorist violence together and focusing on media responsibility, as much of the literature does, are mistakes.

A few studies suggest that media coverage supports terrorism. Weimann (1983) found that subjects' evaluations of terrorists and terrorism were enhanced somewhat after they read press clippings, taken from Israel's leading daily newspaper, on two different violent acts. But, as he notes, the evaluations remained quite negative. Recently, Weimann (1990) completed a more elaborate version of this experiment. While there was no change on some evaluative dimensions (e.g., kind-cruel or valuable-worthless), and subjects in the experimental groups remained disapproving, Weimann observed substantial change on several scales (brave-cowardly, just-unjust, good-bad) (p. 22). Agenda-setting and status conferral also occurred: "Subjects who were exposed to press reports of terrorist incidents tended to see the issue as more important, to believe that an international solution is desirable, and to hold that media coverage and public attention were merited"

(p. 23). Weimann suggests that the stories may have produced these effects through rationalizing terrorism, labeling it positively, and depicting the terrorists as underdogs.

### Hinders Terrorism

Picard (1986) has caustically reviewed and rejected the contagion effect argument, finding that no cause-effect relationship between coverage and increased incidence of terrorism has been established. However, that was before publication of the more recent studies cited above. He also has dismissed attempts in the literature to link research on the effects of televised violence and crime on viewers to effects of coverage of terrorism, saying that the violence research is far from reliable, and that transferring its tentative conclusions is "dubious science." Arguments based on polls of public and law enforcement officials are similarly unreliable, for such people can hardly be regarded as dispassionate sources.

Contagion aside, most studies indicate that media coverage does terrorists no favors. Kelly and Mitchell (1981) content analyzed media coverage of 158 incidents of transnational terrorism in the *New York Times* and *London Times*. They conclude: "While transnational terrorism does generate a considerable amount of press attention, the particular type of coverage it receives would appear to undermine the effectiveness of terrorism as a communications strategy" (p. 269). Analyzing coverage in three U.S. newspapers of the 1985 TWA hostage crisis, Nacos, Fan, and Young (1989) conclude that while the terrorists received considerable attention and had their causes and grievances reported, "they had only limited success in gaining coverage that might have helped their efforts to gain respectability and legitimacy" (p. 107).

A few studies have examined the sources relied upon by the media. Paletz, Fozzard, and Ayanian (1982, 1983) analyzed the content of *New York Times* and television network news coverage of three terrorist groups. The stories relied on authority sources and did not legitimate the terrorists' causes. Coverage emphasized violence and destruction, ignoring the movements' motives, objectives, and goals. Moreover, over the July 1, 1977, through June 30, 1979, period studied, violence had to become more dramatic and extensive to be reported.

A related study by Knight and Dean (1982) showed that coverage of terrorist events by two Canadian dailies tended through the use of myth to legitimate and sanctify use of violence by the government. By creating and invoking particular rules or cues concerning the relevant actors, the newspapers made governmental violence appear natural, inevitable, and necessary.

The most significant study of the failure of terrorists to acquire legitimacy through media coverage comes from Crelinsten's (1987a) thoughtful analysis of the battle for media coverage and concomitant reporting of the conflict between the terrorists of the Quebec Liberation Front (FLQ) and the federal and state governments of Canada during the October 1970 negotiations over the FLQ's hostages and programmatic demands:

> The terrorists had forced their way into the communication network by means of kidnapping and threat of murder. They had dominated public discourse for almost two weeks by manipulating media hunger for news and the competitive search for scoops. . . . When the traditional criminal justice model was finally abandoned by the authorities, in recognition of the fact that it was no longer effective in denying political legitimacy to the terrorists and their political goals, the war model . . . achieved the desired goal. The terrorists were expelled from the communication network, the media became most reluctant to let them back in, public support was silenced and the focus of discussion was drawn away from the terrorists' political programme to that of the Government. (pp. 444-445)

### Justice

One study stands apart in showing the benefits of a free press not for or against terrorism, but for justice. In "Preserving Liberty in a Society Under Siege: The Media and the 'Guilford Four,' " Miller (1990) chronicles the ultimately successful efforts of courageous journalists to obtain the freedom of four men falsely convicted and incarcerated for IRA bombings and deaths in England. For Miller, the case shows "how responsible, vigilant and free media provide an independent, institutional base of power that can help reunite democratic aspirations and practice" (p. 305). While acknowledging the basis for Miller's conclusion, we would note that the men's vindication resulted from the efforts of a very few intrepid journalists working for years against the disinterest if not active opposition of most of the press. Nor does Miller discuss the possibility that the media, particularly the tabloids, were guilty of bludgeoning the police into charging and the court into convicting.

### DIFFERENCES AMONG MEDIA

Some studies have uncovered intriguing differences among media. Delli Carpini and Williams (1984) compared coverage on the evening news programs of the U.S. television networks with that of the *New York Times* of the seizure of the Dominican Republic's embassy in Bogotá in 1980. They conclude that the *Times* coverage was much more detailed and balanced than television news about the background, intentions, and actions of perpetrators of violent acts. Television news tended to portray the terrorists "as, at best, inscrutable and, at worst, lunatics or common . . . criminals" (p. 120). Coverage is "erratic, oversimplified, morally unambiguous and misleading" (p. 120). Television, with a much larger audience than the *Times*, did not favor the terrorists.

Schlesinger, Murdock, and Elliott (1983) found that production constraints, combined with the public identities of news programs, yielded "systematic variations" in coverage of political violence on British television (p. 35). Fiction programming tends to be more open to alternative viewpoints and interpretations. The authors challenge both sides of the question of media coverage influence: Television is consistently a friend neither of insurgents nor of the state.

Relatedly, Altheide (1987) has shown how TV news formats (news practices and perspectives) produced different visual and thematic emphases in British and U.S. television news coverage of two IRA bombings. "News formats of the *event type* associated with regular evening newscasts in both countries focused on visuals of the aftermath and tactics of terrorism, while *topic type* formats associated with interviews and documentary presentations included materials about purposes, goals, and rationale" (p. 162). As a result, although the news reports were "not uniformly narrow and negative . . . much of the news media coverage about terrorism promotes the symbolic legitimacy of established leaders" (p. 164).

*Implications*

These three studies highlight an important fact often overlooked by the media indicters: Neither terrorism nor the media are monolithic. The media include television, radio, print, and so on. Some media outlets are privately owned, others are publicly owned. They are more or less insulated from government control or influence. Their contents, encompassing fiction, nonfiction, and various formats, can differ both within and between countries. Similarly, "terrorism" comprises various types of people, motives, and deeds (Schmid, 1988). As Schmid and a few others remind us, ethnic, nationalist, and social revolutionary terrorists are not synonymous. The extent to which any of them uses or benefits from media coverage likely depends upon many factors, not all of which have been adequately explored in the literature.

The different audiences of the different media also need to be considered. Terrorists may care most about the readers of elite newspapers, because included among them are powerful policymakers. They may count on mass sentiment to pressure policymakers, and thus seek favorable television coverage. But the impact of media coverage may be ambiguous: Scenes of destruction shown on television that produce fear in some people could outrage others, leading them to support retaliation.

### MEDIA IN CONTROL

A few studies suggest that the media cover terrorist events in such a way as to reinforce their own power to transmit "reality." Picard and Adams (1988) studied reports on terrorist activity in the *Los Angeles Times, Washington Post,* and *New York Times* over the period 1980-1985. The vast majority of characterizations of perpetrators and their actions (82%) were nominal, that is, "straightforward descriptions with as little judgmental qualities about the acts or perpetrators as possible" (p. 1) and without much connotative meaning. The coverage was not sensationalistic. Moreover, 94% of all characterizations in the stories were made by the media themselves; few were from officials of any kind or witnesses. This indicates that the print media are not conduits for the characterizations of terrorist events by either terrorists or government.

An earlier study obtained similar findings for television news. Based on their textual analysis of CBS news coverage of the aftermath of a Palestinian raid near Tel Aviv, Barton and Gregg (1982) conclude that the program's imposition of certain features and manipulation of time, information, and visuals supported the network's authority and perspective.

### SUMMARY

The actual research evidence tends to support the argument that media coverage does not much help terrorists. In particular, micro-level data on the content of coverage indicate, if anything, that it supports Western governments against terrorism. However, there are two fundamental problems with drawing conclusions from this research. First, it is generally confined to analyses of media content. Few studies try to pursue the actual effects of media depictions by relating coverage to public opinion data or focused interviews, or through experimental research. Second, the studies rarely analyze media coverage of terrorism, and public reaction to it, in terms of the specific arguments made by the indicters: Miller's contention, for example, that for terrorists "the value of the propaganda lies in their getting the public to be so amazed at their description of reality that it will begin to question its own assumptions about morality and about the political system" (p. 4). Of course, it could be argued that rather than arguments to be tested, some of the indicting assertions are "truths" impervious to empirical verification. Thus if publicity is the terrorists' goal, any and all media coverage of their activities, no matter how hostile in content and tone, by definition benefits, helps, facilitates, or at least encourages them.

## Conclusions and Research Suggestions

With notable exceptions (e.g., Schlesinger et al., 1983; Schmid & De Graaf, 1982; see also Crelinsten's studies and Picard's research), the bulk of the literature on the relationship between the media and terrorism is dismaying. Some of it is blatantly propagandistic, consisting of shrill jeremiads, exhortations, tendentious examples, and undocumented assertions. Unexamined assumptions abound, terms go undefined, and arguments are untested. Works suggesting solutions to perceived problems place overwhelming responsibility on the media. Few writers discuss the necessity for other participants to alter their behavior if terrorism is to be curtailed, controlled, ended to everyone's satisfaction. There is little available on terrorists' viewpoints, or on their own reasoning as to strategies and tactics. The attitudes and actions of authority holders, the measures they take, their strategies and tactics, are neglected. There are few assessments of the impact of coverage on audiences, let alone how that impact varies by media, program format, verbal and visual content, and numerous other factors. Even the best academic journal dealing with terrorism, *Terrorism and Political Violence*, is sometimes vulnerable to reproach: The three pieces on media and terrorism in its winter 1990 issue are by a British diplomat who had been kidnapped by terrorists, by the former vice chancellor of London University and chairman of the Committee on the Future of Broadcasting, and by the managing director of the BBC World Service.

How can we explain the relative dearth of serious inquiry and research in comparison with the abundance of repetitive fulminations? Most obviously, the subject is inherently politicized and highly contentious (see Crelinsten, 1987b, pp. 3-6, for other factors). Authority and power at the highest and lowest levels are linked to definitions of and responses to terrorism. A confrontation on the U.S. Public Broadcasting Service's *MacNeil-Lehrer*

*News Hour* on December 6, 1990, illustrates the situation. Senator Joseph Liebermann (D-CT) wrangled with a representative of the PLO over the issue of U.S. dialogue with the Palestinian organization. Liebermann invoked the "terrorist" acts of a PLO leader as a block to talks; the PLO representative stressed Israeli military violence against "women and children." He wanted this violence categorized as "terrorism," which Liebermann consistently resisted. Both men, and the institutions they represented, understood the centrality of the definition of terrorism to their debate: It automatically influenced, even determined, their statements, responses, and conclusions.

All the while, the media are participants in the struggle, shaping in ways as yet not fully specified or understood the terms of debate and the impressions, if not reactions, audience members in and out of power form of the state and insurgents. Clearly, media coverage of terrorism can affect five different elements (see also Crelinsten, 1989b). First, there are the terrorist perpetrators, other actual and potential members of these organizations, and their counterparts in other countries. Second, the coverage can influence the behavior of government officials about whether and how to deal with a particular event and with terrorists in general. Third are the effects of the coverage on the public, particularly as registered in opinion polls. Fourth, the coverage can determine the fates of victims, particularly any held hostage, and can affect the lives of their families, relatives, and friends. Fifth, media coverage can influence decisions about process and content made by media personnel in covering subsequent terrorist activities.

Obviously, these factors are often interconnected. Coverage affects public opinion, which constrains or perhaps emboldens public officials, who in turn try to influence coverage. The relations can work in many ways. Complicating the situation, none of these elements—government, terrorists, media, or even victims—is monolithic. The public, in particular, consists of people variously sympathetic, hostile, neutral, and ambivalent toward, or ignorant about, any terrorist group. People are also likely to differ widely in their trust in the media and in their belief in the reliability of television coverage of terrorism. (See Wolfsfeld, 1991, for an illuminating study using a transactional model to explain the roles and effects of, and on, the mass media in situations of political protest and violence.)

Future research can specify and test for possible media influences much more carefully by examining source reliance, verbal and visual content, program formats, fiction versus nonfiction programming, audience exposure patterns and reactions, terrorist goals and strategies, and state interests and responses. Comparative studies of coverage in different types of states throughout the world would be especially revealing about media processes and imperatives, as well as about government influence.

Certainly there is little need for more complaining symposia. Urgently required is serious research that gathers, assesses, and tests credible information from all sides of the conflict. In the process, nothing should be assumed as self-evident: not authority holders' purposes, terrorists' intentions, or journalists' motives, and certainly not the public's reactions to the coverage. This book is a singular step in that direction.

# References

Alali, A. O., & Eke, K. K. (Eds.). (1991). *Media coverage of terrorism.* Newbury Park, CA: Sage.

Alexander, Y. (1977). Terrorism and the media in the Middle East. In Y. Alexander & S. M. Finger (Eds.), *Terrorism: Interdisciplinary perspectives* (pp. 166-206). New York: John Jay.

Alexander, Y. (1984). Terrorism, the media and the police. In H. H. Han (Ed.), *Terrorism, political violence and world order* (pp. 135-150). New York: University Press of America.

Alexander, Y., & Latter, R. (Eds.). (1990). *Terrorism and the media.* Washington, DC: Brassey's.

Allen, T. H., & Piland, R. N. (1976). Bungling assassins rate page one. *Journal of Communication, 26*(4), 98-101.

Altheide, D. L. (1987). Format and symbols in TV coverage of terrorism in the United States and Great Britain. *International Studies Quarterly, 31,* 161-176.

Atwater, T. (n.d.). *Network evening news coverage of the TWA hostage crisis.* Boston: Emerson College, Terrorism and the News Media Project.

Barnhurst, K. G. (1991). The literature of terrorism: Implications for visual communications. In A. O. Alali & K. K. Eke (Eds.), *Media coverage of terrorism* (pp. 112-137). Newbury Park, CA: Sage.

Barton, R. L., & Gregg, R. B. (1982). Middle East conflict as a TV news scenario: A formal analysis. *Journal of Communication, 32,* 172-185.

Bassiouni, M. C. (1982). Media coverage of terrorism: The law and the public. *Journal of Communication, 32,* 128-143.

Bassiouni, M. C. (1983). Problems in media coverage of nonstate-sponsored terror-violence incidents. In L. Z. Freedman & Y. Alexander (Eds.), *Perspectives on terrorism* (pp. 177-200). Wilmington, DE: Scholarly Resources.

Brosius, H.-B., & Weimann, G. (1991). The contagiousness of mass-mediated terrorism. *European Journal of Communication, 6,* 63-75.

Catton, W. R., Jr. (1978). Militants and the media: Partners in terrorism? *Indiana Law Journal, 53,* 703-715.

Chafets, Z. (1985). *Double vision: How the press distorts America's view of the Middle East.* New York: William Morrow.

Clawson, P. (1990). Why we need more but better coverage of terrorism. In C. W. Kegley, Jr. (Ed.), *International terrorism* (pp. 241-244). New York: St. Martin's.

Clutterbuck, R. (1983). *The media and political violence* (2nd ed.). New York: Macmillan.
Cooper, H. H. A. (1977). Terrorism and the media. In Y. Alexander & S. M. Finger (Eds.), *Terrorism: Interdisciplinary perspectives* (pp. 141-156). New York: John Jay.
Crelinsten, R. D. (1987a). Power and meaning: Terrorism as a struggle over access to the communication structure. In P. Wilkinson & A. M. Stewart (Eds.), *Contemporary research on terrorism* (pp. 419-450). Aberdeen: Aberdeen University Press.
Crelinsten, R. D. (1987b). Terrorism as political communication: The relationship between the controller and the controlled. In P. Wilkinson & A. M. Stewart (Eds.). *Contemporary research on terrorism* (pp. 3-23). Aberdeen: Aberdeen University Press.
Crelinsten, R. D. (1989a). Images of terrorism in the media: 1966-1985. *Terrorism, 12,* 167-198.
Crelinsten, R. D. (1989b). Terrorism and the media: Problems, solutions and counterproblems. *Political Communication and Persuasion, 6,* 311-339.
Crenshaw, M. (1990). The logic of terrorism: Terrorist behavior as a product of strategic choice. In W. Reich (Ed.), *Origins of terrorism* (pp. 7-24). Cambridge: Cambridge University Press.
Czerniejewski, H. J. (1977). Guidelines for the coverage of terrorism. *Quill, 65*(7), 21-23.
DeBoer, C. (1979). The polls: Terrorism and hijacking. *Public Opinion Quarterly, 43,* 410-418.
Delli Carpini, M. X., & Williams, B. A. (1984). Terrorism and the media: Patterns of occurrence and presentation, 1969-80. In H. H. Han (Ed.), *Terrorism, political violence and world order* (pp. 103-134). New York: University Press of America.
Delli Carpini, M. X., & Williams, B. A. (1987). Television and terrorism: Patterns of presentation and occurrence, 1969-1980. *Western Political Quarterly, 40*(1), 45-64.
Dowling, R. E. (1986). Terrorism and the media: A rhetorical genre. *Journal of Communication, 36*(1), 12-24.
Frey, B. S. (1987). Fighting political terrorism by refusing recognition. *Journal of Public Policy, 7*(2), 179-188.
Gallimore, T. (1991). Media compliance with voluntary press guidelines for covering terrorism. In Y. Alexander & R. G. Picard (Eds.), *In the camera's eye* (pp. 103-117). Washington, DC: Brassey's.
Gerbner, G., Gross, L., Signorielli, N., Morgan, M., & Jackson-Beeck, M. (1979). The demonstration of power: Violence profile no. 10. *Journal of Communication, 29*(3), 177-196.
Hacker, F. J. (1976). *Crusaders, criminals and crazies: Terror and terrorism in our time.* New York: W. W. Norton.
Herman, E. S. (1982). *The real terror network: Terrorism in fact and propaganda.* Boston: South End.
Herman, E. S., & O'Sullivan, G. (1989). *The "terrorism" industry: The experts and institutions that shape our view of terror.* New York: Pantheon.
Hoge, J. W. (1982). The media and terrorism. In A. H. Miller (Ed.), *Terrorism: The media and the law* (pp. 89-105). Dobbs Ferry, NY: Transnational.
Hooper, A. (1982). *The military and the media.* Brookfield, VT: Gower.
Jaehnig, W. B. (1978). Journalists and terrorism: Captives of the libertarian tradition. *Indiana Law Journal, 53,* 717-744.
Jenkins, B. (1981). *The psychological implications of media-covered terrorism* (Rand Paper P6627). Santa Monica, CA: Rand Corporation.
Johnpoll, B. (1977). Terrorism and the mass media in the United States. In Y. Alexander & S. M. Finger (Eds.), *Terrorism: Interdisciplinary perspectives* (pp. 157-165). New York: John Jay.
Kelly, M. J., & Mitchell, T. H. (1981). Transnational terrorism and the Western elite press. *Political Communication and Persuasion, 1,* 269-296.

Knight, G., & Dean, T. (1982). Myth and the structure of news. *Journal of Communication, 32*(2), 144-161.

Kramer, M. (1990). The moral logic of Hizballah. In W. Reich (Ed.), *Origins of terrorism* (pp. 131-160). Cambridge: Cambridge University Press.

Kupperman, R., & Trent, D. (1979). *Terrorism: Threat, reality, response.* Stanford, CA: Hoover Institution Press.

Laqueur, W. (1977). *Terrorism.* Boston: Little, Brown.

Leeman, R. W. (1986). Terrorism as rhetoric: An argument of values. *Journal of Political Science, 14,* 33-42.

Levitt, G. M. (1988). *Democracies against terror: The Western response to state-supported terrorism.* New York: Praeger.

Livingston, S. (in press). *Violent spectacles: The U. S. press, terrorism, and political power.* New York: Harper Collins.

Livingstone, W. D. (1986). Terrorism and the media revolution. In N. C. Livingstone & T. E. Arnold (Eds.), *Fighting back: Winning the war against terrorism* (pp. 213-227). Lexington, MA: D. C. Heath.

Martin, J. L. (1985). The media's role in international terrorism. *Terrorism, 8*(2), 127-146.

Methvin, E. H. (1984). [Statement]. In S. Midgley & V. Rice (Eds.), *Terrorism and the media in the 1980's* (pp. 16-18). Washington, DC: Media Institute.

Midlarsky, M. I., Crenshaw, M., & Yoshida, F. (1980). Why violence spreads: The contagion of international terrorism. *International Studies Quarterly, 24,* 262-298.

Miller, A. H. (1980). *Terrorism and hostage negotiations.* Boulder, CO: Westview.

Miller, A. H. (Ed.). (1982). *Terrorism: The media and the law.* Dobbs Ferry, NY: Transnational.

Miller, A. H. (1990). Preserving liberty in a society under siege: The media and the "Guilford four." *Terrorism and Political Violence, 2,* 305-324.

Murphy, P. V. (1982). The police, the news media, and the coverage of terrorism. In A. H. Miller (Ed.), *Terrorism: The media and the law* (pp. 76-88). Dobbs Ferry, NY: Transnational.

Nacos, B., Fan, D. P., & Young, J. T. (1989). Terrorism and the print media: The 1985 TWA hostage crisis. *Terrorism, 12,* 107-115.

Netanyahu, B. (Ed.). (1986). *Terrorism: How the West can win.* New York: Farrar, Strauss, & Giroux.

Nossek, H. (1985). The impact of mass media on terrorists, supporters, and the public at large. In A. Merari (Ed.), *On terrorism and combating terrorism* (pp. 87-94). Frederick, MD: University Publications of America.

Paletz, D. L., Fozzard, P. A., & Ayanian, J. Z. (1982). The I.R.A., the Red Brigades, and the F.A.L.N. in the "New York Times." *Journal of Communication, 32*(2), 162-171.

Paletz, D. L., Fozzard, P. A., & Ayanian, J. Z. (1983). Terrorism on TV news: The IRA, the FALN, and the Red Brigades. In W. C. Adams (Ed.), *Television coverage of international affairs* (pp. 143-165). Norwood, NJ: Ablex.

Paust, J. J. (1978). International law and control of the media: Terror, repression and the alternatives. *Indiana Law Journal, 53,* 621-677.

Picard, R. G. (1986). News coverage as the contagion of terrorism: Dangerous charges backed by dubious science. *Political Communication and Persuasion, 4,* 385-400.

Picard, R. G. (1989). Press relations of terrorist organizations. *Public Relations Review, 15*(4), 12-23.

Picard, R. G. (1991). Journalists as targets and victims of terrorism. In Y. Alexander & R. G. Picard (Eds.), *In the camera's eye* (pp. 65-71). Washington, DC: Brassey's.

Picard, R. G., & Adams, P. D. (1988). *Characterizations of acts and perpetrators of political violence in three elite U.S. daily newspapers* (Paper No. 5). Boston: Emerson College and California State University, Fresno, Terrorism and the News Media Research Project.

Quester, G. H. (1986). Cruise-ship terrorism and the media. *Political Communication and Persuasion, 4,* 355-370.

Redlick, A. S. (1979). The transnational flow of information as a cause of terrorism. In Y. Alexander, D. Carlton, & P. Wilkinson (Eds.), *Terrorism: Theory and practice* (pp. 73-95). Boulder, CO: Westview.

Said, E. W. (1981). *Covering Islam.* New York: Pantheon.

Scanlon, J. (1989). The hostage taker, the terrorist, the media: Partners in public crime. In L. M. Walters, L. Wilkins, & T. Walters (Eds.), *Bad tidings: Communication and catastrophe* (pp. 115-130). Hillsdale, NJ: Lawrence Erlbaum.

Schlesinger, P., Murdock, G., & Elliott, P. (1983). *Televising terrorism: Political violence in popular culture.* London: Comedia.

Schmid, A. P. (1988). Goals and objectives of international terrorism. In R. O. Slater & M. Stohl (Eds.), *Current perspectives on international terrorism* (pp. 47-87). New York: St. Martin's.

Schmid, A. P., & De Graaf, J. (1982). *Violence as communication: Insurgent terrorism and the Western news media.* Beverly Hills, CA: Sage.

Stohl, M. (1983). *The politics of terrorism* (2nd ed.). New York: Marcel Dekker.

Tan, Z. W. C. (1988). Media publicity and insurgent terrorism: A twenty-year balance sheet. *Gazette, 42,* 3-32.

Terell, R. L., & Ross, K. (1988). Terrorism, censorship and the U.S. press corps. *Gazette, 42,* 33-51.

Terell, R. L., & Ross, K. (1991). The voluntary guidelines' threat to U.S. press freedom. In Y. Alexander & R. G. Picard (Eds.), *In the camera's eye* (pp. 75-101). Washington, DC: Brassey's.

Wardlaw, G. (1982). *Political terrorism.* Cambridge: Cambridge University Press.

Weimann, G. (1983). The theater of terror: Effects of press coverage. *Journal of Communication, 33*(1), 38-45.

Weimann, G. (1987). Media events: The case of international terrorism. *Journal of Broadcasting and Electronic Media, 31*(1), 21-39.

Weimann, G. (1990). "Redefinition of image": The impact of mass-mediated terrorism. *International Journal of Public Opinion Research, 2*(1), 17-29.

Wolfsfeld, G. (1991, June). Media, protest, and political violence: A transactional analysis. *Journalism Monographs, 127.*

Woodward, B. (1987). *Veil.* New York: Simon & Schuster.

# 3

# Terrorists' Perspectives: Memoirs

## Robin P. J. M. Gerrits

In this chapter I will attempt to provide insight into the way terrorists utilize the means of publicity. Publicity encompasses more than just the modern mass media. Although newspapers, radio, and television do play the most important part in the "public relations" of political terrorists, there remain other ways for terrorists to attract the attention they seek. Publicity in general is an important element in terrorist strategy, which raises the question of whether terrorist groups can be suffocated by being denied the "oxygen of publicity," to use the metaphor of former British Prime Minister Margaret Thatcher (*New York Times*, June 16, 1986).

Before proceeding to a discussion of the uses of the media by terrorists—discussion based predominantly on the descriptions of terrorists themselves—it is important to look at the place of publicity in terrorist strategy.

## Terrorist Strategy

Starting from the definition given by Schmid, Jongman, et al. (1988) in their book *Political Terrorism*, a fundamental triangular relationship can be seen in terrorist strategy among the terrorist, the target of the terrorist violence (the victims, such as British soldiers in Northern Ireland, the hostages in a plane, a killed banker), and the actual targets of the action, whose minds terrorists try to affect with their violence. Such "targets of attention" may be a certain country's government, which the terrorists want to coerce, or the public in general or a sector thereof, which is put in a state of apprehensive interest or fear.

In contrast with state-practiced terrorism, insurgent terrorists actively seek publicity (Schmid & De.Graaf, 1983, p. 16). Researchers agree on this point, but when it comes to the question of the extent to which terrorists use the media, they tend to disagree. Some writers hold that terrorists seek the mass media because they depend on it, as a result of their chosen mode of action. Others stress the skillful and professional way in which terrorists actively use or, in their words, manipulate the media.

A strong expression of the latter position is contained in the often-heard theater metaphor. William Catton, Jr. (1978), for example, states: "Terrorist activity is basically a form of theater. Terrorists play to an audience. Without the mass media they would seldom be able to reach audiences as large as those from which they do now gain attention" (pp. 712-713; see also Bell, 1978; Tugwell, 1981, p. 18).

Terrorism is a method of violent action that has been applied to pursue different ultimate goals, which could vary from striving for a Marxist-Leninist revolution to working for the expulsion of a colonial power from a certain country or region. In their pursuit of such ends, terrorists employ psychological strategies. M. Cherif Bassiouni (1981, p. 17) subsumes these in five categories:

1. Demonstrate the vulnerability and impotence of the government.
2. Attract broader public sympathy by the choice of carefully selected targets that may be publicly rationalized.
3. Cause a polarization and radicalization among the public.
4. Goad the government into repressive action likely to discredit it.
5. Present the violent acts in a manner that makes them appear heroic.

Other authors also refer to such psychological goals. Carlos Marighella (1972), for example, the much-cited Brazilian urban guerrilla, says: "The war of nerves is an aggressive strategy, in which information, spread by the mass media and orally, is meant to demoralize the government" (p. 161).

Several researchers have identified "demoralization" or the "discouraging of the authorities," in contrast with the boosting of the terrorists' supporters or the people at large, as an important psychological goal of terrorism (Schmid & De Graaf, 1983, pp. 12, 19). The concept of a shift "from asset to liability," introduced by British antiterrorism expert Maurice Tugwell (1981), points in the same direction. Tugwell describes the Irish terrorist strategy as one in which terrorists try, by constantly harassing the troops of the government, to modify the attitudes of their opponents or their supporters. This change of attitude should ultimately lead to a decision on the part of authorities to withdraw from a region that only causes difficulty. Propaganda, especially violent propaganda, is, according to Tugwell, the most suitable means to bring about this change (p. 17).

All the terrorist strategies mentioned so far are fought on a psychological battleground: They are meant to bring about changes in the attitudes or feelings of the public and/or opponents. Probably this is the reason some authors call terrorism the "weapon of the weak"—the strategy does not aim at a military victory, but at a psychological defeat of the enemy.

Terrorists commit violent deeds such as bomb attacks or acts of hostage taking to achieve psychological results, which, in turn, are expected to bring the final goals of the movement closer to realization. In order to achieve massive attitude changes, terrorists seek publicity, and they do this with carefully chosen tactics. The amount of publicity, especially mass media publicity, that terrorists manage to achieve with their deeds will often be seen as the criterion for the success or failure of an action.

This does not mean, however, that the ways in which terrorists are portrayed in the media are of no importance. There is no agreement in the literature on this point. Bell (1979) has said that terrorists don't care how hostilely they are portrayed in the media, as long as they get the publicity they need. Other authors, however, assume that terrorists must often feel "used" by the media, especially when the media spread word of terrorists' violent deeds, for the sake of their news value, but leave out the political messages contained in accompanying terrorist communiqués (Alexander, 1977, p. 189; Clutterbuck, 1981, p. 136; Schmid & De Graaf, 1983, p. 27; Schmid, De Graaf, et al., 1982, pp. 71, 79).

### TACTICS OF PUBLICITY

What tactics do terrorists employ to obtain badly needed publicity? What do terrorists do to receive the maximum attention of the print and broadcast press? Schmid and De Graaf (1983, pp. 33-54) provide a long list of active and passive uses of the news media by insurgent terrorists. Although the list, with its 22 active and 10 passive uses, looks fairly complete, I would like to propose a different list. The problem with Schmid and De Graaf's original list is that, in the analysis of terrorist uses of publicity, the psychological strategies and the specific tactics used to reach the public are enumerated next to each other. For example, Schmid and De Graaf mention in succession "inciting public against government" and "occupation of broadcasting stations to issue message." These two strategies should be separated, because the second activity may serve the first. Analytically speaking, they belong to two different phases in terrorist strategy. In this chapter, the former will be classified under psychological aims, and the latter under specific ways to obtain publicity.

The ways of reaching the necessary means of publicity can be grouped in another categorization:

1. planning actions for *their news value*
2. undertaking *supporting propaganda and recruitment activities*
3. choosing the *most favorable time and place* for publicity for actions and movement
4. issuing *statements*
5. keeping in *contact with the press* and giving *interviews*
6. claiming *responsibility* for terrorist actions
7. issuing messages through *the meaning or symbolism of the target or the deed*

In my perception, these seven tactics serve the psychological strategies that in turn are supposed to bring about the final goals of the (terrorist) movement. This is illustrated in Figure 3.1. It should be noted that, in principle, *each* tactic of publicity may serve *each* of the psychological strategies (Gerrits, 1989, p. 39).

Generally speaking, the terrorist is seen as someone who employs all possibilities to obtain publicity in a most purposeful and rational way, weighs them carefully, and selects a strategy in the first place with the publicity he or she can win in mind. Yet most terrorists are not aiming at publicity for its own sake. The publicity obtained is *instrumental* and serves the final aim of the terrorist movement. However, there might also be cases in which the *means* are raised to the level of a *goal* of the strategy (Schmid & De Graaf, 1983, p. 20). This said, we can now turn to the terrorists' own stories, as reflected in their personal recollections.

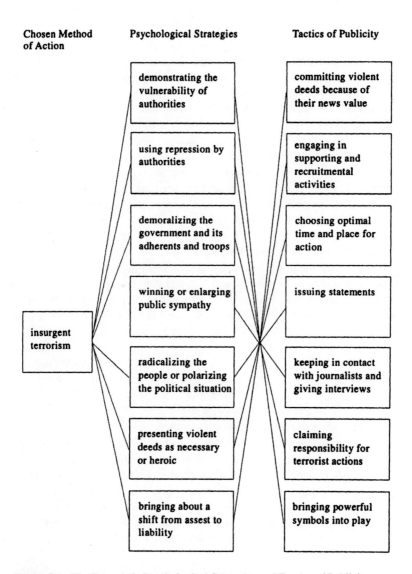

**Figure 3.1.** The Terrorist's Psychological Strategies and Tactics of Publicity

## Personal Documents of Terrorists

To learn something about the attitudes of terrorists toward the employment of publicity and the media, it is important to find a source that does not, like many studies of a (semi-)scientific nature, concentrate on the subject from the outside, but renders insight into the minds and motivations of terrorists (Rapoport, 1988). Within terrorist writings a distinction can be made between personal documents (autobiographies, memoirs, diaries, letters) and material that is written with a predominantly political-ideological aim (pamphlets, proclamations). For this investigation, the second type of document is of less interest than the first. Pamphlets and treatises are generally produced by groups or movements as a whole, and reveal little or nothing of the actions, thoughts, and motivations of individual terrorists. Personal documents, on the other hand, can reveal these aspects (Bertaux, 1981, pp. 225-234; *Tijdschrift voor Geschiedenis*, 1970, pp. 238-239).

The personal documents of terrorists that are known are nearly all memoirs, occasionally in the form of autobiography. In this study, the following documents are investigated. For the Provisional IRA, Seán MacStiofain's *Revolutionary in Ireland* (1975) is one source. MacStiofain was chief of staff of the Provisional IRA from 1969 to 1973. In the same period, Maria McGuire was also active in the armed Republican movement. She tells her story in *To Take Arms: A Year With the Provisional IRA* (1973). Gerry Adams, president of Sinn Fein, offers the third personal source for the Irish terrorists. He is the author of, among other works, *Falls Memories* (1982) and *The Politics of Irish Freedom* (1986). Though neither of these is a memoir in the true sense, both are informative about the actions of the Irish terrorists. The second of the two is the source used here. From the West German *Stadtguerrilla* (urban guerrillas) I studied two memoirs: *Wie Alles Anfing* (*How It All Began*) (1976) by Michael (Bommi) Baumann, and Hans-Joachim Klein's *Rückkehr in die Menschlichkeit* (*Return to Humanity*) (1979). Furthermore, I have analyzed two revealing sources from recent Palestinian history: Abu Ijad's *Heimat oder Tod* (*Fatherland or Death*) (1979) and Leila Khaled's *My People Shall Live: Autobiography of a Revolutionary* (1973).

All of the above works are from the recent past. There are many interesting examples from earlier periods as well, such as the works of Boris Savinkov, Vera Figner, Five Sisters, Stepniak, Tom Barry, Menachim Begin, and George Grivas. These have not been utilized for the present chapter, however.

Although memoirs are often interesting and useful, they have certain shortcomings of which the reader should be aware. The foremost problem is the bias of the source, which can be the result of a number of factors. An author's account of past events can serve a present goal, such as the support of an ideology. This can lead to the phenomenon of a writer purposefully relating certain events extensively, such as the violence of the "oppressing" opponent, while leaving out other things, such as the violence practiced by the terrorist group itself.

There is another goal that can be served with bias: The writings of Klein, Baumann, and McGuire, for instance, are clearly meant to deter other people from joining terrorist groups. This bias may lead an author to emphasize the ruthlessness of ex-comrades in his or her memoirs (Bertaux, 1981, p. 65; *Tijdschrift voor Geschiedenis*, 1970, p. 176). We also see that when a terrorist leaves a group, he or she is likely to describe group life in dark colors, while using bright colors to describe the period thereafter. Another thing to keep in mind is that memoirs often serve as a justification of the deeds of the author, both to readers and to the author him- or herself. Another difficult problem is the question of how representative a given source may be. Only a few members of any given movement write memoirs. It is hard to determine whether their accounts represent the attitudes and motives of the others in the group.

On the other hand, there is no other document that can shed as rich and interesting a light upon behaviors, actions, and motivations of terrorists, seen from their perspectives. And that is what is important in this case. In the following discussion of terrorist strategies, different aspects will be illustrated with many quotations and examples from the memoirs, in order to describe the participants' attitudes and thoughts.

## Psychological Strategies and the Purpose of Violence

Let us turn to the different ways in which terrorists utilize publicity to pursue their psychological strategic aims. Needless to say, this analytical division into six categories is not an absolute one. In reality, all six categories blend into and are complementary to one another.

DEMONSTRATION OF THE MOVEMENT'S STRENGTH
AND EXPOSURE OF THE VULNERABILITY OF AUTHORITIES

The first psychological strategy is a very important element in terrorism. Insurgent terrorists show their power preeminently through deeds that embarrass their more powerful opponents. There are several ways to embarrass the opposing authorities. Terrorist deeds can cause a loss of face for the government, they can demonstrate the possibility of (armed) resistance, and they can show that those in power are more vulnerable than was commonly assumed. Violent deeds also underline the strength of the terrorist group. These outcomes are all dependent on publicity to achieve a psychological effect. Terrorists want people to see something, and the media are the means by which news of such shows of force is disseminated.

Let me illustrate this with some examples. In the memoirs of nearly all terrorists and their spokespersons, we find the embarrassment of the government in the eyes of the public to be a goal. Maria McGuire (1973), who was active in the Provisional IRA in its early years, summarizes the result of a series of bombings by claiming, "The terror we caused demonstrated that the British government could no longer govern" (p. 35). Her superior, Seán MacStiofain, chief of staff of the Provisional IRA from 1969 to 1973, gives another description of how to embarrass the British authorities. It was decided to attack post office vans in Northern Ireland and set them on fire. The aim was, in MacStiofain's (1975) words: "The British could not afford to let it be obvious to senders of mail from countries all over the world that they were unable to deliver it in areas where they were supposed to be in military control" (MacStiofain, p. 249). Since the British would be forced to escort mail vans, this would also offer more targets to the Provisionals, MacStiofain argued. This line of reasoning might seem a bit farfetched, but it demonstrates the clever ways in which actions and strategies are planned.

An example in which the emphasis is on the vulnerability of the authorities is provided by Bommi Baumann (1976), a representative of the West German urban guerrillas. He mentions this strategy in his memoirs as a method to win the workers for armed resistance. When, for example, workers labor under bad conditions in a factory, he says, "you must set their bosses' mansions on fire, show the people: resistance is possible, if you take the right man; the one in that function is a human being and therefore he is vulnerable . . . if you hit him in his private life" (p. 94).

Leila Khaled (1973) explains the goal of demonstrating vulnerability to the passengers of a hijacked plane: "We took you to Tel Aviv as an act of defiance and challenge to the Israelis and to demonstrate their impotence when the Arabs embark on an offensive rather than a defensive strategy." Elsewhere she writes: "As a comrade has said: We act heroically in a cowardly world to prove that the enemy is not invincible. . . . We act as revolutionaries to inspire the masses and to trigger off the revolutionary upheaval in an era of counter-revolution" (p. 142).

Nearly all terrorists emphasize the strength and invincible nature of their movements (McGuire, 1973, p. 100). Gerry Adams (1986), for instance, writes about the bombing of the Grand Hotel in Brighton during the Conservative Party Congress in 1984:

> The full effects of this IRA operation will not become apparent until some British Minister writes his or her memoirs. But the fact is that Oglaigh na h-Eireann [the name of the IRA in Gaelic] almost wiped out the British Cabinet and that fact awakened the government to the urgent need from their point of view to address themselves to the issues of Ireland and the IRA. (p. 105)

In February 1991, the Provisionals made a new attack on the British cabinet when a mortar shell nearly killed members of the war cabinet during a meeting at 10 Downing Street. Again this was meant as a demonstration of their power and strength.

The strength of the terrorists is, however, often exaggerated not by the opponent but by the terrorists' own constituency. Abu Ijad (1979) admits that this pursued effect might turn against the interest of the movement. The expectations of the constituency can rise too high. Following some propaganda successes in the Arab and Western media, he warned: "As a consequence of the Arab news—in some cases also foreign broadcast news—the size and extent of our operations got so exaggerated that the dangerous illusion arose that we were really capable of liberating Palestine" (p. 87).

### UTILIZATION OF REPRESSION BY THE GOVERNMENT

Repression by the authorities of the opposing forces is important to terrorists for several reasons. First of all, repression (actual or perceived) can make (future) terrorists decide to take up arms and join the active resistance. Second, there is hardly any other group that has to cope with repression as terrorists have to, because of the simple fact that authorities often go out of their way to neutralize resistance. Finally, through repression terrorists' opponents show their darkest side, which also becomes visible for the rest of the citizens. Therefore, a terrorist movement can, on the basis of the reaction of the people to the repression of the government, find out to what degree there is popular support for the movement. One positive effect of repression is that it can supply the movement with new volunteers.

In the documents reviewed here, I found references to positively experienced alienation of the people from the authorities. Repression then results in an increase in the ranks of the armed resistance. In some cases, the provocation of repression by terrorists is deliberate. In such cases the importance of publicity does not emanate directly from the terrorist violence, but from the spreading of news about widespread repression. Adams (1986), for example, explains the change that took place in the 1960s in the United Kingdom as a consequence of the introduction of television. Authorities could no longer act as they wished, he argues, because anyone could see their outrage:

> The RUC [Royal Ulster Constabulary] action on 5 October was not the first action of its kind by any means, but it was the first time that such brutality had been enacted in front of television cameras. . . . The killing of John Downes was different because it was seen by the media. The fact was that in the electronic age Unionism and later the British could not cover up all that was happening. (p. 25)

Adams describes this as profitable for the movement.

All of the memoirs consulted mention repression. In nearly every document, the possible positive effect of repression for the terrorists is recognized. McGuire (1973), for instance, comments on the policy of internment introduced by the British on August 9, 1981: "The British could have thought of no more effective way of helping to recruit members for the Republican movement if they had tried" (pp. 23, 27). Adams (1986), in turn, says, "Recruitment to Sinn Fein used to occur primarily in the wake of such events such as the 1969 pogroms, internment, Bloody Sunday and the hunger strikes" (p. 150).

### DEMORALIZATION OF THE OPPONENT AND RAISING OF THE MORALE OF THE TERRORIST GROUP AND ITS SUPPORTERS

Although this aspect is important for any group in any political struggle, for terrorists the effects that violent deeds have on different sides are crucial. A movement can address itself to both the lowering of the opponent's morale and the boosting of the self-confidence of its own constituency. Such effects can also be achieved with ancillary activities, other than terror. Publicity matters here as well: To have any effect on people other than those immediately involved, the event will have to be made public by the mass media. MacStiofain (1975), for instance, stresses the effect of terrorist attacks in Northern Ireland on the constituency of its opponent. He quoted a national poll taken by the *Daily Mail* in September, which indicated that 59% of the respondents wanted the British troops brought home from Ireland (Mac-Stiofain, p. 215). This example is an illustration of Tugwell's concept of a shift "from asset to liability."

McGuire (1973) offers an example of morale boosting with the Irish constituency: "Hitting the British army helped morale in the movement both in the Six and in the Twenty-six Counties, and there was always admiration for fine examples of marksmanship" (p. 35). Adams (1986) not only mentions this effect, but implies that the IRA pursued it by reacting to claims of the opponent: "When Prime Minister Faulkner said things like 'We have them [the IRA] on the run' and the IRA came back the next day with a devastating series of operations, the effect that had in lifting people's morale was enormous" (p. 54).

Ijad (1979) describes how his group deliberately tried to raise the morale of its supporters with its deeds, while also seeking other effects:

> Our operations in the occupied territories were most diverse. We mined streets, we laid ambushes, carried out attacks with bombs, grenades, antitank weapons and rockets. Our goals were modest: we wanted to raise the morale of the Arab masses, to drive the enemy into the corner, to force him always to be on his guard, and—in the best case—bring damage to the Israeli economy. (p. 87)

## GAINING OR ENLARGING SYMPATHY AMONG THE PEOPLE FOR THE MOVEMENT

The existence of a constituency, or at least a degree of public sympathy, is of great importance to terrorists. Apart from the pressure that public opinion can bring to bear upon the authorities, it can provide the movement with a feeling of legitimacy.

Public opinion is composed of several segments, such as more or less militant adherents of the terrorists, followers of the opponent, and "world opinion," which, in turn, can be divided into peoples, international media, and foreign governments.

In the documents studied, there are several indications of the importance of public sympathy to terrorists. Seán MacStiofain (1975) very often, and not without pride, mentions in his memoirs examples of massive support among the Irish, as for instance at the annual commemoration at the grave

of Wolfe Tone, the father of Irish nationalism. Commenting on the Bodens-
town commemoration in June, which was attended by at least 14,000 people
(9,000 more than the year before), he said: "After that huge turnout, nobody
could mistake how the movement was growing, North and South" (Mac-
Stiofain, p. 172).

The president of Sinn Fein, Gerry Adams (1986), emphasizes the impor-
tance of public opinion when referring to the hunger-striking IRA member
Bobby Sands, who succeeded in winning a seat in the national Parliament of
Westminster:

> His victory exposed the lie that the hunger-strikers—and by extension the IRA
> and the whole republican movement—had no public support. . . . It had a
> particular impact to British MPs simply because of the status that the parlia-
> ment at Westminster enjoys: a man had been elected on a massive popular vote
> who was, according to their views, a terrorist and a criminal who was offering
> the people nothing. (pp. 80, 156)

Abu Ijad (1979) calls attention to the growth of the movement, and notes
with satisfaction: "In thousands, nay in tens of thousands, the young and also
the old wanted to join Fatah. . . . The movement of the Fedajin went through
a boom never experienced before. And because our commandos in the
occupied territories possessed the active sympathy of the people there, they
could extend and intensify their actions" (p. 93).

Another testimony to the importance of public sympathy is the frequently
heard remark that the support of the movement grows when many terrorist
deeds are carried out, and, vice versa, that support decreases when little or
nothing is done. This reasoning can be found in one form or another in
practically all of the memoirs studied. This comes as no surprise, however,
since it forms the basis of the existence for insurgent terrorists.

MacStiofain (1975) reiterates again and again: "While they [the British]
kept up their repression in any area, they had to be hit, because if they weren't,
the IRA would start to lose the tremendous support it had built up in the
communities" (p. 165; see also pp. 289, 219). Leila Khaled (1973) makes
the same point when she speaks of the effects of the struggle against the
forces of King Hussein of Jordan in 1970: "The masses were not de-
ceived. They knew who the enemy was and applauded our actions when
we valiantly defended our fortresses in the camps with courage and without compromise on the negotiation table. The Front and its deeds became
synonymous" (p. 174).

Ijad (1979) demonstrates the way this urge to act is felt among the movement and its supporters: "In our view now was the moment to enter armed struggle. The masses of the Palestinian people . . . were easily impressed by our will to act and our firmness. Only by the experience of armed struggle, we argued, could Fatah become a massive movement" (p. 71). Adams (1986) wants his readers to believe that not the IRA itself but its constituency calls for violence: "The IRA eased back on operations during the hunger-strike. But by the time a number of hunger-strikers had died there was a considerable popular demand for the IRA to take punitive action" (p. 86).

Nevertheless, some authors are aware of the negative effect terrorist deeds can have on public sympathy. In McGuire's book and, to a lesser extent, in MacStiofain's and Klein's, we find warnings that especially the killing or wounding of what the public perceives as innocent people may lower support. McGuire (1973), who in the summer of 1972 quit the IRA for that very reason, warned: "There was a clear risk, as I reported to Dave [O'Connell], that these killings were proving counterproductive" (McGuire, p. 100). Seán MacStiofain (1975) claimed: "No resistance movement in history has ever succeeded in fighting a struggle for national freedom without some accidental casualties, but the Republican interest in retaining popular support clearly lay in causing as few as possible." (MacStiofain, p. 214).

The concern with reactions of different segments of the public and target groups is, strangely enough, not very prominent in the memoirs. MacStiofain and McGuire show some concern for world opinion at large. They also take into account the feelings of the conservative Irish Roman Catholic population. McGuire (1973, p. 71), for example, recalls that a decision was made not to import condoms (which are forbidden in Ireland), despite their suitability for the ignition of bombs. It was feared that their discovery would be a severe blow for the movement. Hans-Joachim Klein (1979) explains that the action at the OPEC meeting in 1975, in which he participated, was specifically aimed at the Arab countries because of the Palestinian problem (pp. 52-53).

An important question is whether or not terrorists handle the gaining of public sympathy very rationally and purposefully. Some light has already been shed on this through the preceding quotations. It also emerges in a quote from McGuire's (1973) book. She explains the reaction of Dave O'Connell, one of the most important members of the movement at the time, to her warning of the risk of loosing support through violent actions by the Provisionals: "He took my news seriously, for it had always been crucial to our operations that we should retain the support of the local Catholic population" (p. 99; see also p. 71).

MacStiofain (1975) also makes many remarks that indicate a purposeful attitude toward the gaining of sympathy. As an illustration, he mentions the eventual peace proposals of the English prime minister, Edward Heath: "With all the talk of civil war and chaos as the psychological back-up to create a climate of acceptance for Heath's coming proposals, the Republican movement decided to counter with a strong public gesture" (MacStiofain, p. 238). The IRA therefore called for a unilateral truce lasting 72 hours in order to demonstrate its internal control and discipline.

### RADICALIZING THE PEOPLE OR POLARIZING THE POLITICAL SITUATION TO CREATE CHAOS AND FEAR

A situation with many uncertainties and anxieties can be favorable for the strategic aims of terrorists. In addition to demonstrating that the authorities are not fully in control, a chaotic situation can serve to exacerbate a social or ethnic conflict, to polarize different groups, and to pull certain political militants across the threshold of using violence. The psychological aspect in this category is obvious, the terrorists' interest in publicity derives from it.

Most of the terrorist authors examined here, however, have written hardly anything detailed about the purposeful incitement of unrest. MacStiofain and McGuire are relatively explicit: "The intention behind the bombing campaign was to cause confusion and terror," McGuire (1973, p. 34) writes. MacStiofain (1975) notes dryly: "During May alone the British logged 1,223 engagements and shooting incidents, and ninety-four explosions. The sabotage offensive continued to disrupt the day-to-day working of direct rule" (p. 253; see also pp. 42-43).

In the accounts of West German terrorists Hans-Joachim Klein and, especially, Bommi Baumann, the arousal of radicalization is clearly recognizable as a goal. Baumann (1976) writes:

> When negotiations about amnesty were going on, we discussed whether we should try to extort with bombs the amnesty for all leftist people or whether we should try to prevent it with bombs, so that they could say: We won't offer an amnesty to these lunatics. That would have had an advantage for us, that in West Germany about two or three thousand students would have to choose between: illegality or prison, which meant at that time: Will we go on fighting or are we going to give up? (p. 19; see also pp. 40, 53, 55, 60)

Klein (1979, p. 198) even mentions the death of a hunger striker as part of a preconceived plan to radicalize groups of people into violent action.

Klein and McGuire are the only ones in whose memoirs references to polarization in a strategic sense can be found. McGuire (1973) describes, for instance, MacStiofain's reaction to a statement by Sinn Fein's president Ruairi O Bradaigh: "How dare Ruairi take such a soft line, MacStiofain demanded; it was absolutely necessary for the movement to maintain a hard position" (p. 104; see also p. 33).

Klein (1979) is very clear about the question of the purpose of the action in Vienna in 1975, during which all OPEC ministers were taken hostage: "The contradictions in the Arab world had to be sharpened, the Palestinian resistance strengthened" (p. 261). Adams (1986) too mentions this aspect when he recalls the function of the civil rights movement (NICRA) in the 1960s, namely, to bring the contradictions in society to the surface (p. 14).

Since relatively little can be found in the memoirs that deals with the creation of radicalization, chaos, and polarization, one might expect that more could be found about the *use* of these situations. However, only in Leila Khaled's (1973) book do we find a trace of this: "Everyone knew we were deadly serious revolutionaries, not 'revolutionaries' seeking a 'peaceful solution' by diplomatic means and using the fighting as a side show to demonstrate that we could cause trouble" (p. 174).

## STRESSING HEROISM OR THE NECESSARY USE OF VIOLENCE

Terrorism implies the use of violence. In itself, violence is not a (psychological) strategy. But the attitude toward this violence is important: What role do terrorists assign to it? Do terrorists consider the violence they use an ugly but necessary instrument, unfortunately the only way they have of changing the status quo? Or do they consider and present violence as a noble thing, full of beauty and heroism? Or is violence an aim in itself? Do personal motives for the use of violence play a role? If terrorists describe terrorist violence as heroic, this not only tells us something about the attitude of the participants, it can also serve the strategy, for example, to recruit people for the armed struggle or to attain understanding or support among the population. Violence has a central position in terrorism. How do the perpetrators talk about it in their life stories?

All the authors express themselves in such a way that the necessity of terrorist violence is stressed. Sometimes they refer to a (perceived) absence of any alternative. In the perceptions of the Irish authors, violence is legitimated by the simple fact that it is the only thing the British are sensitive to. McGuire (1973) states: "History showed that British control had never been overthrown against its will other than by the use of force. . . . I was prepared to agree with the selective use of force in order to achieve a better system of government" (p. 16). And Adams (1986) notes dryly: "Violence in Ireland has its roots in the conquest of Ireland by Britain" (p. 62). Elsewhere, he stresses that armed struggle is a necessary evil: "In the 6 counties armed struggle is a terrible but necessary form of resistance which is engaged in as a means towards an independent Ireland" (p. 65). And: "They know that . . . dealing with the IRA they are dealing with determined political opponents who are using the only means at their disposal to bring home this message in terms that will be understood and taken seriously enough to result in action and movement" (pp. 66, 68).

West German activists Baumann and Klein offer a similar line of argument. Baumann (1976) says: "Yet on the other side there was the consideration that a revolution without violence is impossible, for a revolution always implies the birth of a new society" (p. 43; see also p. 23). And Klein (1979) states: "The arrangement of this world . . . is based on violence. And the powerful of this earth . . . will never change the existing societal order voluntarily. . . . And then comrades started to put their counterviolence against the state's monopoly of violence. Well, they had my blessing for it" (p. 154; see also pp. 122, 153, 155).

In the minds of many terrorists, violent "resistance" is also something noble, heroic. McGuire (1973) states:

> I agreed with the shooting of British soldiers and believed that the more who were killed, the better. I remember occasions when we heard late at night that a British soldier had been shot and seriously wounded in Belfast or Derry and we would hope that by the morning he would be dead. I accepted too the bombing of Belfast, and when civilians were accidentally blown to pieces, dismissed this as one of the unfortunate hazards of urban guerrilla war. (p. 9; see also pp. 18, 31)

Leila Khaled (1973) is the only author discussed here who speaks plainly and with great pride about the heroic struggle she and her comrades are engaged in: "As a Palestinian, I had to believe in the gun as an embodiment of my humanity, and my determination to liberate myself and my fellowmen. Every self-respecting Palestinian had to become a revolutionary" (p. 87). And about her weapons: "My Russian-made gun, the Seminof, became my companion!" And also, "Blessed be the arms that carry out deeds and the revolutionary brains that conceive the deeds and plan them. We shall be victorious" (pp. 118, 148). Finally she describes the honor that the same violence could bring her and her fellows in the hijacking of a plane: "Our rendezvous with history was approaching: all plans had to be translated into action; history was ours to write; Patrick Arguello was to write it in blood, I was not so honored" (p. 183).

All of the authors examined here share the inclination to present violence as a necessary, or even the only, way to change an abhorrent situation. Some of them emphasize the positive and heroic sides of violent resistance. Most striking is the fact that Seán MacStiofain, very well represented in all the other categories, scores lowest in this category. This comes as a surprise because McGuire and others depict him as a ruthless, fanatical hard-liner, hungry for violence. The omission can therefore not be interpreted as an absence in this case.

With regard to the other authors, it is striking that while there is much in their memoirs about their attitudes toward the violence used, they say hardly anything about the role this violence should play in terrorist strategy. Probably they take this for granted.

## Publicity Tactics

As we have seen, psychological aims play an important part in terrorist strategy, and publicity is a condition for realizing these goals. Yet the interesting question concerns how this publicity is achieved. In the following pages the concrete ways in which terrorists approach publicity will be discussed.

In the list of seven categories of publicity tactics, a distinction can be recognized between tactics aimed at catching public attention and tactics that are meant predominantly to explain the message of the terrorist group to the public at large or a smaller subgroup. Again, this is an analytical distinction; in reality, tactics overlap and serve one another.

### COMMITTING VIOLENT DEEDS BECAUSE OF THEIR NEWS VALUE

In fact, the perpetration of terrorist deeds for their news value implies that terrorists have to commit only deeds in which the media are interested. The publication of such deeds would subsequently be left to others. Many contemporary authors start from the idea that terrorists apply this tactic in a very conscious, rational way. Bell (1978), for instance, writes: "These new transnational gunmen are, in fact, constructing a package so spectacular, so violent, so compelling, that the networks, acting as executives, supplying the cameramen and the audience, cannot refuse the offer" (p. 50).

Yet there are at least three ways terrorists can enhance their actions' news value. One obvious way is the degree of violence applied and, derived from this, the number or the status of the victims. The more people are killed in a bomb attack, or passengers caught in a hijacked plane, the stronger the attention of the media and the interest of the public. The special vulnerability of a category of victims (for example, the children in a primary school in Bovensmilde, taken hostage by South Moluccan terrorists) or their fame (for instance, Lord Louis Mountbatten, a war hero and relative of the royal family, killed by Irish terrorists in 1980) can increase the news value of an act (Schmid et al., 1982, p. 79).

In their memoirs, however, terrorists hardly ever mention such techniques of raising news value. Nowhere in the documents examined was it stated that the decision to undertake an act of violence was made for this particular reason. Nor do the authors of these works generally discuss victimization in these terms. Only Klein gives an example of a possible selection on the mere basis of celebrity status. At a deliberation of the Revolutionary Cells about possible actions, Klein (1979) proposed "to kidnap the princess of Monaco, because in those days in the German magazines a lot was written about Caroline, that only needed to be verified" (p. 212).

A second way to make deeds attractive to media and public is based on the use of symbolism. If actions are carried out at a time or place with a special meaning for the movement or the attacked country, they will attract extra attention. National holidays as times for victimization or the offices of foreign airline companies as locations have always been very popular with terrorists for this reason. Bommi Baumann (1976) gives a very obvious example of symbolic timing, namely, the choice of the anniversary of a Nazi pogrom that took place in 1938: "It was a prize for the press, because of all people, it had to be Germans again, who planted a bomb in a Jewish Synagogue in the Kristallnacht" (p. 64). Klein (1979) mentions a planned act of hostage taking in an embassy on the national holiday of that specific country that was meant to have a similar effect.

A third way to increase news value lies in the performance of very spectacular or special deeds likely to appeal to the media. To give one example: In 1970, the PFLP (Popular Front for the Liberation of Palestine) managed to hijack not just one but three airplanes simultaneously. They were brought together on a desert airfield in Jordan, where they were blown up before a rolling camera (Schmid & De Graaf, 1983, p. 29).

Terrorist spectaculars need not always be violent. MacStiofain and McGuire mention several spectacular escapes from prisons and internment camps that also won favorable publicity. McGuire (1973) writes: "Two days later came the most dramatic escape of all from the Six Counties, fully worthy of any British POW [prisoner of war] film. . . . The Maidstone escape, once again, was a superb propaganda coup for us, appealing directly to all that was most romantic and adventurous in the Irish Republican tradition" (p. 37).

An indication that the attention of the press is important to the goals of a terrorist movement can also be found in many proud statements in the memoirs that the attention of the whole world was gained by a particular event. Adams (1986) explains the rationale behind this: "The tactic of armed struggle is of primary importance because it provides a vital cutting-edge. Without it the issue of Ireland would never even be an issue. So, in effect the armed struggle becomes armed propaganda" (p. 64).

The strategic importance of publicity can also be deduced from the following line of reasoning: Though a particular action may have failed militarily—for example, the selected victim was not killed in the attack—it can be called successful because of the publicity it attracted. McGuire (1973) refers, in the same vein, to a cargo of Czech arms intercepted at Schiphol Airport in the Netherlands in 1971: "A spectacular operation which put the Provisional IRA on the front pages of the world's newspapers—even though the operation ultimately failed" (p. 37; see also pp. 25, 58, 62). MacStiofain (1975) hates to talk about failures, but from his account of the British military occupation of the Republican-controlled areas in Belfast and Londonderry, the same appreciation can be found: "The no-go areas were a bluff. . . . The whole world had heard about the Bogside and the other no-go areas. From a political and publicity point of view they had been of tremendous value" (pp. 297, 307). Apparently the terrorists know not only success or failure; there is also a third outcome of action: the "glorious failure" in which the propaganda success compensates for the actual failure.

Several authors offer their insights into the ways the news is spread or how news value is exploited. McGuire (1973) gives us a view of the way the movement learned how to make use of publicity when an important and well-known member of the IRA, Joe Cahill, was taken into custody for some time at the customs office in the United States: "Even so, the publicity the case attracted helped the movement. . . . Until then, the Provisionals had tended to operate more by stealth; now they saw the use that could be made of personal publicity" (p. 36; see also pp. 79, 102). Later, when she talks of a near confrontation between British and Republican units, she already dreams about the possible headlines: "Not that such a confrontation would be against our interest—it would attract press and television coverage and would also crystallize the issues facing us: Armed Troops Repel Demonstrators at Republican Prison Camp, and so on" (p. 139).

The best examples of sophisticated media use can be found with the Provisional IRA. For instance, McGuire (1973) refers to British government reports published at the time of presumed violations of human rights by the British authorities in Northern Ireland, following the internment measure of 1971:

> In the wake of this report, we knew that a press conference with the seven men who escaped would be powerful propaganda, and so we arranged it for the next Wednesday, 25 November. . . . Although the six who did turn up were nervous at the television cameras, the conference was effective and well-covered. (p. 79)

Seán MacStiofain also gives several striking examples. He stressed that the prisons were another revolutionary front. By nominating prisoners as candidates for public office, they could be kept in the public eye. At a certain moment two Irish militants, imprisoned in Belfast, gained a seat in the Westminister parliament. According to MacStiofain, this was "an embarrassment for the British" (MacStiofain, p. 73).

Hunger strikes were, because of the empathy generated by self-victimization, attractive for the Provisionals. In Gerry Adams's (1986) words: "We were all aware that a hunger strike such as was proposed would demand exclusive attention, would, in fact, hijack the struggle" (pp. 79-80). The slow but potentially irreversible nature of hunger strikes could hardly be refused as a news item. As MacStiofain (1975) states: "That stretches out the period of the hunger-strike until even the establishment media have to report the number of days you have been on it. If they don't the regime has even more problems with rumours" (p. 91; see also p. 171).

In Germany, Baumann (1976) was also willing to admit the lust for media attention characteristic of his and other West German groups. However, in retrospect he judged this to be a big mistake:

> We took a great interest in the press. We always immediately looked how the newspapers, especially in Berlin, reacted to our actions, and how they explained them, and thereupon we defined our strategy. But this is wrong. For the way the bourgeoisie behaves to revolutionary actions is obvious, you

shouldn't tune your own actions to it. . . . Then already, too much importance
was attached to the media. (p. 94)

About the RAF, Baumann says: "The RAF has said, this revolution will not
be built up by political work, but through headlines, through its appearances
in the press, which reports again and again that guerrillas are fighting here
in Germany" (p. 129, German edition). Looking back, Baumann was critical
about the media focus of the German revolutionaries. Indirectly this was,
however, a testimony to the centrality of the media in the terrorists' tactical
arsenal.

### SUPPORTING RECRUITMENT AND PROPAGANDA

In his memoirs, Bommi Baumann (1976) refers to the role of propaganda
and recruitment for the armed struggle: "On one side pamphlets, demonstrations, stickers, local work, so as to build up Red Help and address the
problems in youth centers as well. And on the other side a secret cell, that
wouldn't reach the surface, and from which the cadre would undertake
hit-and-run actions and thereby support the massive actions" (p. 94). Various
statements from terrorists indicate that they exploit the media attention
created by a violent incident. Khaled (1973) mentions meetings, speeches,
posters, pamphlets, radio broadcasts, and political literature as vehicles for
public attention. After her first plane hijacking, she traveled through the
Persian Gulf and Iraq: "The purpose of the tour was to spread revolutionary
propaganda as well as to collect funds for the Front. It was a tremendous
success. We not only reached and communicated with the Arab masses, but
we learned a good deal of their concerns" (pp. 50-60; see also p. 168).

The role of propaganda is highlighted by the fact that an organization such
as Sinn Fein has a director of publicity. MacStiofain (1975) mentions the
Irish Republican Publicity Bureau and the newspapers *An Phoblacht* and
*Republican News* as outlets for propaganda (pp. 91, 171). Adams (1986)
refers to the work of a separate department called Republican Publications:
"Educational pamphlets, a number of small books, collections of poetry,
policy documents, posters, an annual calendar and a republican diary are but
some of the items produced and distributed by a small group of voluntary
workers" (p. 163).

Smaller terrorist organizations do not have specific propaganda sections.
Neither Baumann nor Klein mentions a section that takes care of the activities
of recruitment and propaganda. From their memoirs it appears that these
tasks were carried out by those members of the radical left movement that

were not yet militarized and had not gone underground. In particular, the Red Help groups, originally coming into existence on behalf of imprisoned members of the movement, were used as a pool for recruitment.

### CHOOSING OPTIMAL TIME AND PLACE FOR ACTION

Terrorists' choices of times and places for their actions are closely linked to the goal of achieving maximum psychological advantage. These choices constitute one of the most purposefully planned elements of terrorist strategy. Let us first take a look at the choice of place for terrorist deeds.

Terrorist groups tend to make use of concentrations of the press. Bomb attacks in cities can produce more publicity than can attacks in the countryside. One of the leaders of the Algerian FLN, Abane Ramdane, asked the rhetorical question: "Is it better for our cause to kill ten of the enemy in the countryside of Telergma, where no one will speak of it, or one in Algiers, that will be mentioned the next day in the American press?" The presence of foreign press correspondents determined in this case at least in part the place of the struggle. Relatively small-scale violence witnessed by many people can have more impact than large-scale violence that is seen by only a few (Clutterbuck, 1981, p. 136; Schmid & De Graaf, 1983, pp. 9, 19).

Another explication of the same principle is to plan attacks to take place when and where media are already gathered for a spectacular event. In this way, terrorists do not have to create all the news themselves; they can make use of already-existing "media events." The best-known example of this is the hostage taking of the Israeli team by Palestinian terrorists during the 1972 Olympic Games in Munich. Abu Ijad (1979) describes the strategic goals: "Firstly, the existence of the Palestinian people would be underlined; secondly, the international press, that was present in great numbers in Munich, would be used to give our cause worldwide attention, either positively or negatively" (p. 156; see also Schmid & De Graaf, 1983, pp. 30-31).

Another way to attract attention by a specific choice of place was revealed by one of the most influential spokesmen of Sinn Fein, Dave Morrison. In a television interview triggered by the IRA attacks on British soldiers in Limburg in May 1988, Morrison identified the anticipated effect as a causal factor. To the reporter's question about why the IRA commits terrorist acts outside the United Kingdom, Morrison answered: "Exactly the reason you are here, and why many reporters now come here" (reported in AVRO's *Televizier Magazine*, June 2, 1988). The out-of-area attacks attracted the attention of foreign journalists, forcing them to discover and describe the problem of Northern Ireland.

Just as some locations lend themselves better than others to terrorist acts, timing is also an important consideration. Terrorists can, for instance, react to the peak hours of the media. Clutterbuck (1981, p. 92) gives examples of how the IRA has had bombs go off at such a moment that they would get maximum publicity on the big 6:00 p.m. news show. With careful timing for the bombings, the IRA has the opportunity to release a prepared statement that will get on the air at 6:00, while British police and army cannot meet the deadline.

Schmid and De Graaf (1983, p. 51) mention that the Red Brigades in Italy preferred to stage their actions on Wednesdays and Saturdays, aware of the fact that Italian newspapers are larger and have a wider circulation on Thursdays and Sundays. Moreover, by releasing their statements just before the papers' deadlines, the Red Brigades gave the editors little time to change or select their messages.

McGuire (1973) also indicates the deliberate way time was used to the IRA's advantage: "The reason why MacStiofain was so anxious there should be no delay became clear; on a pre-arranged schedule our statement was to be issued at 2 p.m. I went round to the Kevin Street Office and phoned it over to the Press Association, the three broadcasting stations RTE, BBC, and UTV . . . and the Dublin newspapers." And after a reaction from the British had arrived, "MacStiofain had his statement responding to Whitelaw's reply all ready, and I hurried back to Kevin Street to phone it through" (p. 130).

Another reason to perform a certain deed at a certain time lies in the desire to react to political events, actions, or statements by other parties to the conflict. Khaled (1973) relates how she explained to the passengers of a hijacked plane that the reason for the hijacking was a speech by the American president, Richard Nixon, in which he pleaded for the regional military superiority of Israel. Elsewhere she gives an example of consciously planned timing in order to make a powerful impression. The hijackers of three different airplanes would release a statement at the same time: "The hijack proclamations were supposed to have been simultaneously announced at twelve-thirty" (p. 127; see also p. 187).

The Irish provide several other examples of time-linked statements issued by the IRA. Adams (1986, p. 28) notes that Sinn Fein published in 1986 many comparisons between Northern Ireland and South Africa, between the IRA and the ANC, because at that time the well-covered violence in South Africa was a political issue from which the Republicans wished to profit.

Yet another reason to act at a particular time is to deflect the attention of press and public from things unfavorable to the movement. McGuire (1973) relates how the new commander of the British troops in Ulster was "welcomed" by the IRA. He was to give his first press conference on December 20, 1971: "And so, on 19 December, we held our own press conference in Dublin, in which we said that our organization had not been seriously affected by Internment, our supplies of arms and ammunition were still intact and that the British Army was powerless to prevent our operations." General Sir Harry Tuzo felt obliged to react to this challenge by his opponents and said in his own press conference that the British Army was about to defeat the IRA. McGuire goes on: "His statements did not get the coverage he must have hoped for. We drove him off the front pages of the *Belfast Evening Telegraph* with a dozen bomb explosions in Belfast, demonstrating very clearly just who was winning in the Six Counties" (p. 80; see also pp. 30, 24, 127).

### TACTICAL USE OF ISSUED STATEMENTS

A terrorist act invariably calls for an explanation. To provide meaning to otherwise often inexplicable violence, statements or communiqués are issued. These enable the terrorists to present their own well-considered stories, without the intervention of interviewers. Since the public may interpret the symbolic meaning of a deed incorrectly, a statement by the terrorists is often mandatory.

The importance of self-issued statements is therefore considerable: It is the obvious way to acquaint people with the ideas of the terrorist group, and with the justification of the action. McGuire (1973, pp. 3, 33-35, 91, 109), MacStiofain (1975, pp. 2, 152, 166, 210, 239, 296, 332), Baumann (1976, pp. 25, 67, 88), Klein (1979, pp. 199, 210), and Ijad (1979, pp. 51, 88) frequently refer to the use of such proclamations.

Terrorists, by the way, do not issue statements only *after* attacks. Some communiqués are explicitly meant as warnings. MacStiofain (1975), for example, when presenting the Provisional IRA's "peace proposals," concluded with a kind of ultimatum, saying that a rejection of the proposals would lead to an intensification of the campaign (p. 152).

McGuire and MacStiofain provide many illustrations of statements that are produced for reasons other than the explanation of their own violent deeds. They refer to attacks by other groups, to statements by politicians, to their own goals or peace proposals, to the prisoners of the movement, to economic policy, to the propaganda of the government, to hunger strikes, and so on. Such statements on subjects other than the immediate violence or terror seem to indicate that the IRA attaches a great deal of importance to publicity as a part of its struggle and goals (e.g., see MacStiofain, 1975, pp. 171, 172, 174, 239, 267, 278, 289, 300, 323, 332, 355, 363; McGuire, 1973, pp. 29, 82, 100, 104, 111, 136, 140, 159).

Statements may be issued in a number of ways. A statement or communiqué may be printed and spread by the movement itself or its adherents. They can do this by posting proclamations in the city, giving speeches at funerals and other gatherings, organizing press conferences, reading out statements in court, handing out pamphlets at pop music concerts, printing communiqués in their own or sympathizing weeklies, or broadcasting on illegal radio stations (Schmid & De Graaf, 1983, p. 29).

A second way to issue statements is by offering the press a prepared communiqué and having the media print or broadcast it. In these cases, statements are often prepared in such a way that the press can reproduce them at full length.

A third way to issue statements is to demand the publication or broadcast of a communiqué under the threat of violence (e.g., killing hostages, the explosion of a bomb). In cases of kidnapping or acts of hostage taking, such demands are often made. The South Moluccan train hijackers in 1975 and 1977 demanded not only the publication of their statements in newspapers and weeklies, but broadcast airtime for their leaders in the Netherlands and a statement by the Dutch government on television (Schmid et al., 1982, pp. 73, 80; see also Schmid & De Graaf, 1983, p. 23; Wilkinson, 1978).

Hans-Joachim Klein took part in the taking of hostages at the OPEC meeting in Vienna in 1975. He quotes the explanation of "Carlos" while preparing the action:

> Phase one, secondary for the commando: The capture of all the OPEC ministers and every other person with them. The demand to have a statement read out on radio at prescheduled times. . . . Then the release of the oil ministers, one after the other in his own country, but only when this particular country published a pro-Palestinian statement in writing, in sound and vision beforehand. That's all that will be required. If this condition is not met, immediate departure and death of the minister. (Klein, 1979, p. 57; my translation; see also p. 282)

Klein later gave a rationale for such coerced statements: "One produces that damned propaganda because they know or presume that some comrades will believe that shit, spread it and have themselves recruited some day" (p. 51; my translation).

A fifth way for terrorists to reach the mass media is by keeping in contact with journalists and granting interviews to representatives of the print or broadcast press. Interviews are attractive for terrorists because they decrease the distance to the public and often provide them the opportunity to make unedited political statements. This is especially true of live interviews. According to Clutterbuck (1981, pp. 92, 109), this is the most productive kind of publicity (see also Schmid et al., 1982, p. 71). Between 1971 and 1979 at least six interviews with IRA members were broadcast by the BBC, which produced great friction between the broadcasters and the Westminster government and led to discussions in British Parliament. Subsequently such interviews were forbidden.

Journalists and editors are the gatekeepers to mass audiences. Depending on the nature of the contacts with (sympathizing) journalists, terrorists will be able to count, to a larger or smaller degree, on the publication of their ideas. As Adams (1986) puts it: "The media demand special attention because of their importance in influencing their audiences' opinion and values" (p. 147).

In both McGuire's and MacStiofain's memoirs, many references to interviews with journalists can be found. When Maria McGuire joined the IRA, she immediately became an object of an interview: "Quite soon afterwards Seán [Brady] sent along a reporter from the London Observer, Colin Smith, to interview me as an example of the new type of middle class members the movement was attracting" (p. 19; see also pp. 69, 74, 85, 104, 115, 138, 140, 144, 150, 151). Contacts with British and foreign governments could, at times, bring badly needed benefits of a different sort. When McGuire and her colleague Dave O'Connell were on the run from the authorities in France after an arms deal had gone wrong, they called on a friendly correspondent of the *Irish Times* in Paris, who gave them shelter.

A less questionable use of the media is when terrorists simply call a press conference. The memoirs studied here contain numerous references to news conferences. For example, McGuire (1973) says, "It took me all of Tuesday and much of Wednesday to telephone all the newspapers we wanted to invite to the press conference, to insure that all our nominated representatives would be there" (p. 133; see also pp. 23, 70, 126). MacStiofain (1975), after having announced a press conference at short notice, says: "When we walked into the hall there were around thirty pressmen and three or four television crews waiting, which was about the attendance we could expect on that notice" (pp. 262, 361). For the Palestinians the press conference is also a well-known instrument. Immediately after her release following her second hijacking, Leila Khaled gave a press conference in Beirut, and many interviews with journalists followed afterward.

Sometimes terrorists go further than just inviting journalists to press conferences. Khaled (1973) writes, for example: "The Al-Hadat photographer, who was parachuted by the Front to film our landing and the explosion, was so excited he forgot to remove the lens cap from his camera" (p. 141). Baumann (1976) recalls how his group made an arrangement for the presence of a journalist at a meeting: "We had sold the rights previously to a reporter from Quick, the exclusive rights for the pictures" (p. 75).

## CLAIMING RESPONSIBILITY FOR TERRORIST ACTIONS

Perhaps the most direct way to catch the attention of the media is by means of claiming responsibility. After a bomb explosion or another terrorist incident, by phone or in writing, the terrorist group makes it known to the world who was responsible. In most cases newspaper offices, radio and television broadcasting stations, or news agencies are chosen for transmitting such announcements.

Maria McGuire (1973) makes several interesting remarks about the attitude of terrorists toward such announcements. Referring to a huge bomb blast in Belfast, which cost the lives of 6 people and injured another 146, she says:

> I believed at the time, and still do, that the Provisionals did not cause the casualties intentionally. . . . Even so, despite blaming the security forces, the movement "accepted responsibility" for the explosion and it was a curious thing that the Provisionals felt that by doing so they somehow atoned for the casualties, as if they had gone to Confession and asked forgiveness. I admit that at the time I did not connect with the people who were killed or injured in such explosions. I always judged such deaths in terms of the effect they would have on our support and I felt that this in turn depended on how many people accepted our explanation. (p. 103)

Elsewhere in her book she tells of a bomb that exploded in a luggage depository inside a police station. It later emerged that the bomb had probably been brought there by a policeman who had discovered it elsewhere. The claiming of responsibility for the bombing allowed the IRA to obtain credit for smuggling a bomb into a police station. Later she would admit: "Maybe it was one of the rare occasions when our claim of responsibility was based more on hope than on fact" (p. 123; see also pp. 34, 91).

MacStiofain (1975) makes few claims of responsibility. In those cases where he does, and where civilians were killed, he always stresses that in the claim it was very clearly stated that there had been ample warnings beforehand. The casualties were in fact caused by the British or Northern Irish authorities, he implies, since they transmitted the warnings too late or not at all. MacStiofain also relates that he personally phoned newspapers when the IRA was accused of a bomb attack it did not commit (p. 171).

More common than rejection of responsibility are multiple claims of responsibility. Baumann (1976) is most clear about this way of making use of publicity and the effect it has:

> At that time, there were about ten or twelve attempts on judges, public prosecutors, prison officials and all sort of people. Each time, a pamphlet joined the attempt, and it was delivered at the Deutsche Presse Agentur, each time signed with a different name. So, from one day to another, there were twenty groups. That had to give the impression that a huge people's army had risen, which was now striking. It had to confuse the police and show the people that there were a great many of us. But of course it was the same group of about ten people all the time. (p. 67; see also p. 61)

### BRINGING POWERFUL SYMBOLS INTO PLAY

Symbols are used to bring home a certain message. The choice of a particular person as a target of attack can tell a great deal about the aims of a movement, as can the name a terrorist group chooses for itself.

Symbolic meaning can relate to various things: The deed can carry symbolism in itself, or the place, time, or date can have a certain meaning. In addition, the way a deed is carried out can be symbolic; for instance, the choice of a particular number of victims can be meaningful. Furthermore, the meaning of the target or the victim can be explained in different ways. Does the movement consider the action revenge or punishment (that should also warn others, who share the same characteristics)? Does the group regard the target in military terms—in other words, as a link that must be hit in the chain to the final victory? Or is the value of the victim or target symbolic, conveying a primarily political message? In reality these three motivations for target selection are often intertwined.

MacStiofain (1975) recalls how IRA fighters are buried with military honors: tricolor on the coffin, guard of honor, and salutes over the grave.

Adams (1986) also mentions the carrying of the "tricolor" in demonstrations in Ulster, "as a symbol of Irish nationalism, despite the ban." McGuire (1973) mentions several important gatherings that were held in Dublin in front of the General Post Office, "one of the most renowned locations of Irish Republican mythology," because it was on that particular spot where the 1916 rising started on Easter Monday, on which day speeches still are organized throughout the country every year (see pp. 23, 45, 88, 105, 107, 126).

Baumann (1976) explains why the media are so important for the success of the meaning of actions:

> At that time, we were already very much on that media trip. . . . It was always great when those actions were planned. You could have a good laugh. They were really well put together, so that the symbolism would appear. And when all went well, you had great fun. We would go home and watch it all on the telly. That was great. (pp. 55, 23; my translation; see also p. 25)

The choice of a name of a terrorist movement also has a symbolic meaning. As Baumann (1976) puts it:

> We chose that name to distinguish us from the RAF. . . . Also "2. Juni," because the press had to mention in each news item "the 2nd of June, the day the student Benno Ohnesorg was killed by the cop Kurras." They have to mention it in every article in the papers, even now. With that name, we could demonstrate: You were the first to shoot at us. When we fight back, it's your own fault. That was the symbolism of that name. (p. 93; my translation)

In the same vein, MacStiofain (1975) remarks: "The term 'Provisional' caught the public's attention immediately. It rang a bell in the memory of the Irish people. The men of 1916 had signed the Proclamation as the Provisional Government of the Irish Republic" (p. 142).

Symbolism is not only expressed in self-labeling, it is also very important in the choices of targets or victims. Generally speaking, there are three kinds of targeting: individualized targeting, "military" counterforce targeting, and symbolic targeting. The first category refers to victims that are hit for revenge or as punishment for their deeds. In these cases the attacks are meant to be lethal. By assassinating one particular person, the terrorist, however, usually also wants to intimidate others. Individualized assassinations of opponents, then, are meant as revenge and retribution. Klein (1979), for instance, explains an RAF attack in the summer of 1972 in these terms: "The bomb attacks in Augsburg and Munich against cop quarters were explained as actions of revenge for RAF members Petra Schelm and Tommy Weisbecker, who had been shot" (p. 166; my translation).

Seán MacStiofain legitimates himself with the same principle of retribution. He concludes, after an extensive summing up of rising cruelties on the part of the British: "It was time to move into a far more determined phase of retaliation, one of anti-personnel operations." Adams (1986), referring to the death of an Irish hunger striker, writes: "Francis Hughes died on 12 May [the second death, just after Bobby Sands]. On 19 May the IRA killed five British soldiers with a land mine in South Armagh" (p. 83).

Apart from revenge or retribution, there can also be "military" reasons to attack a target. In this case the primary aim is the disruption of the functioning of the enemy's organization. MacStiofain (1975) often uses this military justification for the choice of a target. The use of military terminology thereby seems to serve a legitimating function. For example, he writes: "The next phase of Republican strategy was largely intended to force them to extend the saturation policy to non-Nationalist areas, offering more targets still, while tying down their strength on static duties" (p. 206; also see pp. 207-208, 238, 243, 254).

In the context of this inquiry, however, we are more interested in the selection of victims for their symbolical value. By deliberately selecting a person, the message of the terrorist movement can be transmitted to the public, to opponents, and/or to the group of which the victim is a part. McGuire (1973) gives us a glimpse of symbolic reasoning when she justifies IRA attacks on individual British soldiers. These young men, she argues, stand for the British Army as a whole, which in turn represents the British presence in Ireland (pp. 145-146). Adams (1986) explains the reason for attacks on British soldiers:

> The people of Britain should be interested in what their government is doing in Ireland and in what their army is doing here. Sadly this interest is only aroused when the problem involves them directly. . . . Meanwhile British soldiers and Irish civilians are dying on Irish streets, Irish prisoners have died and are ill-treated in British jails and there have been periodic bombings in England itself. The English people must therefore concede, regardless of the confusions of facts, that their government has not brought peace to Ireland. (p. 165)

Abu Ijad (1979), in turn, explains the significance of a victimized person for the movement in these terms: "The prime minister of Jordan was a symbol of the treason to the Palestinian case . . . a stimulating view for those responsible for the assassination attempt and [a warning to] all those in the Arab world who would be tempted to sacrifice the rights and interests of the Palestinian people" (p. 143; my translation).

The "best" victim of an act of terrorism is one who epitomizes the values and hopes of the other side in a political confrontation. It is no accident that people who have become symbols run a special risk of being targeted. Spiritual leaders, economic leaders, and even sports heroes are utilized to bring terrorists' messages home to all those who see the victim as "one of us."

## Conclusion

In real life, the seven types of tactical uses of publicity take place in an integrated way. This very fact can turn terrorism into a powerful weapon. This discussion of concrete publicity tactics makes it clear that several contemporary terrorist groups use the mass media and publicity in general in a very purposeful way. The Provisional IRA is definitely the most skillful group, but the West German urban terrorists and the Palestinian liberation movements also reveal a mastery in the use of the media.

However, one should not exaggerate the admittedly large role the media play in terrorist strategy. By way of concluding this chapter, I would like to make some comments on the sometimes rather hasty conclusions drawn by some authors who discuss the relation between terrorism and the media.

First, it seems to me that the study of terrorists' personal documents presented here demonstrates that exclusive attention to terrorists' manipulation of the mass media is not justified. Terrorists do not depend exclusively on radio, television, and newspapers to accomplish their psychological aims. They spend a great deal of time and energy on other ways of promoting their movements and ideals. Gatherings, as well as self-made brochures, pamphlets, and periodicals, remain important in the dissemination of information on movements and their ideas. The mass media are an important and attractive instrument, but not the only vehicle for terrorist propaganda.

In the second place, there are significant differences in the degree of "professionalism" with which terrorists handle the instrument of publicity. Different political and historical circumstances in the countries concerned account for this. A tradition of political violence, for instance, seems to be important. The fact that, of the groups under investigation here, the Provisional IRA turns out to be the most sophisticated terrorist movement can be at least partly explained by the movement's long history, going back to at least the Easter Rising in 1916. Experience gained from long years of struggle also shows in the Palestinian armed resistance. The IRA and the Palestinian terrorists have always been more in touch with their constituencies than the RAF, the RZ, and the June 2nd Movement. In the memoirs this shows in a less arrogant attitude toward supporters in (Northern) Ireland and Palestine. Characteristically, the extent of publicity tactics directed at the people in those two areas has been larger than in the German Federal Republic, where this aspect was given less attention in favor of the (inter)national audience.

In conclusion, I wish to emphasize that while the role of the mass media in terrorist thinking is undeniably great, one cannot ignore the fact that publicity in all the instances studied remains an instrument, a means to achieve other ideals. Many researchers who stress the role of the media neglect the political motivations of terrorists. Sincerely felt anger about what the terrorists consider unjust is a far more important factor in their choice of strategy than the availability of highly developed and sophisticated mass media technology. Margaret Thatcher and Roy Hattersley can, by banning interviews with members of Sinn Fein and the IRA, indeed deprive the terrorists of an important instrument, but they will not be able to destroy thereby the political fanaticism that forms the basis of (armed) resistance. Gerry Adams (1986) seems to illustrate this when he writes that censorship alone will certainly not paralyze the movement: "Despite the censorship of Section 31 of the Broadcasting Act, the combined campaigns of harassment and black propaganda by the Dublin and London governments and our own organizational weaknesses, Sinn Fein is a growing force in Irish politics" (p. 149). And also: "The effects of Section 31 of the Broadcasting Act pose a considerable problem, not so much in terms of support for Sinn Fein specifically, but in terms of disinformation" (p. 156; see also p. 153).

Despite his lack of democratic credentials, Adams makes an important point. The media may provide insurgent terrorists with a good dose of the "oxygen of publicity," but censorship can provide a government with the "narcotic of secrecy," which is an even bigger danger to democracy.

# References

Adams, G. (1982). *Falls memories.* Dingle, Ireland: Brandon.
Adams, G. (1986). *The politics of Irish freedom* (2nd ed.). Dingle, Ireland: Brandon.
Alexander, Y. (1977). Terrorism and the media in the Middle East. In Y. Alexander & S. M. Finger (Eds.), *Terrorism: Interdisciplinary perspectives* (pp. 166-206). New York: John Jay.

Bassiouni, M. C. (1981). Terrorism, law enforcement and the mass media: Perspectives, problems, proposals. *Journal of Criminal Law and Criminology, 72,* 1-55.

Baumann, M. (1976). *Hoe het allemaal begon* [translated from German, Wie Alles anfing; How it all began]. Amsterdam: S. Landshoff.

Bell, J. B. (1978, May/June). Terrorist scripts and live-action spectaculars. *Columbia Journalism Review, 17,* 47-50.

Bell, J. B. (1979). *The secret army: The IRA 1916-1979* (2nd ed.). Cambridge: MIT Press.

Bertaux, D. (1981). *Biography and society: The life history approach in the social sciences.* Beverly Hills, CA: Sage.

Catton, W. R., Jr. (1978). Militants and the media: Partners in terrorism? *Indiana Law Journal, 53,* 703-715.

Clutterbuck, R. (1981). *The media and political violence.* London: Macmillan.

Gerrits, R. P. J. M. (1989). *Huiver en Luister! Een verkennend, kwalitatief onderzoek naar het gebruik van publiciteit door terroristen in Europa, 1875-1975.* Unpublished master's thesis, Erasmus University, Rotterdam, Netherlands.

Ijad, A. (1979). *Heimat oder Tod. Der Freiheitskampf der Palästinenser.* Düsseldorf: Econ.

Khaled, L. (1973). *My people shall live: Autobiography of a revolutionary.* London: Hodder & Stoughton.

Klein, H.-J. (1979). *Rückkehr in die Menschlichkeit. Appell eines ausgestiegenen Terroristen* [Return to humanity]. Reinbek: Rowohlt.

MacStiofain, S. (1975). *Revolutionary in Ireland.* Farnborough: Gordon Cremonesi.

Marighella, C. (1972). *Minihandbuch des Stadtguerilleros.* Hamburg: Latein Amerika Kollektiv.

McGuire, M. (1973). *To take arms: A year with the Provisional IRA.* London: Macmillan.

Rapoport, D. C. (1988). The international world as some terrorists have seen it: A look at a century of memoirs. In D. C. Rapoport (Ed.), *Inside terrorist organizations.* London: Frank Cass.

Schmid, A. P., & De Graaf, J. F. A. (1983). *Violence as communication: Insurgent terrorism and the Western news media* (2nd ed.). London: Sage.

Schmid, A. P., De Graaf, J. F. A., et al. (1982). *Zuidmoluks terrorisme, de media en de publieke opinie.* Leiden: COMT.

Schmid, A. P., Jongman, A. J., et al. (1988). *Political terrorism: A new guide to actors, authors, concepts, data bases, theories and literature* (2nd rev. ed.). Amsterdam: North-Holland.

*Tijdschrift voor Geschiedenis.* (1970). [Special issue devoted to the study of personal documents as a historical source]. Vol. 83, No. 2.

Tugwell, M. A. (1981). Politics and propaganda of the Provisional IRA. *Terrorism, 5*(1-2), 13-40.

Wilkinson, P. (1978). Terrorism and the media. *Journalism Studies Review, 3,* 2-6.

# Terrorists' Perspectives: Interviews

## Cynthia L. Irvin

The burgeoning literature on the relationship between terrorism and the media leads one to believe either that the media are the unwitting accomplices of terrorist organizations, easily manipulated by skilled propagandists, or that the media, recognizing the public appeal of violent acts, are willing actors in the theater of terrorism.

Eoghan Harris (1987), a former editor for Radio Telefis Eireann (RTE), writing in an internal report, *Broadcasting and Terrorism*, which accompanied a video role-playing exercise for RTE reporters who might confront supporters of the Irish Republican movement, clearly expresses the former perspective. In the report he strongly affirms his support for Section 31, the legislation that forbids live interviews with representatives of the IRA or Sinn

Author's Note: I would like to thank Professor David Paletz, Duke University, for his comments on the original draft of this chapter and his support for this project. I would especially like to thank Sean MacManus, Richard and Chrissie McAuley, and Takolo for their assistance with this study and particularly for their patience and willingness to take on my seemingly endless list of questions. I am also grateful for the financial support received from the Center for International Studies, Duke University, which awarded me Tinker Field Research Grants for study in the Basque country during the summers of 1987 and 1988. Research for this project was also funded by a Duke University dissertation travel grant and a predissertation fellowship from the Council for European Studies.

Fein on Irish radio and television. He does so on the grounds that the Provos (i.e., members of the IRA and their supporters) could always draw and often "win" any interview, even should the interview take place within minutes of the airing of film of the most appalling IRA atrocity. Indeed, the public relations skills of such Sinn Fein spokespersons as Gerry Adams, Danny Morrison, and Richard McAuley, among others, are so highly reputed that the Sinn Fein press office is widely regarded as the Saatchi & Saatchi of "terrorist" publicity departments. Certainly, the British government is fond of portraying the Republican Press Center in Belfast as a well-financed, well-staffed propaganda machine. In reality, as I discovered during my stay in Belfast, the center operates on extremely limited financial resources, in very cramped quarters, and with a minimal, if highly skilled and dedicated, staff. Such an image, however, does not suit the propaganda campaigns of the well-financed and efficient British and Irish press machines in the battle for hearts and minds. Hence it remains largely obscured.

Bassiouni (1983) articulates the latter perspective delineated above, which places greater responsibility on journalists for the "contagion" of terror incidents. In his discussion of problems associated with media coverage of terror-violence incidents, he remarks:

> Reporters do not merely report the news; they are often subjective participants in it. They are, in essence, the actors, the script writers, and the idea behind each story. Terrorists take advantage of this situation in their attempts to manipulate the media. (p. 191)

From both perspectives, the perpetrators of the violent acts are the clear winners.

## Insurgents and the Media:
## Winners or Losers?

The central questions I wish to raise are as follows: First, do, in fact, the perpetrators of acts of insurgent "terrorism" always perceive themselves as victors when they obtain media attention? Or, contrary to conventional wisdom, is there a recognition by the insurgents that media coverage of acts perpetrated by them can impede rather than advance their cause? Second, of the various aims attributed to insurgent "terrorists'" use of the media, which do the insurgents themselves view as most important, and do those aims change during the course of an insurgency? In addressing these issues I have relied on press releases and documents issued by Sinn Fein and the IRA, Herri Batasuna and ETA, and the PLO, as well a series of interviews I conducted with party activists and elected representatives of Sinn Fein and Herri Batasuna. The majority of these interviews took place between October 1988 and January 1990, while I was engaged in dissertation research in Ireland and the Basque country. The PLO interviews were carried out in the Palestine Affairs Center in Washington, D.C., in October 1990. My study will focus primarily on the Irish and Basque cases and is limited to an analysis of what Christopher Hewitt elsewhere in this volume refers to as "nationalist terrorism"—that is, acts of political violence committed by insurgent organizations seeking to achieve the withdrawal of foreign troops and national independence (see Chapter 9). It should be made clear that while I accept that the insurgent organizations analyzed in this chapter may, in some instances, use terrorism as a strategy, I do not view them as terrorist organizations. For this reason, representatives of the IRA, ETA, PLO, and their political wings are referred to as *insurgents* in this study.

Numerous experts on terrorism have written on how terrorists perceive the role of the media in society and on the various ways in which they can use the media to publicize and advance their causes (Alexander, 1976; Alexander & O'Day, 1984; Bassiouni, 1983; Bell, 1978; Clutterbuck, 1983; Jenkins, 1975, 1981; Laqueur, 1977; Lodge, 1981; Schlesinger, 1984; Schmid, 1984, 1990; Schmid & De Graaf, 1982; Stohl, 1988; Wardlaw, 1989; Wilkinson, 1977). Schmid (1990, p. 6), for example, lists 38 different ways in which terrorists can use the media. However, empirical insurgent-based research, particularly from a comparative perspective, is clearly lacking.

This lacuna in the existing literature is, certainly, partly due to the difficulties related to interviewing spokespersons for insurgent organizations. However, I would argue that it is better explained by constraints imposed upon journalists and researchers by the prevailing paradigm of the media-terrorist relationship that dominates in official government circles and among conservative journalists, academics, and counterinsurgency theorists. This paradigm maintains that by giving any coverage to "terrorists," particularly in a format that allows them to voice their views directly to the public (i.e., live interview), investigators grant them legitimacy and strengthen their position. This perspective was clearly articulated by then Home Secretary Douglas Hurd (1988) in his announcement of the Thatcher government's October 1988 decision to ban live interviews with members, supporters, and elected representatives of Sinn Fein:

> For some time broadcast coverage of events in Northern Ireland has included the occasional appearance of representatives of paramilitary organizations and their political wings, who have used these opportunities as an attempt to justify their criminal activities. . . . The terrorists themselves draw support and sustenance from having access to radio and television and from addressing their views more directly to the population at large than is possible through the press. The Government has now decided that the time has come to deny this easy platform to those who use it to propagate terrorism. (p. 1)

According to this "official" perspective (Schlesinger, Murdock, & Elliott, 1983), if the media refuse to cover acts of terrorism, terrorists will disappear. Denying the political legitimacy of the grievances voiced by insurgent terrorists, this perspective emphasizes the criminal aspects of political violence and maintains that the cause of terrorism is terrorists and those who supply them with the "oxygen of publicity." Indeed, some proponents of this perspective, such as Professor Jose Desantes Guanter (1980), a Spanish expert on information law, view those who report terrorist propaganda as engaging in an activity almost as criminal as those whose actions they are reporting:

> Terrorism today is an "information crime"; it cannot operate without the modern social communications media. . . . Terrorist violence is merely the springboard for real terrorism which is communicated terrorism. (p. 2)

Even those who seek merely to provide explanations for the actions of terrorists are viewed as contributing to the legitimation of the terrorists and as encouraging them to engage in further acts of violence.

The reply by Dr. Conor Cruise O'Brien—who, as Irish minister of posts and telegraphs, in 1976 introduced legislation to prohibit even the reports of interviews with Republican spokespersons—to a 1983 New Year's Day editorial in the *Guardian* titled "The Year of the Terrorist" aptly illustrates the official view that to attempt to explain terrorism is to encourage and legitimate terrorist activities. In response to the suggestion that the political motivations of the IRA need to be recognized if a solution to the Northern Ireland conflict is to be found, O'Brien (1983) stated:

> When we are summoned to make an effort to understand them, I don't think this is really a call to cognitive effort. Rather it is a way of deflecting indignation and preparing surrender—"know thine enemy" may be a first stage in giving in to him. . . . It is an invitation in fact to acquiesce in legitimating terror. . . .

The IRA must interpret public endeavors to understand them and recognize their motives as a sign of cracking will. What can that do except to encourage them to greater efforts.

One regrettable result of this official consensus has been the imposition of self-censorship by journalists and academics who investigate political violence and terrorist organizations. In a political climate in which merely offering possible explanations for the actions of a terrorist organization is to leave oneself open for attack as being sympathetic to that organization, it clearly becomes increasingly difficult and costly to pursue research projects that require contact with representatives of terrorist organizations or that merely attempt to portray their point of view. The fate of Jo Thomas, a former correspondent in the London bureau of the *New York Times* who was removed from her post as a result of her attempts to investigate controversial shootings by the British army of unarmed IRA members, provides a good example. Writing in the *Columbia Journalism Review*, Thomas (1988) states:

A senior editor, who kept a home in London as well as New York and who had been enthusiastic about my initial dispatches from Belfast, began telling me to stay out of Northern Ireland. A high-ranking British official, who in the past has had close ties to the intelligence community in Northern Ireland, took me to lunch and suggested I drop my investigation in exchange for a lot of access to the secretary of state for Northern Ireland, the British official who administers the place. . . . I refused. Several American colleagues in London suggested I leave the difficult investigations to the local press: if there really were a story, British and Irish reporters would be on top of it. In fact, they were not—but some of them began treating me as if I were a member of the IRA. Then, too, the mail at my house in London started to arrive opened. (p. 32)

One noticeable consequence of this practice of official and self-censorship is the glaring gap in empirically based research regarding the media-terrorist relationship from the insurgent "terrorist's" point of view. This gap in the existing literature, my data will show, has allowed an exaggerated view of the benefits of media coverage of acts of insurgent terrorism for insurgent organizations to flourish with few challenges.

Among those who have challenged the conventional wisdom (e.g., Hewitt, in Chapter 9 of this volume; Paletz, Fozzard, & Ayanian, 1982, 1983; Schlesinger et al., 1983; Schmid, 1990), most have argued that media coverage of acts of political violence has a limited, and generally negative, impact on public attitudes toward terrorist organizations. However, these studies have relied primarily on secondary sources of information regarding insurgents' perceptions of the impact of media reports on their struggle. Little evidence regarding the positive or negative value of media coverage of acts of political violence for insurgent organizations has been introduced that relies on the insurgents' own accounts of that coverage.

In this chapter, data obtained from members and supporters of insurgent organizations show that, contrary to the conventional wisdom, insurgents do not always view media coverage as beneficial to their struggle. Indeed, the data show that these organizations are more likely to perceive the media not as their "best friend," as Laqueur and other proponents of the official perspective argue, but as a hostile, if necessary, commentator on their struggle. The following excerpt from an internal Sinn Fein (n.d.) education department document from the 1980s, on the role of officers, including press officers, in the party illustrates this uneasy relationship:

> While always remembering that in the main the media are hostile to our position, and therefore less likely to honestly and objectively record our views, it is of great benefit if one can build up a personal relationship with journalists. (p. 8)

Indeed, much of the attention devoted to publicity by propagandists for these groups is spent on combating and correcting, when possible, distortions and inaccuracies in the coverage they receive, as is illustrated in the same document:

> Complaining about bad media coverage is a vital part of the process of getting good media coverage. . . . A letter of factual correction, or one pointing out unfairness, is not going to convert sloppy and/or right-wing reporters into paragons of radical, painstakingly accurate journalism; but it will sow seeds of doubt that will make them a bit more careful in the future about republican stories. (p. 14)

In general, the representatives of the political wings of insurgent organizations whom I interviewed perceive the media as an integral element of the capitalist, hegemonic state that generally conspires with government to suppress alternative political views, especially radical or socialist viewpoints. The media are seen not so much as a medium through which the prevailing order can be attacked, but as one that assists in the perpetuation of the political status quo and the capitalist exploitation of the masses.

Richard McAuley, director of the Sinn Fein Publicity Department for Northern Ireland, neatly summarized this perspective in response to a question regarding Sinn Fein's perception of the role of the media in society:

> In different societies there are subtle differences in the role of the mass media. However, it remains in principle an advocate of the status quo, occasionally questioning, but rarely confronting. . . . In Ireland, our experience of the media is one in which the media is the guardian of British values and interests. There is ample evidence of both direct and indirect censorship at work to ensure that the images of the conflict reflect the political analysis of the state. In our case, the colonial backdrop, partition, and the structured political, cultural, and economic discrimination which flow from it is ignored. (personal communication, October 11, 1991)

The following excerpt from *Askatzen*, the international affairs bulletin of Herri Batasuna, reveals a similar perception of the press on the part of the radical Basque activists.

> An important facet of the Spanish State's aggression against Herri Batasuna is the continuous news distortion which has various aims: to sow confusion in the ranks of the MLNV, to create a climate of opinion hostile to the MLNV, to present a false image of HB, and to cover up the arbitrary action of the state. (*Askatzen*, no. 6, p. 14)

Indeed, the issue of propaganda offensives by the establishment press against their movements is frequently raised by spokespersons for the insurgent organizations in interviews as well as in movement documents. In the series of interviews I carried out with representatives and supporters of Sinn Fein from October 1988 to May 1989, and with Herri Batasuna militants from September to December 1989, this issue was described as "very important" by 48 out of 54 respondents in the Irish case and by 32 out of 36 respondents in the Basque case.

The importance attached to this anti-Republican government propaganda offensive is particularly acute in the Irish case. Since the Thatcher government's imposition of a ban on live interviews with Sinn Fein in October 1988, Sinn Fein is virtually excluded from media coverage in both Ireland and Britain. In March 1989 the Republican Press Center in Belfast reported that inquiries from broadcast journalists had dropped by 75% since the ban went into effect. In Sinn Fein's *Political Report*, published for its most recent party conference (February 1-3, 1991), there are numerous references to the party's need to redouble its publicity efforts and to counter its isolated status. The following excerpt is taken from a section of that report headed "Censorship."

> The last 12 months saw a continuation of political censorship against our party. The censorship laws have been described as similar to those of Turkey and South Africa by the International Federation of Journalists. . . . Section 31 is being extended by RTE, not just to prevent our party giving our view on current events, but to try to deny the reality of our party's involvement in other political, community and trade union struggles. Therefore, not only the government but the RTE management have a case to answer in their implementation of political censorship. Despite the court cases being taken by our party, and others, much more must be done if political censorship is to be ended. Censorship is the most significant factor distorting political discussion in Ireland. . . . We need to mobilize public opinion to force both governments to end political censorship. (p. 16)

Priorities set by the party membership in the report for 1991 reflect its concern with the effects of censorship on its organization:

> The priorities for Sinn Fein in the year ahead are to develop and strengthen our party organization, to improve our publicity output and to overcome the effects of censorship. . . . As we try to overcome censorship it is essential for republicans to confidently assert our role in the struggles for basic democratic rights. . . . We are consistent in demanding civil rights, precisely because we are also demanding national, democratic rights. (p. 29)

While much attention has been focused on insurgents' use of the media to intimidate the public, the ability of the media to intimidate the public from which insurgents hope to draw support has been relatively ignored. As the following comments illustrate, there is considerable concern within each of the insurgent organizations considered in this study regarding the media's potential to demoralize the insurgent organization's support base and to discredit the political dimension of the organization. As Gerry Adams (1990), president of Sinn Fein, stated in his address to the 85th Sinn Fein Ard Fheis:

> Propaganda, enhanced by the censorship of this party, is a key element in the full frontal assault on us and our supporters. Again and again and again we have been told that we cannot win. . . . The aim of all this implacable no-can-win nonsense is obvious of course. It is aimed not only at IRA Volunteers. It is aimed at us. It is aimed at the republican base. (p. 23)

Similar statements have been made by Basque and PLO activists in regard
to the Spanish campaign against ETA and Herri Batasuna and the pro-Israeli
campaign against the PLO.

> I think that it would be difficult for the PSOE and its "radio" to better achieve
> its goals of distortion and manipulation of HB. They do not use the inflamma-
> tory rhetoric of Hitler, nor the total censorship of Franco, but still they
> succeed . . . through innuendo, through half-truths, through phrases with dou-
> ble meanings, in suggesting that the representatives of HB merit assassination,
> that they are ETA. (ITZAL, 1989)

> Zionist propaganda is waging a war of defamation against its arch-enemy, the
> Palestinian people as a whole, and has succeeded in isolating this victimized
> people and their political vanguard, the Palestine Liberation Organization. It
> has succeeded in equating the initials P.L.O. with blood, terror, murder and
> destruction. . . . This is one of the most effective weapons deployed by the
> Zionists and it has contributed to the creation of a negative Palestinian image
> on the world scale. (PLO, 1981)

Numerous references to the negative impact of censorship legislation and
negative media coverage on the Republican movement can be found in
internal Sinn Fein strategy discussion papers. The following excerpts are
from internal party reports on movement strategy written after Sinn Fein's
decision in 1986 to participate in Irish parliamentary elections and to expand
its electoral activity.

> No serious or penetrating examination of our policies has ever been undertaken
> by any section of the media and the malicious campaign of propaganda against
> us has been so concentrated and sustained that many sympathizers regard us
> as more of a demolition gang than a building team.
>     Section 31 is not only a bar or distorting factor on news reporting, it helps
> generate the atmosphere in which people are afraid to be seen as associated
> with Sinn Fein. Section 31 can be undermined to some extent even at present,
> by getting Sinn Fein spokespersons on pirate radio and interviews in local
> press. (Sinn Fein, 1986, p. 2)

The recognition of the threat posed to the Irish Republican movement by
this ideological bombardment from the establishment press is evident in the
importance attributed to the task of countering its effect in the description of
a press officer's duties as described in the Sinn Fein briefing document
distributed to each of the local cummain (i.e., party organizations):

Anti-Republican propaganda should be challenged aggressively wherever it appears—this would require the building of very active press centers and PRO's at every level. Positive news about Sinn Fein activities should be equally pushed. (Sinn Fein, n.d., p. 2)

A similar assessment of the importance of ideological struggle was apparent in my interviews with Herri Batasuna¯activists, in which 30 of 36 respondents characterized ideological struggle as one of the most important elements of the Basque struggle for national liberation. According to one Herri Batasuna activist who wished to remain anonymous:

This need to fight against the total boycott by the media of any information, except, of course, ETA operations, means that we must continually take our struggle to the streets, where we again encounter the repression of the state. Despite our marches being legal, seldom do all our militants return home unscathed. Time that would be better spent preparing for electoral campaigns or for expanding our involvement in other political areas must be constantly devoted to fighting back against Madrid and its media's attempt to isolate us, to make us a nonissue.

For insurgent political organizations that must raise operating funds from a membership with generally limited financial resources, this need to devote considerable resources, both human and economic, to countering the state's propaganda offensive against their movements has often meant that political activities that might further movement goals have had to be postponed or forgone. As Pedro Ibarra (1989), who has written numerous works on the political strategy of ETA and Herri Batasuna, has noted:

This [propaganda] offensive of the State forces ETA, and especially its civilian support groups to concentrate all its forces . . . on the fight against isolation. Working externally with the objective of increasing its popular support, they must seek new solidarities; internally, they must reinforce their civilian structures and organizations, above all rendering the movement ideologically impervious in face of ideological bombardment of the State and its strategy of isolation. (p. 150)

While the above excerpts testify to the fact that insurgents, clearly, do not always perceive the media as sympathetic, or as providing support for their struggles, an even stronger refutation of the official perspective's claim that all publicity is good publicity for terrorists can be made based on responses by insurgent organizations to press coverage of acts of terrorism in which civilians are killed. In response to the British and Irish coverage of the Enniskillen tragedy in November 1987, in which 11 civilians were killed in a badly planned IRA operation, Gerry Adams commented in an interview published in *An Phoblacht/Republican News* (November 19, 1987):

> Since Enniskillen there has been an unprecedented propaganda onslaught on the Republican movement. The dead and the injured have been utilized as the basis for that campaign and there has been a massive effort to convert the natural revulsion of ordinary people about what happened in Enniskillen into anti-republican sentiment. . . . they have tried to invalidate the entire struggle on the basis of the Enniskillen tragedy. . . . [Many] pronouncements have been aimed at eroding the republican base. . . . the British have seized on the Enniskillen tragedy because they believe that the emotional response will be to their benefit. It is no exaggeration to say that the British administration with the aid of the media . . . have manipulated the events of Enniskillen in such a way as to expedite repression. . . . we accept the fact that the Enniskillen bombing has had the most serious consequences for the Republican movement.

Similar comments were made by representatives of Herri Batasuna in the aftermath of the ETA bombing of a supermarket in Barcelona in June 1987 that killed 18 shoppers in a working-class district that, only a few days earlier, by giving 40,000 votes to the Herri Batasuna candidate for the European Parliament, Txema Montero, clearly contributed to his election. Montero, for example, referred to the bombing as "un crimen multiple." In a press release issued the day after the bombing, the leadership of Herri Batasuna publicly decried the "cost in human lives and in the injured which resulted from this attack" and expressed its "most energetic criticism of this type of attack which posed enormous risks for the civilian population and which, in this case, had resulted in this tragic outcome . . . which inevitably will be used propagandistically." The Herri Batasuna leadership, fearful of the public reaction to the bombing, was later widely reported to have issued a directive to ETA that "another operation like that of Hipercor will not be tolerated or condoned."

I was in the Bilbao office of Herri Batasuna to arrange a series of interviews the morning after the Hipercor bombing in Barcelona. Among those present, there was widespread disbelief as to ETA's responsibility for the attack, given the role of that area in securing the election of Txema Montero. Those present expressed deep concern and anger both for the lives lost and for the expected negative consequences of the attack for the political struggle.

This question of the value of media coverage of acts of political violence carried out by the military wings of the political organizations examined here is, perhaps, one of the most debated topics in the media-terrorist literature. While proponents of the official perspective generally argue that any coverage benefits both the terrorists and those who support them, others who propose alternative views often argue that media reports have limited or no impact on the actions of terrorists, their supporters, and the public. Although this question has often been answered for the insurgents by those writing on the media-terrorist relationship, seldom have the actual responses of insurgents been sought. To address this issue, I specifically asked several national party officials to comment on the value of media coverage of armed operations by the military wings of their organizations. The first excerpt below is taken from a conversation with Sean MacManus, national spokesperson for Sinn Fein, 1983-1990; the second is from an interview with Richard McAuley.

In general, I would say media reports of IRA actions have a limited impact on our movement. Certainly, for example, when an operation goes wrong and civilians are killed, the morale of Republican supporters is dampened. But I would say our supporters, especially our core base, understand that tragic mistakes will be made in the course of any war. Certainly, condemnations of IRA actions by those outside the Republican movement would have no effect on our support for the IRA. You must understand that media reports of IRA actions, irrespective of whether they are actions its supporters would view as successful, such as the mortar attack on Downing Street, or those such as Enniskillen which went horribly wrong, will be negative publicity for our movement. I suppose the only way you could say it is beneficial is that it is better than no coverage at all.

What is particularly frustrating, however, and certainly it is a deliberate action on the part of the media, is the constant emphasis on IRA actions. For example, whenever Sinn Fein attempts to hold a press conference to discuss its political initiatives, the media always attempt to switch the issue to Sinn Fein's position on the most recent IRA operation. This is obviously extremely frustrating. The same questions are always asked, Does Sinn Fein condone or condemn this or that IRA operation? Is Sinn Fein ready to abandon its support for the IRA? Is their a split between hard-liners and moderates in Sinn Fein? Will there be a cease-fire? Hardly ever are the political issues which Sinn Fein is trying to put forward discussed. (MacManus, personal communication, June 3, 1991)

IRA actions which result in civilian casualties can have a politically damaging impact on the struggle. British propaganda is reinforced, people become confused and morale can be damaged. . . . Even when Republicans express regret at such events this is used by the media to criticize the struggle. If Republicans express no regret at all, this too is held up as an example of our insincerity and callousness. However, within the north, among Nationalist and Republican supporters, there is an awareness of the bias with which the media covers actions by one side or the other. (McAuley, personal communication, October 11, 1991)

To contrast responses by Sinn Fein and the IRA, the next excerpt is taken from a statement by a member of the IRA General Headquarters staff to the Republican newspaper *An Phoblacht/Republican News* (June 28) regarding its attack on London's Carlton Club, a popular meeting place for members of the Tory establishment. In response to a question regarding whether or not the IRA sees elements of the media being involved in a deliberate campaign to undermine nationalist morale, the IRA spokesperson stated:

It is difficult to quantify, but the British have a very sophisticated and well financed publicity network, especially internationally. Their methods of pro- pagandising and spreading disinformation are legion. . . . It has been part of their modus operandi for many years to feed certain journalists stories when they seek to float an idea, undermine individuals, sow dissension, prepare the ground for proposed repressive legislation or simply to confuse their oppo- nents. Censorship also plays a large role, preventing a creditable reply to the British line being heard. (p. 2)

When asked specifically about media reports of splits between Sinn Fein and the IRA as a result of disagreements over the IRA war effort, the IRA spokesperson responded:

Well, such speculation and claims are ridiculous. There have been so many "hawks" and "doves" let loose it is a wonder we can walk the street for bird droppings. Sinn Fein has stated on numerous occasions that its stance is one of critical support for the right of the Irish people to wage armed struggle against British occupation. We welcome this support from our comrades in Sinn Fein and from any anti-imperialist group or individual. We do not and would not demand that those who support the right to engage in armed struggle must support every IRA action. It is in the interests of the whole Movement and community that IRA operations function solely to undermine the will of the British to remain in Ireland. . . . Quite simply, the deaths of innocent civilians are unacceptable; they are tragic in themselves and do not advance our cause or bring closer the day of victory. (p. 2)

In comparing the Sinn Fein and IRA statements, it is apparent that similar issues are addressed by both groups. Each group, however, has a different, if related, criticism of media coverage by the establishment press. In the Sinn Fein statements, criticism is focused on how government restrictions and hostile press coverage restrict the political debate, as well as affect the morale of its support base, while the IRA focuses on the attempts of the press to lower morale and sow dissension in the Republican movement. Given the different needs and tactical objectives of each group, this finding is not surprising. It does, however, weaken the conventional argument that terrorists always benefit from media coverage of terror incidents.

That the issues addressed by the IRA and Sinn Fein are common to other insurgent organizations is clearly evident in the following remarks of Inaki Pinedo, a member of Herri Batasuna's national executive:

> Looking at the newspapers you would think that Herri Batasuna and ETA are one and the same. Of course, that's a deliberate ploy of Madrid and the national media to exclude us from the political debate, when it's obvious we are at the center of that debate in the Basque country. With few exceptions the only time the media want to speak with us is when ETA has carried out an operation. They don't want to hear what we have to say about the environment, about social issues, about our proposals to resolve the conflict, all they want to hear is what we think about this or that ETA action. So, I would say that media reports of ETA actions, while keeping the public aware that there is a serious political conflict here which won't go away, and which certainly won't be repressed, which is obviously very important, have a limited impact on our day-to-day political struggle. What it does do is place our political representatives and supporters at risk of assassination by those death squads who see no difference between ETA and Herri Batasuna. (Pinedo, personal communication, November 1989)

Similarly, in response to the worldwide condemnation of the *Achille Lauro* incident, the PLO admitted soon afterward that "events prove . . . that terrorist acts committed outside the occupied territories harm the cause of the Palestinian people and tarnish their just struggle for freedom" ("PLO News and Views," 1985, p. 2). The issue of the negative impact of the *Achille Lauro* incident and other operations in which civilians are killed was discussed at length by Khalil Foutah of the Palestine Affairs Center:

> Of course, the media give more attention to operations in which civilians are killed. For this reason any civilian casualty is not for our benefit, because of

that we try hard to avoid civilians but sometimes they get caught in the middle. . . . Even now when you see any interview or any clipping with Abul Abbas the first thing they say is, this is Abul Abbas who did the *Achille Lauro* operation. Why, because an older Jewish man, a civilian, was killed. So every time Abul Abbas is mentioned in the media, they bring up the *Achille Lauro* operation. They always try to publicize this issue and put it in the front, therefore Abul Abbas is always the terrorist, the killer of civilians, and that is all the people hear. Whatever he says, there is no credibility. (Foutah, personal communication, October 1990)

That violent acts attract media attention clearly cannot be disputed. However, the claim that such coverage is always beneficial to the perpetrators is one that may be better assessed in view of the different stages of development of an insurgent organization. In the following section I demonstrate how both the tactics for obtaining publicity and the type of publicity sought by insurgent organizations change during different stages of the movement.

## The Media: Insurgent Organizations' Aims, Audiences, and Stages of Development

Within the existing literature on insurgent "terrorists'" uses of the media, the majority of the case studies of terrorist-media relationships treat those relationships as static rather than dynamic. A more useful framework for the analysis of these relationships, I propose, is one that focuses on the roles the media play in the various stages of an insurgent organization's development.

Larson (1973) asserts that there are four major stages in the development of a social movement:

1. the creation of internal and external identities
2. the establishment of legitimation and sufficient resources for survival
3. institutionalization through achieving participation and developing unity among supporters
4. penetration of society (i.e., obtaining acceptance by others)

Within each of these stages, my research would suggest that both the publicity aims and target audiences of the insurgents vary greatly.

Schmid (1990) distinguishes a minimum of six possible target audiences for terrorists:

1. world opinion
2. the national majority that is opposed to the goals of the terrorists
3. the national minority or social class for which the terrorists claim to fight
4. the national government that is the direct opponent of the terrorists
5. rival political movements, both terrorist and nonterrorist
6. the terrorists and their direct supporters

Examined in a framework that integrates Larson's stages and Schmid's categories of target audiences, my data provide a more detailed picture of the dynamic nature of the media-terrorist relationship.

### IDENTIFICATION AND LEGITIMATION

During these early stages, in which movements attempt to gain recognition, draw attention to their demands, and establish credibility, acts of political violence are clearly recognized by insurgent organizations as an effective means of securing media coverage. Foutah (personal communication, October 1990) notes, "Of course the media play a great role in shaping the public opinion toward any nationalist movement or any people that are trying to achieve something, especially in this age of mass communication." And McAuley (personal communication, October 11, 1991) states, "I think the IRA sees all of its actions as having a political impact. Media coverage would play an important role in increasing or lessening that impact. Armed actions are seen by the IRA as armed propaganda."

In the case of nationalist insurgencies, these acts are designed to attract worldwide attention, to establish credibility among their own supporters as well as their enemies, and, in particular, to obtain recognition as a legitimate political force by the national government that they oppose. Comments by an IRA spokesperson in *An Phoblacht/Republican News* (1979) on the British media's response to the August 27 execution of Mountbatten by the IRA confirm these aims:

> Through such operations we have raised the Irish liberation struggle to a new international level, one which it has not reached for several years, giving the IRA the chance to explain itself, to make sense of a war we have been fighting for the past ten years or more. . . . Demanding recognition for political status

is all a piece of the war we are fighting, and you can measure its importance by the fact that London refuses to give it to us with such tenacity.

At this stage, as former British Home Secretary William Whitelaw noted in his response to the Mountbatten assassination,

> terrorists and terrorist organizations seek and depend upon publicity. A principal object of their acts of violence is to draw attention to themselves and to gain notoriety. . . . they bomb and murder their way into headlines. (cited in Hoggart, 1979)

Statements by spokespersons for the insurgent organizations clearly support this position:

> The tactic of armed struggle is of primary importance because it provides a vital cutting edge. Without it, the issue of Ireland would not even be an issue. So, in effect, the armed struggle becomes armed propaganda. (Adams, 1986, p. 4)

> The media? Well, no reporter can ignore a terror incident, an operation in which there are killings. They can't ignore this. . . . In the 70s when we started hijacking planes, I mean the Palestinian movement, well they were trying to publicize the cause and were asking the media to come and cover the cause. What they did in Munich, for example, they did it for the newspapers, probably, because during that time, before 1982, there was only one side of the story presented. Nobody mentioned us. Nobody knew who are the Palestinians. We were just numbers, figures over there. We had no face, no clothes. (Foutah, personal communication, October 1990)

What matters for the insurgents, at this point in their struggle, is that their name and cause are placed prominently on the public platform, as the following exchange illustrates: "Why did you kill a harmless old man like Mountbatten?" asked a reporter calling Sinn Fein's Belfast press center. "Why are you calling from New Zealand?" came the reply from Belfast (Kelley, 1982, p. 306). And again, the response in *An Phoblacht/Republican News* by a member of the IRA Army Council to the worldwide condemnation of the Mountbatten murder is particularly illuminating:

> Killing this man had the aim of making the world understand—and first and foremost the British—that there is a state of war in this country. Given his personal importance there was inevitably going to be enormous publicity attached to this operation. . . . we had no hatred for him as a person. It is the

society, the military and the political machine he symbolized that we were aiming at.

Continued acts of violence in the later stages are, however, likely to constrain participation in the political wings of the insurgent organization and the organization's further penetration of society.

### PARTICIPATION AND PENETRATION

In the case of insurgent organizations seeking to achieve political objectives through both military and political action, acts of "terrorism" in these later stages often deflect attention from political initiatives. Indeed, the very appeal of violent acts that can propel an organization into the media headlines becomes an obstacle to media coverage of the movement's nonviolent political issues, as the media, well aware of the dramatic appeal of violent acts, continue to focus on those acts as opposed to less dramatic political pronouncements and initiatives. Also, the early identification of key political figures with support for, or actual participation in, acts of violence often limits the effectiveness of those leaders as they seek to advance their political initiatives. For example, as prominent Palestinian intellectual Edward Said (1986) has noted:

> Roughly speaking, there are a small handful of essential thematic clusters in today's media coverage of the Middle East. [Among them is] . . . the Middle East as the fons et origo, the hatching ground, of the gratuitous evils of the PLO. Yasir Arafat, whose poor media image is probably beyond repair, is the ranking figure in this cluster of motifs whose basic message is that, if they exist at all, the Palestinians are both marginal and entirely to blame for their misfortunes. (pp. 88-89)

Indeed, the violent acts carried out in the early stages of a movement may well contribute to an "immunization effect" as the public becomes increasingly familiar with the horrific results of political violence. Philip Elliott (1977), for example, in his study of the coverage of Northern Ireland in the British media, has pointed out that even during the periods of the most intense constitutional political activity, the stories were predominantly ones of irrational violence, lacking in any historical background, and largely based upon official sources. This immunization is likely to require acts of even greater violence to attract attention during the later stages of movement development, precisely when such actions are more likely to increase public opposition to the cause and erode gains made in the expansion of the base of support.

Although media coverage of armed operations achieves a certain, if negative, status for insurgent organizations, this focus on violence also often precludes media coverage of more pressing political initiatives as the insurgent movement expands politically. The frustration with the media's unwillingness to focus on the political aspects of the Republican movement is clearly expressed in the following remarks by Sinn Fein President Gerry Adams to journalists on the day the Thatcher government introduced the current media ban on interviews with Sinn Fein spokespersons. In response to claims that interviews with Sinn Fein representatives had been censored on the grounds that Sinn Fein championed the armed struggle of the IRA and hence should be banned, as is the IRA, Adams commented:

> If that is the perception, it is because that has been the issue on which the media has concentrated down through the years. Eighty percent of all press statements issued through Republican press centers have been on social, economic and political issues in particular, most of which, incidentally, have been ignored. . . . The British government challenged Sinn Fein to contest elections, which we did. We put forward a very wide range of views. The media tended to concentrate on our position on armed struggle. (quoted in Morrison, 1989, pp. 8-9)

While effective at securing the world's attention to their cause, a rhetoric of violence, once established, limits the ability of the insurgents to introduce an alternative rhetoric of reasoned argument. Attempts by the political representatives of insurgent movements to shift public attention from the narrow issue of armed struggle to the broader social and political issues necessary to further their penetration in society are rendered more complex and difficult by their early, and continued, linkage in the media to acts of political violence.

> The media image of the armed struggle in the 26 Counties has had a negative effect on Sinn Fein in the context of people joining Sinn Fein. We need to look at how we can change people's perceptions of SF. (Sinn Fein, 1986, p. 2)

> Since the 1970's there has been a concerted campaign to politically isolate both the IRA and Sinn Fein. This campaign takes on a whole range of forms from censorship to hostile reporting in the media. . . . People are afraid to let it be known that they support Sinn Fein. This campaign has been most successful in the 26 counties because of the almost unchallenged and distorted picture

> that people have regarding what is happening in the north and the bad image they get of IRA actions. . . . The war is undoubtedly the main feature of Sinn Fein's image. . . . to break out of isolation and grow is a formidable task because it means taking on the major opinion forming bodies and reversing their hold on the minds of the general public. (Sinn Fein, 1986, p. 4)

Perhaps as important, this linkage also limits the insurgents' struggle for international legitimacy and impedes attempts to expand the domestic base of support.

> IRA actions which result in civilian deaths or injuries are usually seized upon by the media in an effort to reinforce their prejudiced presentation. Internationally this can be especially damaging. (McAuley, personal communication, October 11, 1991)

The importance placed by Sinn Fein on international recognition and support is well illustrated in the following comments by Ted Howell, head of Sinn Fein Foreign Affairs Bureau, to the Sinn Fein membership at its 1990 party conference:

> The importance of international work, of positively influencing international public and political opinion and of generating interest and the adoption of positive political positions and actions, has long been recognized as an integral and crucial part of the struggle for Irish independence. . . . The reality for many years has been that most international media correspondents with few exceptions report the conflict in Ireland from the confines of London. . . . we have to move to a situation where we are enabled to put our position, in a timely fashion, on the desks of London based correspondents. . . . in tandem with the International Publicity and Information Committee, the Foreign Affairs Bureau . . . [provides] activists on Ireland in Britain, the USA, Canada and Europe with facts, statistics and arguments on a wide range of issues on a weekly basis.

The insurgents, as they advance politically in their struggle, increasingly recognize that the audiences whose attention and support they wish to attract are unable, unwilling, or afraid to listen. As a result, armed operations during these later stages are likely to be confined, where possible, to targets of considerable importance to the government in power and to the domestic military concerns of the insurgents. Rather than maximum exposure, the aims of actions in the later stages will be to place enough pressure on official government and military personnel to bring them to the negotiating table.

Public statements by groups during these advanced stages will certainly place greater emphasis upon the political as opposed to the military aspects of the campaign. For example, in reference to ETA's operations during 1988, an article in Herri Batasuna's foreign affairs bulletin claims:

> ETA's military offensive was the prelude to a peace drive, aimed at unblocking the situation and advancing towards a genuine negotiation, which is considered by all sensible individuals as the only possible solution leading towards peace and freedom for the Basque People and the other oppressed peoples of the Spanish State. (*Askatzen*, no. 7, p. 2)

Although spokespersons for insurgent organizations recognize that there is little they can do to counteract, particularly under strict censorship controls, this intimate association of their political and military wings, strategies are adopted to minimize this linkage. Perhaps the most noticeable attempts to project a more political, less violent image have been made in party newspapers and documents prepared for external circulation. Whereas documents from the early periods of intense armed struggle emphasize the military capabilities of the insurgents and the impact of bombings and other operations on government policy, those from later periods tend to place more emphasis on social and political initiatives and electoral achievements of the political wing. In particular, whereas photographs of armed militants in action or of demolished buildings appear prominently in documents from the early periods of the ETA and IRA campaigns, such photos are less in evidence in later publications, except in cases of major military operations such as those carried out by the IRA against Thatcher in Brighton in 1984 and the attack on Downing Street in 1991. One particularly good example of an attempt at an image shift can be seen in the international news briefings prepared by Sinn Fein's Foreign Affairs Bureau and first published in January 1989. Whereas previous news briefings had carried considerable coverage of IRA operations, this publication, conceived as a means to overcome what was perceived by Sinn Fein as an international media blackout of events in Ireland, focuses far more attention on social issues and Sinn Fein political initiatives and merely includes a chronology of IRA operations.

In my discussions with Chrissie McAuley, convener of Sinn Fein's International Publicity and Information Committee and editor of the committee's international news briefs, the issue of how to focus attention on the politics of Sinn Fein rather than the armed struggle of the IRA was raised on numerous occasions. In general, she agreed that there are no easy ways to do this. However, some strategies suggested by the international publicity committee to minimize the association have included the more frequent and prominent display of photographs of Sinn Fein councillors engaged in local political initiatives and increased coverage of national social and political issues in the Republican newspaper *An Phoblacht/Republican News* and the widespread use of leaflets outlining Sinn Fein policy positions on current social, cultural, and political issues for distribution in the local communities.

During these later stages, when insurgent organizations are attempting to increase participation and further their penetration in society by broadening their base of supporters, it is clear that the relative merits of violent or nonviolent tactics are considered by the insurgents before they adopt a particular strategy. Based on the data gathered for this study, I maintain that the value attributed to each set of tactics during these later stages can be significantly affected by the attitudes and policies of the media toward insurgent organizations.

If political solutions to the conflicts being waged by the groups examined here are sought by participants on both sides, this will entail openly examining, discussing, analyzing, and directly addressing the political positions and tactics adopted by these groups and their public spokespersons. It will require persuading those who now support such groups that there are either alternative, better goals or more effective nonviolent means of achieving the desired goals, and, as Article 19 (1989), the London-based human rights organization, has noted, it will require "allowing those who speak for all groups, but *especially* those who now communicate through violence, to put their case on television, on the radio and in the print media and allowing their arguments to stand or fall on their merits in open interplay with the views advanced by the many opposing and competing political forces" (p. 101). It will require that the media that placed the violence and insurgents in the headlines look as intently at the political, nonviolent strategies of the insurgents to end the violence. Ignoring positive moves by insurgent organizations in the political sphere may well encourage their return to acts of terrorism that they have seen will generate attention.

## Conclusion

Contrary to the conventional wisdom that "all publicity is good publicity" for "terrorists," selective media coverage of acts of political violence can impede, as well as advance, the aims of insurgent "terrorism." An examination of the statements and internal documents of three insurgent nationalist organizations provides empirical support for the claim that insurgent "terror-ists" are more likely to view the media as, at best, reluctant allies and, at worst, hostile and powerful enemies. This study also suggests that analysis of the media-terrorist relationship could be improved through the application of a dynamic rather than a static framework.

Perhaps most important, this chapter has revealed the need for more empirical insurgent-based research regarding the role of the media in the strategy of insurgent "terrorist" organizations if we are not to fall into the practice of seeing only what we wish to see in this relationship, with the dangerous result of elaborating counterproductive policies based on faulty perceptions. To encourage this research is also to encourage a significant shift within official government and intellectual circles regarding the motives of those who pursue it. It must be made clear that the decision to research insurgent "terrorism," to attempt to understand the motives and strategies of terrorists, or to defend the right of dissident political organizations to have their opinions aired and challenged by the media on the same basis as mainstream organizations does not necessarily imply sympathy for either the aims or the tactics espoused and adopted by the insurgent organizations.

## References

Adams, G. (1986). *The politics of Irish freedom.* Dingle, Ireland: Brandon.

Adams, G. (1990, February). *Presidential address.* Speech given at the 85th Sinn Fein Ard Fheis, Dublin.

Alexander, Y. (Ed.). (1976). *International terrorism.* New York: Praeger.

Alexander, Y., & O'Day, A. (Eds.). (1984). *Terrorism in Ireland.* London: Croom Helm.

Article 19. (1989). *No comment: Censorship, secrecy and the Irish troubles.* London: International Centre on Censorship.

Bassiouni, M. C. (1983). Problems in media coverage of nonstate-sponsored terror-violence incidents. In L. Z. Freedman & Y. Alexander (Eds.), *Perspectives on terrorism* (pp. 177-200). Wilmington, DE: Scholarly Resources.

Bell, J. B. (1978). *A time of terror: How democratic societies respond to revolutionary violence.* New York: Basic Books.

Clutterbuck, R. (1983). *The media and political violence* (2nd ed.). New York: Macmillan.

Desantes Guanter, J. M. (1980, November). *Relationship between freedom of press and information and publicity given by the mass media.* Paper presented at the Conference on Defence of Democracy Against Terrorism in Europe, Parliamentary Assembly, Council of Europe, Strasbourg.

Elliot, P. (1977). Reporting Northern Ireland. In UNESCO (Ed.), *Ethnicity and the media.* Paris: UNESCO.

Harris, E. (1987). *Broadcasting and terrorism.* Dublin: Radio Telefis Eireann.

Hoggart, S. (1979, July 17). Neave broadcast episode dropped. *Guardian.*

Hurd, D. (1988). *Broadcasting and terrorism.* London: Home Office.

Ibarra, P. (1989). *La evolucion estrategica de ETA.* San Sebastian: Kriselu.

ITZAL. (1989, December 14-28). [Editorial]. *Punto y Hora, 561,* p. 54.

Jenkins, B. (1975). *International terrorism.* Santa Monica, CA: Rand Corporation.

Jenkins, B. (1981). *The psychological implications of media-covered terrorism* (Rand Paper P6627). Santa Monica, CA: Rand Corporation.

Kelley, K. (1982). *The longest war: Northern Ireland and the IRA.* Dingle, Ireland: Brandon.

Laqueur, W. (1976). The futility of terrorism. *Harper's, 252*(1510), 104.

Laqueur, W. (1977). *Terrorism.* London: Weidenfield & Nicholson.

Larson, C. U. (1973). *Persuasion: Reception and responsibility.* Belmont, CA: Wadsworth.

Lodge, J. (1981). *Terrorism: A challenge to the state.* New York: St. Martin's.

Morrison, D. (1989). *Ireland: The censored subject.* Dublin: Sinn Fein.

O'Brien, C. C. (1983, January 9). Terrorism and the liberal fallacy. *Observer,* p. 7.

Paletz, D. L., Fozzard, P. A., & Ayanian, J. Z. (1982). The I.R.A., the Red Brigades, and the F.A.L.N. in the "New York Times." *Journal of Communication, 32*(2), 162-171.

Paletz, D. L., Fozzard, P. A., & Ayanian, J. Z. (1983). Terrorism on TV news: The IRA, the FALN, and the Red Brigades. In W. C. Adams (Ed.), *Television coverage of international affairs* (pp. 143-165). Norwood, NJ: Ablex.

PLO. (1981). [Editorial]. *PLO Information Bulletin, 8*(1), 69.

PLO news and views: Arafat condemns terrorism. (1985). *Palestine Perspective.*

Said, E. (1986). The MESA debate: The scholars, the media and the Middle East. *Journal of Palestine Studies, 16*(1).

Schlesinger, P. (1984). Terrorism, the media, and the liberal-democratic state: A critique of the orthodoxy. In Y. Alexander & A. O'Day (Eds.), *Terrorism in Ireland.* London: Croom Helm.

Schlesinger, P., Murdock, G., & Elliott, P. (1983). *Televising terrorism: Political violence in popular culture.* London: Comedia.

Schmid, A. P. (1990, March 7). *Terrorism and the media: Freedom of information vs. freedom from intimidation.* Paper presented at the University of California, Irvine.

Schmid, A. P., & De Graaf, J. F. A. (1982). *Violence as communication: Insurgent terrorism and the Western news media.* Beverly Hills, CA: Sage.

Sinn Fein. (1986). *The needs and demands of the struggle* (internal briefing document). Dublin: Author.

Sinn Fein. (1991). *Political report.* Dublin: Author.

Sinn Fein. (n.d.). *The role of officers.* Dublin: Author.

Stohl, M. (1988). *The politics of terrorism* (3rd ed.). New York: Marcel Dekker.

Thomas, J. (1988). Bloody Ireland. *Columbia Journalism Review, 27,* 31-37.

Wardlaw, G. (1989). *Political terrorism: Theory, tactics and counter-measures.* Cambridge: Cambridge University Press.

Wilkinson, P. (1977). *Terrorism and the liberal state.* London: Macmillan.

# 5

# Governments' Perspectives

Jennifer Jane Hocking

> The variable modalities of meaning that attend terrorism are the products of socially constructed realities.
>
> *Greisman, 1977, p. 303*

In the relatively brief contemporary resurgence of the concept of "terrorism," Greisman was one of the first theorists to recognize an essential contestability. Replete with implied moral opprobrium, a socially assigned value and meaning, an imputation of illegitimacy and outrage, "terrorism" can never fit the apparently value-neutral typologies much used in the social sciences (see, for example, Sloan, 1978).

The phenomenon of reification, the ascription of a phantom objectivity to a social meaning, Greisman (1977) uses to explain "a paradox that follows acts of terrorism: individual, or non-state, terrorism, is generally seen as evil, while official, or legitimate, terrorism, is relatively accepted" (p. 304). That *terrorism* is, in its essence, a politicized term has been argued elsewhere (Hocking, 1984). The power of the discourse of terrorism lies particularly in the ability to define its application, and this is as much the case for "counterterrorism" as it is for "terrorism."

The orthodox literature on terrorism, however, has invariably reduced the development of counterterrorism measures to the unproblematic reaction to acts or threats of terrorism. Counterterrorism, rather than being considered a discrete phenomenon worthy of analysis in its own right, has commonly been defined only in terms of its apparently reactive relationship to "terrorism." The question of terrorism's relation to the media is no exception.

The relationship between terrorism and the media has been characterized as one of "symbiosis," in which terrorism's primary aim is media coverage (Bell, 1978). The perception of terrorism as aimed primarily at publicity rather than at the resolution of specific political demands locates its success not in the meeting of those demands but in the generation of publicity. "Media recognition is absolutely crucial; the success of a terrorist act depends mainly on the media coverage it enjoys" (Frey, 1987, p. 181).

Bell (1978) carries this argument further, claiming that media coverage is crucial to the tactical success of a terrorist attack such that "the quality of coverage is quite immaterial to the terrorist's purpose; only the intensity and quantity of coverage matter" (p. 50). This enables Bell to claim that an act of terrorism may yet be considered "successful," in this publicity sense, even if in political and tactical terms it fails. "Once a terror-event is launched before the camera, the drama by definition is a success. Operationally, all those involved may be killed . . . or captured and imprisoned. . . . Still, the impact exists; and in fact the impact may be greater because of the violent failure" (p. 49).

The perception of a symbiotic relationship between terrorism and the media fails to accommodate any independent role of the state in that relationship. This is a singular failure given that from this perception follows a prescription of counterterrorism measures by the state that includes at its heart a controlling of the alleged media/terrorism symbiosis. The orthodox approach to terrorism has been mirrored in a corresponding strategy of counterterrorism. An orthodox pattern of counterterrorism has developed in tandem with this particular conception of terrorism, persistent with what Stohl (1983) has described as "eight myths" found in the orthodox literature on terrorism (for a more detailed discussion of the orthodoxy within the literature on terrorism, see Hocking, 1984; Schlesinger, 1981). Stohl lists these myths as follows:

1. Political terrorism is the exclusive province of antigovernmental forces.
2. The purpose of political terrorism is the production of chaos.
3. Political terrorism is the province of madmen.
4. Terrorism is criminal, not political, activity.
5. All insurgent violence is political terrorism.
6. Governments always oppose nongovernmental terrorism.
7. Terrorism is exclusively a problem relating to internal political conditions.
8. Political terrorism is a strategy of futility. (pp. 5-6)

To these eight a further common myth should be added: that terrorism depends for its success on media coverage (Bell, 1978; Frey, 1987). The prescribed counterterrorism measures in liberal democracies have been devised to counter these nine mythical dimensions of terrorism.

A problem of definition arises in the application of all counterterrorism strategies that has enabled these measures to be used in response to actions ranging from those seen as challenging the state to the merely politically marginal (Findlay, 1985; Oppenheimer & Canning, 1979; Schlesinger, 1981; Soulier, 1978). This introduces a central concern of this chapter, that incidents may be responded to as terrorism through the activation of counterterrorism procedures, rather than on the basis of the recognition of determining features in the incidents themselves. That is, incidents are being defined as "terrorism" on the basis of a counterterrorist reaction to those incidents. This, of course, turns the orthodoxy on its head, for no longer is counterterrorism defined by its relationship to terrorism; rather, terrorism is defined by its relationship to counterterrorism: Terrorism is defined only by a reaction to it. This underscores Soulier's (1978) argument that the terrorist is, "in the last analysis, whoever is classified and prosecuted as such" (p. 30).

## Media Management

Of crucial importance in contemporary counterterrorism techniques has been the development of a detailed framework for media "cooperation" or "voluntary restraint" in reporting incidents of terrorism. In using the media as part of the battle against terrorism, "cooperation" rather than "control" is the operative approach.

> Few governments have yet learned to make positive and effective use of the mass media.... This does not mean government control of news and comment, which rebounds by killing its credibility. It means helping reporters and cameramen to get to the scene of events, to meet those responsible, to get the facts and to report what they see and hear. (Clutterbuck, 1973, p. 257)

This strategy had been adopted by the London Metropolitan Police under Sir Robert Mark in the early 1970s, and it provided the blueprint for the implementation of media cooperation in Australia. Mark had visited Australia early in 1978, following an unclaimed bombing outside the Sydney

Hilton hotel during the first Commonwealth Heads of Government Regional Meeting. Despite the absence of any indication that this bombing was indeed an act of terrorism, it was widely presented as Australia's "first terrorist incident." Mark was asked to conduct an inquiry into counterterrorist resources and training. His report and general approach to counterterrorism remain the basis for the current policy of "voluntary restraint," and for the critical importance given by security officials to controlled media coverage in the resolution of terrorist incidents.

Mark's view on military aid to the civil power in the resolution of terrorist incidents emphasizes the importance of the media in establishing public awareness of, and support for, the limited use of troops on such occasions. During a lecture at Leicester University in March 1976, Mark (1977) argued that "the confidence and support of the people on whose behalf we act [are] the most essential weapons in our armory" (p. 24). It was Mark's acute awareness of the importance of the media to the police that made the relationship between the police and the media a central feature of his term as commissioner. Mark made frequent use of his successful personal rapport with senior media representatives to publicize his views on political issues and his plans for restructuring the British police force, and to generate public confidence in these moves (Chibnall, 1979). Mark's (1978) approach to the media was based on his often-expressed view that

> the operational effectiveness of the force is to a very large extent dependent upon the goodwill, co-operation and support of members of the general public. . . . public backing can be obtained or strengthened . . . by means of publicity given to the activities of the force in the press and on television and radio. (appendix G)

To this end, one of Mark's early priorities was to improve relations between the police and the media.

There were two main strands to Mark's media strategy: the establishment of direct personal links between higher police officials and media executives, together with the more specific tactic of limiting access to certain information to select journalists (see Chibnall, 1979, p. 140; Kettle, 1980, p. 16). This second strand was achieved through the use of special police press passes—Metropolitan and City Police Press Cards—which have become increasingly exclusive since their introduction in 1973. These cards were initially issued automatically to approximately 8,000 journalists, but by 1975 there were only 2,000 cards available to British press, radio, and television journalists as well as to members of the foreign press (Bunyan, 1977, p. 91). The major newspapers, for instance, were usually allocated 4 passes each, with the editors then nominating particular journalists to receive the passes. These names were then relayed to Scotland Yard. "Journalists 'approved' in this manner are the ones who must cover certain trials, large demonstrations, and the visits of foreign dignitaries—they are also afforded special briefings by the police" (Bunyan, 1977, p. 91).

In 1978 Scotland Yard informed the London free-lance branch of the National Union of Journalists that free-lance and magazine journalists would not be issued Metropolitan Press Cards, further restricting the privileged coverage of largely political news to the established press. Mark's police circular of 1973, reproduced in his Australian report (Mark, 1977, appendix G), stressed the importance of this privileged treatment as being "of real value" to cardholders: "In normal circumstances card-holders are to be provided with all such information and opportunities for access as can be made available. . . . special facilities cannot be accorded to non-holders." Press cards were introduced by state police forces in Australia in the late 1970s. The police provision of cards was far more limited than that sought by some of the major newspapers. The Melbourne *Age*, for instance, re-quested 20 such cards, for use by several journalists, which the police Media Liaison Unit reduced to 4. After several years of operation the police press card system was abandoned in 1985 and replaced by police recognition of the standard Australian Journalists' Association membership card.

In the specific area of media coverage of terrorism, under Mark's guidance the Metropolitan police developed a system of "voluntary" restraint and cooperation from the media when reporting terrorist incidents. This policy of voluntary restraint in reporting sieges and kidnappings was put to the test several times in 1975, and reached its pinnacle of operational efficiency during the Iranian embassy siege of 1980. The media played a crucial role in the state's counterterrorism strategy, restricting their coverage as specified by guidelines set out by the Metropolitan police, and presenting "live" coverage of the storming of the embassy by SAS troops. However, as Schlesinger, Murdock, and Elliott (1983) note: "The moment when the SAS actually attacked . . . was in fact video-taped, and evidently the decision to hold back on live coverage for some minutes on both channels was the result of an 'understanding' with the authorities" (pp. 115-116).

As in many other areas of policing in Britain, Sir Robert Mark's influence on the police-media relationship has been substantial and enduring. Chibnall (1979) concludes that Mark's legacy in this area is "not so much a well-oiled machinery for the repressive control of the news media but rather the painstakingly established conditions of media support and cooperation vital to any further extension of pre-emptive policing and political control in the 1980's" (p. 149).

On each of the main issues to be considered in his Australian report, Mark held strong and publicly expressed views. These issues included military aid to the civil power, the role of special branches within the police forces, the accountability of the federal police, contingency planning for military-police cooperation in counterterrorism, and relations with the news media. On all these matters, Mark's recommendations were simple reiterations of the views he had been propounding in Britain over the previous 15 years—even to the extent of including as appendices his Leicester University lecture and the 1973 circular on press-police relations referred to above. Despite Mark's (1973) claim elsewhere that "the methods to be adopted in keeping the peace will inevitably reflect the historical, constitutional and political conditions of the community" (p. 1), the brevity of his report (79 pages, of which 50 were appendices reproduced from elsewhere) and the speed with which it was produced (six weeks) indicate that he made no apparent effort to come to grips with Australia's particular needs in the area of counterterrorism. Indeed, his 1978 report begins with the admission that he lacked "extensive knowledge of Australian constitutional and criminal law." "All we can do," he wrote, "is to make recommendations on the basis of our experience of policing under a different political and legal framework" (p. 1).

## Media Management: The Australian Approach

In the Australian context, what has been adopted is a system of "voluntary restraint" by media organizations rather than outright censorship. On November 15, 1979, the first (and only publicly released) review of Australia's counterterrorism arrangements was tabled in Federal Parliament. Justice Hope's Protective Security Review (PSR) was also established immediately after the Sydney Hilton hotel bombing in February 1978.

Although this review was clearly an outcome of the Hilton bombing, by the time of its release events had already overtaken its recommendations. The earlier release of the report by Robert Mark had provided a more immediate focus for the reorganization of Australia's counterterrorism machinery, and with the passage of the Australian Federal Police Act and the Australian Security Intelligence Organization Act earlier in 1979, the major legislative changes in this area had already taken place. The PSR was therefore more a descriptive than a policy document, and has provided the most comprehensive examination to date of all aspects of protective security in Australia.

Justice Hope's (1979) review outlines the benefits of the orthodox approach to media reporting of terrorist incidents: "Rather than impose information control on the media, it is preferable to foster close liaison between government, police and the media in an effort to establish guidelines which would operate in relation to a crisis incident" (p. 120). The later review conducted by Justice Hope clearly built on Mark's recommendations. In assessing the role of the media in Australia's crisis management network, it is instructive to examine the view of the relationship between terrorism and the media on which the recommendations were based.

Hope's view of the relationship between terrorism and the media is given in his citing of an article by Chalmers Johnson titled "Terror":

> Equal to or greater in importance than new weaponry in the growth of terrorism is the global expansion of mass media of communications. Since public attention to his cause is usually one of the terrorist's key objectives, advances in communications have been critically valuable to him. Media contribute to publicity for a particular terrorist cause, the contagious triggering of other terrorists' decisions to act, the training of terrorists through a media-fed pool of experience and inspiration, and international linkages among terrorist organizations. (Johnson, 1977, pp. 119-120)

Chalmers Johnson specifically rejects direct causes, such as socioeconomic deprivation or political grievances, as determining factors in the terrorism of the 1970s. Instead, he argues that "the rise in international terrorist incidents is due almost entirely to changes in the permissive causes," which he describes as being the existence of new targets, new technology (weapons and media), and new "toleration" (p. 50). As contributors to this new toleration, Johnson includes "France and Switzerland, which have become involuntary hosts to all manner of foreign dissident groups because of their heritage of strong rights of political asylum and of protection of democratic freedoms" (p. 51).

With such a perspective on the causes of terrorism, which rejects any political basis to actions as diverse as those of the Tupamaros in Uruguay to those of the Baader-Meinhof group in West Germany, Johnson's (1977) solution to the problem of terrorism follows accordingly: "Terrorism can be suppressed through 'special powers,' but these inevitably entail a temporary curtailment or suspension of certain liberties. For example, censorship and detention without trial may be necessary" (p. 52). The PSR uncritically accepted this perspective on terrorism, and the correlating view of the role of the media, in its suggested counterterrorism strategy. Robert Mark's approach to counterterrorism also clearly paralleled Johnson's, and the PSR adopted Mark's cooperative system of media-security liaison during terrorist incidents.

Hope (1979) recommended, in terms that closely follow the recommendations of Mark's report, that in the event of a terrorist incident,

> rather than impose information control on the media, it is preferable to foster close liaison between government, police and the media in an effort to establish guidelines which would operate in relation to a crisis incident. There have been instances overseas where the media have co-operated with the police and actively assisted the police to conclude cases successfully. (p. 120)

Stressing the need for media cooperation, Hope suggests that "as far as possible police and government should enlist media support and confidence to enable it to report responsibly" (p. 121). Moves have been made toward the implementation of this cooperation, following the strategy adopted by the London Metropolitan Police. The major counterterrorist organization in Australia, the Protective Services Co-ordination Centre (PSCC),

> has convened discussions between State and Commonwealth officials on liaison with the media on counterterrorism. As a result of these discussions PSCC is implementing with the States a program of briefing media organizations throughout Australia. PSCC has appointed an experienced journalist as a media liaison officer to participate in this briefing program which is aimed at developing machinery for close co-operation between the media and Government in the event of terrorist incidents. . . . No doubt PSCC will be taking into account recent overseas experience in relation to media co-operation. . . . In the event of a terrorist incident a Commonwealth press centre would be established . . . to be the contact point with media representatives. (Hope, 1979, p. 121)

This description of the PSCC's moves toward media cooperation gives an unequivocal indication that Hope accepted the British approach to media control, and that by 1979 this approach had already been adopted into the Australian counterterrorism strategy.

The aspect of this approach to media control that is seen as particularly sinister by some observers is the PSR's suggested action against media organizations that do not cooperate with government and security guidelines (Halliday, 1980, p. 9). If the media use their own equipment to monitor police and other official communications, the police "must have the necessary technical resources and capacity to counter such monitoring," Hope advises. Further, Hope (1979) contends that since direct communications between terrorists and the media may frustrate police negotiations, the police must be able to disconnect telephones immediately and to jam radio transmissions between terrorists and the media (p. 122).

Specific media guidelines in Australia for reporting terrorist incidents are similar to those used in other Western countries, and include the following, which were presented at a 1988 PSCC media briefing:

1. No live coverage of terrorists, in order to avoid providing them with an unedited propaganda platform.
2. Avoidance of inflammatory catchwords and phrases.
3. Reporting of any demands should be free of propaganda and rhetoric.
4. Media representatives should avoid making themselves part of the story.
5. No telephone calls should be made to the terrorists.
6. Media representatives should do nothing to further endanger the lives of hostages.

The mythical "terrorist incident" referred to during such briefings is an ongoing one in which hostages have been taken. Australia has no history of any such terrorist incidents, and reports consistently indicate that the level of threat from this type of incident remains extremely low. Indeed, a detailed report of a study on Australia's counterterrorism machinery conducted in 1986 within the Department of the Special Minister of State was highly critical of this concentration on a particular type of violence of which Australia has no history. Although a similar report on Australia's counter-terrorism developments was released in 1979, this later report was unreleased for "national security" reasons (R. Holdich, personal communication, 1987). Nevertheless, the Australian strategy has continued to be tightly developed on the basis of the occurrence of such hostage-taking incidents overseas. As with other aspects of counterterrorism developments, this strategy has broadened out from the mythical base (an ongoing hostage incident) to cover a wider range of nonterrorist incidents in practice.

During an incident in Brisbane in 1983, the PSCC's crisis management network was activated and its media control strategy tested. The particular importance of this episode, in which an extortion attempt was made against the major domestic airline, TAA, is that there was no suggestion from security officials that this was in any sense a terrorist incident. Yet the response to it was the mobilization of a counterterrorism strategy that had been developed ostensibly to deal with exceptional incidents of political terrorism. In this case, there was a voluntary news blackout by all of Australia's major media organizations until media briefings were given by official media centers in accordance with the strategy outlined above. There was subsequent widespread criticism by the media of excessive secrecy by police during the episode, especially given that the media blackout had given the public no knowledge of the threat that had been made against TAA, but the Queensland premier had been able to take advantage of his own privileged security information to cancel a flight he had previously scheduled on the airline (Hocking, 1986a).

This incident illustrates how the extraordinary measures that have been developed to deal with terrorism are being gradually extended into the general structure of internal policing. During a 1988 PSCC media briefing, security officials referred to the way in which the strategy of media restraint in reporting acts of terrorism was already operating in all major areas of police work. Recent cases in Australia have witnessed an unprecedented liaison between police and media, with media being given special briefings concerning alleged "criminals," in some cases before charges have even been laid (Freckleton, 1988).

The Code of Ethics of the Australian Journalists' Association includes standards that require that journalists "report and interpret the news with scrupulous honesty by striving to disclose all essential facts and by not suppressing relevant, available facts or distorting by wrong or improper emphasis," and "use fair and honest means to obtain news, pictures, films, tapes and documents." There is no doubt that the practical workings of the strategy of "cooperation and restraint" detailed above involve some compromising of these ethics.

Since the mid-1970s the counterterrorist network, headed by the PSCC, has held regular briefings with journalists to ensure their readiness to slot into that network in practice. In the event of a terrorist incident police would seal off the surrounding area to all people, including journalists. Journalists would be briefed from a central liaison point "outside the inner perimeter but inside the outer perimeter" (PSCC media briefing, 1988). Journalists would be escorted to and from this point by counterterrorist members, and at no stage would they be able to collect information independent of that received from official media releases. Herein lies the capacity for security forces to provide an official construction of a terrorist situation, its context, and its resolution. In this respect the media strategy, which places the media within the state's counterterrorism network, permits an official construction of a particular, contentious, reality. This is the necessary corollary of "voluntary

restraint"—the replacing of independently garnered information with officially sanctioned information. It differs little from the controls of wartime,
with much less fuss. Writing of the Falklands War, Held (1984) notes:

> Through the use of D notices and a whole package of rules, conventions and
> laws pertaining to secrecy . . . the government was able to keep a remarkable
> amount of information to itself, offering only a highly selective impression,
> and making it very hard to discern exactly what was happening and in whose
> interest. (p. 361)

Recent changes to the British approach to terrorism and the media have
clearly put an end to any notions of "voluntary restraint" ensuring apparent
media independence. In October 1988 the Home Office banned all unedited
or live interviews with "terrorist supporters." This change occurred at the
same time as the introduction of curbs on the right of "terrorist suspects" to
remain silent. These British counterterrorism measures have been described
as "part of an attack on civil liberties which [is] unprecedented in peacetime"
(Pienaar, 1988).

The ban on interviews with "terrorist supporters" provides an example of
the definitional problems associated with counterterrorism measures in
general. How is one to determine who are "terrorist supporters"? What of
members of a proscribed organization such as Sinn Fein speaking on a matter
that has no connection with terrorism? The Home Office states that the ban
does not apply to "a member of an organisation . . . speaking in a personal
capacity or purely in his capacity as a member of an organisation not falling
under the notice, eg, an elected council" (Perera, 1988). Despite this quali-
fication, interviews with local councillors over local issues were quickly
dubbed over regardless of their connection with terrorist issues. A confidential BBC memo leaked in November 1988 indicated that the BBC had, under
the guise of the new Home Office guidelines, nominated Labour MP Ken
Livingstone and U.S. Senator Edward Kennedy as two public figures not to
be interviewed on camera, as their criticisms of British policy on Northern
Ireland are well known (Wintour, 1988). Livingstone has claimed:

> Instead of merely closing off the alleged propaganda outlets to Sinn Fein it
> seems that the Government intends to use the ban to apply behind-the-scenes
> pressure to prevent access to radio and TV by those politicians who are critical
> of government policy in Ireland, or who have argued for British withdrawal
> and a united Ireland. (quoted in Wintour, 1988)

## Recontextualizing Counterterrorism

Orthodox perceptions of the relationship between terrorism and the media fail to contextualize adequately either terrorism or counterterrorism measures. The widely held view of the media as providing terrorists with "the oxygen of publicity," as Britain's former Prime Minister Margaret Thatcher has described it, has given rise to the belief that media management is a critical element in counterterrorism planning. Such a view suggests that some control over media reporting of acts of terrorism is essential for the eventual eradication of terrorism in liberal democracies. This of course presents a fundamental dilemma between censorship (prescribed ostensibly to deny terrorists access to media coverage) and the liberal-democratic ideological tradition of free speech. What is required is that these developments be located within a theoretical framework that would enable some hypotheses to be raised not only about the nature of terrorism (and hence about the relationship between terrorism and the media), but also about the nature of counterterrorism measures and their implications for state power and social control.

Domestic counterterrorism measures have focused on five main aspects: the use of exceptional legislation, the maintenance of vast intelligence collections, the development of preemptive controls on political activity, military involvement in civil disturbances, and the development of a strategy of media management in times of crisis. These elements have been described in detail elsewhere (Hocking, 1986b, 1988). Although the practical impact of these techniques has been clearest in the British instance, evidence of this broad approach can be seen in most of the domestic counterterrorism strategies adopted in several countries, particularly Italy, West Germany, South Africa, Israel, and Australia. These elements all have their roots in colonial, military, counterinsurgency techniques. It is in this context that the development of a media strategy as just one aspect of contemporary counterterrorism thought can best be understood.

## Counterterrorism as Counterinsurgency

Counterinsurgency writings grew out of the colonial struggles of Britain and France in the 1950s and early 1960s.[1] This background provides the determining "colonial antecedents" of counterinsurgency thought. As a result, Ahmad (1973) argues, "the biases of incumbents are built into the structure, images and language of contemporary Western . . . literature on the subject. We have come to accept ideologically contrived concepts and words as objective descriptions" (p. 325).

On a theoretical level, the location of counterterrorism writings within a broader school of "counterinsurgency" thought has provided a framework for analyzing the social and political implications of counterterrorism in practice. There is a clear conceptual relationship between counterterrorism and counterinsurgency thought. The works of British counterinsurgency experts such as Kitson (1971) and Thompson (1966) have provided the conceptual basis not only for the more recent writings on terrorism from Clutterbuck, Crozier, Moss, and Wilkinson (whose *Political Terrorism* [1974] Schlesinger [1978] describes as "counterinsurgency doctrine masquerading as political science" [p. 117]), but also for the development of specific counterterrorism strategies.

Indeed, Lowry (1977) suggests that it is possible to make sense of the U.K. Prevention of Terrorism (Temporary Provisions) Act "as a whole" only by examining that act "in the light of Kitson's counterinsurgency theory" (p. 213). Wilkinson's (1976) exposition of counterterrorism strategy for liberal democratic states, for example, is explicitly grounded in the adaptation of counterinsurgency theory to contemporary conflicts: "It is possible to draw from the recent experience of low-intensity and counterinsurgency operations certain basic ground rules which should be followed by liberal democracies taking a tough line against terrorism" (p. 10).

The importance of this theoretical link between counterterrorism and counterinsurgency writings is that counterterrorism has provided a domestic, peacetime, adaptation of strategies developed to deal with the essentially wartime exigencies of a colonial power. Furthermore, in their domestic adaptations, counterinsurgency strategies are being applied to various forms of civil action—to political demonstrations and industrial disputes—and not only to the more extreme violence of "terrorism" in the name of which these strategies were initially adopted.

Counterinsurgency techniques readily lend themselves to such generalized applications largely because they are predicated on a "continuum" view of insurgency. Insurgency is seen as being the final, intended, outcome of a revolutionary campaign that begins with nonviolent political and industrial demonstration and dispute—which Kitson (1971) describes as the "preparatory" and "pre-violent" periods (pp. 4-5, 67-71). Clutterbuck (1973) describes this continuum as "a rising staircase from Demonstration through Disruption to Damage and Death" (p. 38).

The radical alterations in domestic policing and security operations enacted in the name of countering "terrorism" are in this way transferred to similarly cover all violent crime, political violence, and industrial conflict. It is testimony to the rhetorical power of domestic strategies of counterterrorism that these strategies have merged so readily with the more noxious aspects of domestic countersubversion operations, but also (and more disturbingly) with the policing of manifestations of political and industrial conflict (Clutterbuck, 1978, 1984, 1986).

The importance of this theoretical link between counterterrorism and counterinsurgency writings is threefold:

1. Counterterrorism has provided a domestic adaptation of the counterinsurgency techniques that were developed as "the product of Western colonial and imperial expansion and the consequent relations of dominance imposed on the Third World" (Schlesinger, 1978, p. 99). These "relations of dominance" are implicit in counterinsurgency strategies, and are reproduced in the domestic adaptation of such strategies to deal with "terrorism." It is in this sense that Schlesinger (1978) argues that the "consideration of counterinsurgency thinking goes well beyond the area of foreign policy. It is currently highly relevant for an analysis of the *domestic* exercise of state power in numerous Western European states faced with 'terrorism' " (p. 99).

2. Through this link with counterinsurgency thought, counterterrorism is at base a military doctrine, an example of "military intellectual production in contemporary Britain" (Schlesinger, 1978, p. 106). It therefore focuses on militarized responses, the introduction of exceptional legislative measures, and preemptive intelligence collection, all of which involve some compromising of traditional political and legal rights. "The underlying assumption present in current work is that the state needs to anticipate threats. . . . Such views express a particular view of military professionalism which tends to contradict liberal democratic ideology" (Schlesinger, 1978, p. 115).

3. Counterterrorism, as a development of counterinsurgency, places "considerable emphasis . . . on information control" (Schlesinger, 1978, p. 106). Again, the military background of counterinsurgency writers has placed strong emphasis on the control of the media during times of crisis. The development of counterterrorism thought has modified this control into a domestic setting through the advocacy of "voluntary restraint" in reporting incidents of terrorism.

This theoretical approach to counterterrorism has been articulated practically through the adoption of counterterrorism measures that exhibit a remarkable uniformity across nations that have experienced vastly differing forms and degrees of political violence.

How, then, can these developments in counterterrorism be analyzed? Concerning terrorism in a democratic society (which he describes as "that type of regime which formally and practically permits the expression of dissent" [p. 201]), Bonanate (1979a) points to three unanticipated consequences of terrorism: "The more terrorism moves from its more general form to the more specific one, the fewer are its chances of success"; "a society acquainted with terrorism is a blocked one"; and "terrorism unmasks a democracy which is only formal" (p. 208). On the basis of these three consequences comes what Bonanate describes as the "most important of the unexpected consequences of terrorism," that "terrorism ends up involuntarily transforming itself in the opposite of what it wants: that is the *restabilizing* instrument of the existing system" (p. 208).

Bonanate's conceptualization of terrorism as an indicator of a "blocked" society presents an innovative hypothesis for the development of both terrorism and counterterrorism in democratic societies. It represents a significant departure from causal hypotheses that consider terrorism as a product, or itself a cause, of social or economic crises or as part of an "international terrorist" conspiracy in which (as Claire Sterling, 1981, suggests) all roads lead to Moscow. Despite his explicit rejection of these hypotheses as causal explanations for the development of terrorism, Bonanate (1979a) denies that it must therefore be concluded that "terrorism is an irrational, impredictable [*sic*] force which can indifferently hit any society, at any time" (p. 204). Rather, he argues that a different hypothesis can be developed by examining terrorism as an effect rather than as a cause—that is, in particular by analyzing the persistence of terrorism *despite* its argued failure to achieve its objectives.

Bonanate (1979a) posits that

> the presence of terrorism in a society thus becomes an *indicator* that society is (1) too solid to be modified with normal political instruments; and (2) that if, however, it produces terrorism this means that something is going wrong: terrorism then is not the indifferentiated [*sic*] "symptom" of the unease of the crisis of a society, but of the fact that the society is certainly in a particular situation, of solidity but also of immobility and inactivity. A society that knows terrorism is a *blocked society*, incapable of answering the citizens' requests for change but nevertheless capable of preserving and reproducing itself. (p. 205)

Clarifying this concept of blockage, Bonanate (1979a) describes the "blocked situation" as existing

> in a system which has such solid foundations and such solid structural organization that it cannot allow any innovations at all. Terrorism therefore is the symptom—*not* of an imminent collapse, but on the contrary (and in this way it is no longer "obvious") of the fact that the system has entered a phase of self-perpetuating immobility, which instead of damaging its solidarity (at least short or medium-term) makes it so solid that it can neutralize any attack. (p. 205)

If a political system is capable of rebutting demands for political change without itself becoming unstable, "then a block occurs which in turn produces a terrorist answer" (p. 206).

This leads to the third of Bonanate's (1979a) unanticipated consequences, that "societies which have terrorism appear rather undemocratic, or they have the tendency of distorting democratic rules into mere celebrations of formal rituals which are not converted into a substantial democracy" (p. 206). The development of powerful security apparatuses and mechanisms is in fact seen as part of this process of distortion.

> Instruments for social control, the ability to absorb dissent and protests give contemporary societies . . . [the capacity] to limit opposition, even to exploit [it] as a source of legitimization, leaving no room for the autonomous and progressive aggregation of a strong revolutionary movement. (p. 206)

Bonanate's conception of, and causal explanation for, terrorism has an important corollary for the analysis of the relationship between terrorism and the media. If, as Bonanate argues, terrorism indicates the existence of a blocked political structure, then it follows that the most effective way of eliminating terrorism "must lie in an awakening of political life, in an opening up of dynamic possibilities within an antiquated system. It may be suggested that systems which have not experienced terrorism . . . are characterized by a greater mobility than could have been imagined" (p. 208).

Similarly, Bonanate's (1979b) analysis of revolutionary international terrorism ("revolutionary" in the sense that such acts seek to change the existing international political system) presents such acts as

> an attempt to react in the face of the extension of international political-social control. . . . in a world in which national boundaries are less and less important,

not only thanks to a peaceful integration process, but also because of more and more evident interference of certain countries in the affairs of other ones, the terrorist cannot and perhaps doesn't even want to distinguish direct and indirect enemies, and immediate and mediate objectives. (p. 52)

This ascription of a *structural* cause to the existence of terrorism (rather than analyzing terrorism as itself a symptom of crisis) (Bonanate, 1979b, p. 64) has important repercussions for our understanding of counterterrorism at both national and international levels. It follows from Bonanate's analysis that, in countries that have experienced terrorism, the imposition of stringent security measures (and in particular media controls that would deny independent knowledge of the causal factors precipitating violence) will not only fail to resolve the root causes of terrorism, but will also place formidable obstacles in the path of the "democratization" that Bonanate sees as essential for that resolution—thereby exacerbating the already blocked political structure. Second, countries that have had no experience with concerted campaigns of terrorism yet that have nevertheless instituted counterterrorism measures similar to those in other, more conflict-ridden, states risk the development of the very "blocked" situation (through the imposition of this preemptive counterterrorism structure) that can be considered the basic causal link between terrorism and the society in which it occurs.

Not only is it not sufficient, therefore, to introduce stricter security controls over the media in response to terrorism, it may well be generating the structural conditions within which the potential for violence is realized. The ability to expand the definitional basis for the use of counterterrorism measures has enabled their application in controlling a range of civil protests and expressions of dissent. Considering the relationship between terrorism and counterterrorism anew, until democracies broaden their participatory base, enabling a popular and active voice in political life, not only will terrorism never be eradicated, it will in fact be created.

In the development of a counterterrorism strategy theoretically grounded in the colonizing histories of counterinsurgency, we are witnessing the evolution of a new type of state in which the expansion of an increasingly bureaucratic security sector is a critical component. The state's integration of the media into this national security design is, perhaps, an unanticipated consequence of the generality of counterterrorism.

# Note

1. These took place in Cyprus (British, 1955-1969), Malaya (British, 1948-1960), and Algeria (French, 1954-1962).

# References

Ahmad, B. (1973). The theory and fallacies of counterinsurgency. In J. Leggett (Ed.), *Taking state power.* New York: Harper & Row.

Bell, J. B. (1978, May/June). Terrorist scripts and live-action spectaculars. *Columbia Journalism Review, 17,* 47-50.

Bonanate, L. (1979a). Some unanticipated consequences of terrorism. *Journal of Peace Research, 16,* 197-213.

Bonanate, L. (1979b). Terrorism and international political analysis. *Terrorism, 1-2,* 47-67.

Bunyan, T. (1977). *The history and practice of the political police in Britain.* London: Quartet.

Chibnall, S. (1979). The Metropolitan Police and the news media. In S. Holdaway (Ed.), *The British police.* London: Edward Arnold.

Clutterbuck, R. (1973). *Protest and the urban guerrilla.* London: Cassell.

Clutterbuck, R. (1978). *Britain in agony.* London: Faber & Faber.

Clutterbuck, R. (1984). *Industrial conflict and democracy.* London: Macmillan.

Clutterbuck, R. (1986). *The media and political violence* (2nd ed.). London: Macmillan.

Crozier, B. (1976). *Terrorism: The problem in perspective.* London: Institute for the Study of Conflict.

Findlay, M. (1985). "Criminalization" and the detention of "political prisoners": An Irish perspective. *Contemporary Crises, 9,* 1-17.

Freckleton, I. (1988). Sensation and symbiosis. In I. Freckleton & H. Selby (Eds.), *Police in our society* (pp. 57-84). Sydney: Butterworths.

Frey, B. S. (1987). Fighting political terrorism by refusing recognition. *Journal of Public Policy, 7*(2), 179-188.

Gregory, F. (1976, October). Protest and violence: The police response. *Conflict Studies,* No. 75 [special issue].

Greisman, H. C. (1977). Social meanings of terrorism: Reification, violence, and social control. *Contemporary Crises, 1,* 303-318.

Halliday, M. (1980, January). Crisis policy centres (Parts 1-3). *Workers' News, 12, 19, 26.*

Held, D. (1984). Power and legitimacy in contemporary Britain. In G. McLennan, D. Held, & S. Hall (Eds.), *State and society in contemporary Britain* (pp. 299-369). London: Polity.

Hocking, J. J. (1984). Orthodox theories of "terrorism": The power of politicised terminology. *Politics, 19*(2), 103-110.

Hocking, J. J. (1986a). Mixing minimum force with maximum force. *Australian Society, 5*(6), 19-22.

Hocking, J. J. (1986b). Terrorism and counter-terrorism: Institutionalizing political order. *Australian Quarterly, 58,* 297-307.

Hocking, J. J. (1988). Counter-terrorism as counter-insurgency: The British experience. *Social Justice, 15,* 83-97.

Hope, R. M. (1979). *Protective security review report.* Canberra: Australian Government Publishing Service.

Johnson, C. (1977, November/December). Terror. *Society.*

Kettle, M. (1980). The politics of policing and the policing of politics. In P. Hain et al. (Eds.), *Policing the police* (Vol. 2, pp. 9-62). London: John Calder.

Kitson, F. (1971). *Low intensity operations.* London: Faber.

Lowry, D. (1977). Draconian powers: The new British approach to pretrial detention of suspected terrorists. *Columbia Human Rights Review, 9,* 213.

Mark, R. (1977). *Policing a perplexed society.* London: Allen & Unwin.

Mark, R. (1978). *Report on the organization of police resources in the Commonwealth area.* Canberra: Australian Government Publishing Service.

Moss, R. (1977). *The collapse of democracy.* London: Abacus.

Oppenheimer, M., & Canning, J. (1979). The national security state. *Berkeley Journal of Sociology, 23,* 3-33.

Perera, S. (1988, October 31). Channel 4 bows to TV "terror" ban. *Guardian.*

Pienaar, J. (1988, October 22). Government "acting like South Africa." *Independent.*

Schlesinger, P. (1978). On the shape and scope of counter-insurgency thought. In G. Littlejohn et al. (Eds.), *Power and the state* (pp. 98-127). London: Croom Helm.

Schlesinger, P. (1981). "Terrorism," the media and the liberal-democratic state: A critique of the orthodoxy. *Social Research, 48,* 74-99.

Schlesinger, P., Murdock, G., & Elliott, P. (1983). *Televising terrorism: Political violence in popular culture.* London: Comedia.

Sloan, S. (1978). International terrorism: Academic quest, operational art and policy implications. *Journal of International Affairs, 32*(1), 1-5.

Soulier, G. (1978). European integration and the suppression of terrorism. *Review of Contemporary Law, 2,* 21-45.

Sterling, C. (1981). *The terror network: The secret war of international terrorism.* New York: Holt, Rinehart & Winston.

Stohl, M. (1983). Myths and realities of political terrorism. In M. Stohl (Ed.), *The politics of terrorism* (pp. 1-22). New York: Marcel Dekker.

Thompson, R. (1966). *Defeating communist insurgency.* London: Chatto & Windus.

Wilkinson, P. (1974). *Political terrorism.* London: Macmillan.

Wilkinson, P. (Ed.). (1976, January). Terrorism versus liberal democracy: The problems of response [Special issue]. *Conflict Studies, 67.*

Wintour, P. (1988, November 8). Livingstone "ban" denied. *Guardian.*

# 6

# Broadcasting Organizations' Perspectives

David L. Paletz

Laura L. Tawney

As this book demonstrates, the media are the central connection in the terrorism-government-public nexus. Which terrorist activities are reported, how prominently, how framed, with what emphases, and whose views predominate—all influence the behavior of terrorists, the reactions and responses of government officials, and the views of the public. The media, moreover, can often become more than chroniclers of terrorists' actions: They may contribute to or interfere with the resolution of an incident by transmitting terrorists' communiqués; they may become a party to the negotiations; they may even jeopardize the lives of hostages by broadcasting personal information.

We might assume that demands inevitably and inexorably arise, usually from governments, for limitations, constraints, and, most commonly, the creation of guidelines for media coverage of terrorism. As a natural corollary, television, the medium that generates the most controversial, even sometimes inflammatory, coverage and that is usually more subject to government interference than the print media, would be the recipient of most of these pressures.

To ascertain the incidence and effects of such demands, we sent questionnaires to some 80 broadcasting organizations around the world. We requested copies of any codes or guidelines that their news, current affairs, and even entertainment departments use or refer to when covering or depicting terrorist actions and incidents. We asked whether, if used, the codes are considered appropriate and effective, and whether they have caused any problems. We asked about government encouragement or pressure on the broadcasters to devise and deploy such codes. The response rate was approximately 40%. Supplementing our data, Professor Alex Schmid provided us with letters and codes obtained in his research.

Since much of the material we received represents these broadcasting institutions' formal positions, it could be asserted that it is more official than fully revealing. Nor have we empirically determined its accuracy. Nonetheless, the letters and documents do indicate the views of these organizations and their personnel involved in, and in some cases charged with, the responsibility for media coverage of terrorism. In this chapter, therefore, we recount and classify their responses, codes, and guidelines.

## Five Levels

Our data fall, not always comfortably, into five levels, ranging from an absence of guidelines to detailed codes:

- *Level 1:* no rules for covering terrorism; no guidelines, codes, or even approaches
- *Level 2:* no rules, but philosophies or general policies about how to cover terrorism
- *Level 3:* no rules for terrorism, but general programming rules for coverage of violence and civil disorders
- *Level 4:* standardized guidelines
- *Level 5:* detailed rules, codes, guidelines

Only Levels 4 and 5 have guidelines specifically devised for terrorist incidents. However, both Levels 2 and 3 reflect caution and monitoring in covering terrorism, the assumption that it is not a subject to be taken lightly. Our discussion, with examples of which of our respondents typically fell under each category, follows. Unless otherwise indicated, the quotes come from the letters and codes we received.

### LEVEL 1: NO RULES

The broadcasting companies under this category have no formal guidelines or codes. Both the Netherlands Broadcasting Corporation and Portuguese Radiotelevision state that they neither have nor need formal codes. The former explains, however, that Dutch broadcasting has a "very decentralized structure with many autonomous organizations: formal programme guidelines . . . do not fit in this context." As for coverage of terrorist incidents, "general journalistic principles prevail."

The absence of a code does not necessarily mean untrammeled or detached coverage. According to the Ministry of Information of the State of Qatar, the Television Department has no guidelines "because we have not any terrorist activities in our country." Nonetheless, the ministry does rely on international news agencies and networks for coverage, "especially on the terrorist activities of the Israelis in the Arab occupied lands."

### LEVEL 2: NO RULES, BUT PHILOSOPHIES OR GENERAL POLICIES

In this category, the media companies have no guidelines, nor do they acknowledge any governmental pressure to institute them. They do express various philosophies and abstract policies about covering terrorism. For example, the aim of the Television Corporation of the Catholic University of Chile is to "inform of such acts with moderation, in an effort not to publicize them excessively. This is done by the way the news is headed, by the position within the daily newscast and by its length."

In Japan, the Tokyo Broadcasting System bases its coverage on two policies: "Allow no illicit outside exploitation of, or outside manipulation of our broadcasting; be motivated by our fundamental spirit, humanism." Written codes are not considered viable because they are supposedly unable to deal with changing circumstances. Instructions may lead "us to fail in taking the most appropriate measures." There is an in-house committee that studies "possible reactions to new situations."

Similarly, the television department of Danish Radio has not developed any codes or guidelines, for "hardly two terrorist actions would take place in the same way." However, close cooperative relations have been established with the government to deal with the information flow to "relieve any acute life-threatening situation affecting . . . the population." The government has the authority to require the airing of any messages. This has not occurred because, according to our respondent, requests made have been reasonable.

These three companies' philosophies/policies all rest on a strong sense of discretion, combined with a view of terrorism as random and unpredictable in both time and action.

### LEVEL 3: NO TERRORISM RULES; GENERAL PROGRAMMING RULES

Companies in this category depend on their general programming rules to cover terrorism. For Belgium's BRT, these include not to "overreact or to dramatize. Never to stir up emotions . . . one way or the other." Similarly, the Norwegian Broadcasting Corporation responded to our inquiry that "general NRK Rules for Programmes have been considered adequate." NRK has not been asked by the government to establish any codes or guidelines specifically for terrorism coverage.

### LEVEL 4: STANDARDIZED GUIDELINES

At this level, each of the broadcasting companies has an established list of guidelines. Significantly, there is considerable consensus among them about how television should cover terrorism. There are several prominent elements of this consensus: Do nothing to make the sensational event more sensational; paraphrase demands so as to deny the terrorists a political platform; do not provide live coverage of the terrorists unless the head of the news department grants permission. Permission is also required for telephone interviews with terrorists, and, even if approved, such interviews must not interfere with communication by the authorities. In addition, reporters are instructed to be attentive to local authorities and experts for useful phraseology and questions, and to obey all instructions by the police and other authorities. However, they should report any orders that appear to be intended to manage or suppress the news.

Contributing to the presence of guidelines and the consensus on their contents is the fact that most of the broadcasting organizations in this category are North American. They are no doubt responding to their governments' success in placing terrorism high on the agenda of public issues. Particularly controversial incidents of television coverage, as in the 1985 skyjacking of TWA Flight 847, in which hostages were interviewed live and pictures purchased from terrorists, have also added to the awareness of the human dangers and political problems involved in covering terrorism. Indeed, according to William Morgan of the Canadian Broadcasting Corporation, the CBC's "policy concerning terrorism and hostage taking . . . came only after a couple of incidents had happened in Canada."

Ironically, the number of terrorist episodes that have occurred in North America is relatively low, although it increases if the definition is broadened to include incidents involving Americans abroad.

### LEVEL 5: DETAILED RULES, CODES, OR GUIDELINES

The companies in this category have detailed codes, with the British Broadcasting Corporation providing the paradigm. The materials we received from the BBC cover virtually every area from producers' guidelines to detailed instructions for use on the scene as a reporter's ready reference. Reporters are even advised which terms should and should not be used on the air: "Programs should whenever possible avoid terms by which terrorist groups try to portray themselves as legitimate."

John Wilson, controller of editorial policy and originator of the code, justifies it in terms of the BBC's need to be and be seen as a credible and trustworthy provider of information. Moreover, the BBC is particularly equipped to develop these codes because "it has more experience of terrorism than any other broadcasting organization. In the past two decades it has covered many acts of international terrorism and also a persistent campaign of terror in the United Kingdom."

Television New Zealand is subjected to both government and its own regulations. The former begin with the country's International Terrorism Act, which gives the government the right to assume control of what is broadcast in the event of a terrorist act. This includes the power to prohibit the flow of information about the people involved, their identities, and the equipment or techniques being used to try to control the situation. The government has the authority to decide when the emergency state of affairs is over. Broadcasters must adhere to the general journalistic standards of the code of the Broadcasting Standards Authority; for example, that news "should not be presented in a way as to cause unnecessary panic, alarm or stress." The Authority can apply stiff penalties for violations, from fines to shutting down a station for 24 hours.

Television New Zealand also falls under the authority of a document designed by a committee of various branches of the media and the media-specialized branch of the police force specifying journalistic practices for covering terrorism. Among these practices are refraining from serving as a negotiator with the terrorists, not contacting the terrorists without the consent of the authorities, communicating all information obtained from the terrorists to the authorities, and not broadcasting "police movements, plans, staff, disposition or speculation."

Finally, even though Radio Television Hong Kong does not have any formal codes or guidelines, it too falls under the British model and thus under Level 5. It depends on and follows the BBC's guidelines "when dealing with incidents of such nature."

Just as the companies in Level 4 are mainly in North America, those in Level 5 have a strong British background in common. This is the case even though their chances of suffering from terrorist attacks vary widely: Such occurrences are relatively common in the United Kingdom, but rare in New Zealand.

## Conclusion

Several themes run through the answers from our broadcasting respondents at all our levels. There is the need to maintain credibility; as the BBC's John Wilson puts it: "We have to be accepted as trustworthy reporters especially in times of crisis." There is the belief that terrorism is newsworthy and the clear commitment to covering its visible and explosive manifestations, but there is a desire to do so prudently, without sensationalizing the already sensational. There is the determination not to legitimate or even provide a platform for terrorists. There is the concern about avoiding coverage that might endanger hostages or interfere with negotiations for their release.

These themes help explain why so few of our respondents reported encountering any direct governmental pressure to institute guidelines, or much governmental criticism of their terrorism coverage. Yet it is not certain that most governments are satisfied with coverage of terrorism by their countries' television organizations. Public officials and the police forces want coverage (to the extent they want any coverage) that is minimally intrusive and noninflammatory, and that lends no credibility to terrorists. Especially in the heat of a terrorist incident, spurred on at times by competition with other television outlets and different media, television coverage can be quite controversial, even incendiary. So while our respondents may indeed not have experienced much, if any, reaction from public officials to their coverage of terrorism, either in general or to specific incidents, it is also possible that they defined both *government* and *pressure* narrowly, to exclude such communications, or that they may not have considered it appropriate to report candidly to us in writing their relationships with their governments.

# 7

# Editors' Perspectives

Alex P. Schmid

The task of the media is, as ABC anchorman Ted Koppel once said in a television commercial, "to tell the people about what's going on in the world." A good editor, then, ought to present to the public things as they really are. This sounds simple enough. Yet there are, as Cohen, Adoni, and Bantz (1990, p. 10) have pointed out, at least three realms of reality:

- the *real* objective world (whatever is happening "out there")
- the *symbolic* world (mainly the world portrayed and presented in the media)
- the *subjective* world (the world as people interpret it in their minds, what they believe based on a combination of unmediated experiences with the real "things" and "events" as well as with their portrayal on television)

In this chapter the word *editor* is used broadly in the sense of gatekeeper— the person who is active in the "symbolic world" selecting from the temporal and spatial chain of occurrences in the world some considered significant and packaging these according to the media's standard formats for secondary experience by a public. In the chain "attention-seeking terrorist committing a shocking violent incident to appeal to (sectors) of the public"-"event-reporting journalist attracted by the disruptive incident"-"editorial selector and shaper of reported news"-"public audience selectively absorbing the processed news offered, acting or reacting to the presentation," the editor is in a powerful position to give or deny terrorists what they want in terms of publicity. If terrorists intend to create remote nervous shocks in target audiences, they have to get through the editor's switchboard. Ford Rowan, a veteran American journalist, notes that "news is what the newspeople say it is" (quoted in Midgley & Rice, 1984, p. 20). The editor is that newsperson who, in theory, can make or break a terrorist group dependent on publicity by granting or denying it access to mass audiences and by shaping the political communication of the violent news makers, granting or withholding them a degree of legitimacy.

However, the term *newspeople* already indicates a limitation of the power of the editor. If an individual editor denies a terrorist access to mass audiences, his or her news judgment might not be shared by fellow editors. The audience or the advertisers or the marketing manager of the medium might not appreciate an individual editor's reluctance to give (ample) coverage to a terrorist incident.[1] Rival editors with fewer scruples might benefit from the restraint shown by a conscientious editor and gain increased ratings and higher sales. Journalists with a scoop might feel offended by their editor that their "news" is not given all the mileage possible.

There is another limitation to the editor's power to edit. It results from journalism's increased ability to report in real time, as news is in the making. Much of this has to do with the shift from print to electronic media. A century ago, before radio and television entered the picture, there was a considerable time lag between an event and dissemination of accounts of that event— usually time enough for the event to have run its course and time enough to subject it to the editor's news judgment. Today, with the advent of mini-cameras and "birds" (satellite feeds to a network's newsroom), direct electronic transmission of news as it breaks has become routine. The passing of editorial judgment in a live report looks like censorship, and few editors want to be accused of censorship.

Given such constraints on the power of the editor to say no to the terrorist news offer, editors might at times feel that there is not much left of their role as responsible gatekeepers. They might then take an attitude of "Terrorist news is news like any other news"—it has to be reported, independent of the consequences. Other editors might wish to formulate some "guidelines" on how to cover terrorist situations in order to cushion the social impact of terrorist violence. Yet others might have strict rules imposed on them: Various forms of censorship are exercised by authoritarian governments and even by democratic governments in periods of acute conflict. Generally speaking, the lines separating news selection on the basis of professional news judgment, subconscious self-censorship, intramedia standards, and intermedia customs and fashions of reporting considered acceptable within a political culture are far from sharp.

In this chapter I wish to address some problems editors encounter when dealing with terrorism. The chapter is based almost entirely on the answers of 20 editors to a lengthy questionnaire.[2] This is admittedly a very small sample, and the answers cannot be considered representative of Western media (there is not a single North American respondent among them). The findings are, however, illustrative of some currents of thinking within the media. In the final section, I will go beyond the answers to the questionnaire and identify some of the key problems posed by the representation of terrorist violence in the media.

## Editors' Thinking About
## Terrorist Uses of the Media

What do "terrorists" want from the media? Some terrorists (including purely criminal ones) do not claim responsibility for their killings and do not seem to need publicity in order to survive or succeed. The motivations of terrorists are generally broader than obtaining access to the media. The latter might be but a tactical means to such strategic goals as the following:

- provoking the opponent into overreacting
- preparing an opponent for submission by demoralizing the opponent and/or the opponent's constituency
- boosting the terrorists' morale and that of the constituency the terrorists claim to represent

In the terrorist strategy, the media serve a variety of purposes:

- They can offer a platform for the diffusion and amplification of armed propaganda.
- They can aid in the gathering of information and intelligence on the outside world for an underground organization.
- They can (re-)direct attribution of responsibility, leading to possible legitimation of terrorist violence by persuasive guilt transfers in terrorist communiqués.
- They can assist in the coercion and blackmail of a third party.

(See the appendix to this chapter for a more detailed breakdown of terrorist uses of the media.)

Terrorists obviously attribute value to their provocative and shocking deeds, but why should journalists, owners of newspapers, and editors do the same? I tried to give an initial answer to this question 10 years ago in one of the first book-length studies on the subject, published under the title *Violence as Communication* (Schmid & De Graaf, 1982). I pointed out that on a basic level, any type of violence done to human beings—no matter what its context or cause—always demands attention, if not respect, since it can affect our personal survival if we do not respond adequately to it. This basic reflex to signals of violence makes us listen or watch or read even when there is a temporal and spatial distance between the event and ourselves, as during a recorded television feature. On a basic level, editors featuring terroristic news items apparently respond to the archaic mind-set of the audience and its instinctive desire to know. I term it "archaic" because the need to know was real in times when the audience was actually at the scene of violence rather than transported to the scene across space and time by television or radio.

In 1965 Johan Galtung and Mari Ruge published an article titled "The Structure of Foreign News," in which they identified a number of elements that are likely to establish news value. They also tried to explain why nonelite people can break into the field occupied by habitual news makers. Among the intruding elements they identified were the "negativeness of an event" and its "unexpectedness" (see Galtung & Ruge, 1965, 1977). Insurgent terrorist violence striking unexpectedly at "positive" pillars of the social structure fits into such a news value system.[3] However, rather than looking at the interpretations of scholars such as Galtung and Ruge, I was curious about what editors themselves thought. Therefore, I asked them: "Why have acts of terrorism (a high) news value?" The responding editors volunteered a whole series of answers to this question. All but two (respondents 3 and 19 in the list below) accepted the implicit assumption of the question. As the respondents' answers refer to different levels of analysis and show wide diversity, it is difficult to summarize them. They are therefore reproduced verbatim in the following list:

1. Drama rooted in the fact that it could happen to each of us.
2. Because generally they are sensational news events.
3. Have they?
4. Concerning this point I totally agree with the ideas of Brian Jenkins [Rand Corporation]. He suggests ideas like:

Terrorism affronts basic values (e.g., not to kill children).

Terrorism causes public alarm (e.g., Paris in early summer 1987).

Terrorism causes moral dilemmas: to uphold principles and to have a hostage killed or to give in, etc.

Terrorism creates political crisis, etc.

5. Because they often involve civilians and may involve changes of intended events.

6. Bad news is news.

7. They are dramatic and (at least in Western Europe) not yet a daily occurrence.

8. Because they tend to be sudden, unexpected, and disruptive of the regular flow of events.

9. (a) The often cruel and indiscriminate use of violence, (b) their unpredictability, (c) the connection with political situations and possible involvement of countries.

10. Because they are dramatic and theatrically exciting. Readers readily identify with the victims in the same way that they identify with the victims of a road accident or a blunder by a surgeon.

11. They are a major facet of life in Ireland today.

12. Their political and social repercussions, their dramatic effects and sheer ruthlessness, their exposure of security lapses.

13. Simply because they are NEWS, and they are SENSATIONAL.

14. Because they are, on the whole, exceptional events. Because they usually signal dissension.

15. Because they undermine either democracy or dictatorships.

16. Because of their characteristics: bloody, spectacular, blind, often perverse.

17. Because they jeopardize everybody's security.

18. High drama and sensational events like hijackings, kidnapping, and hostage taking have always been newsworthy, whether they were acts of terrorism or not. The same goes for violence, violent death, and serious damage to property, and for anything out of the ordinary. Naturally, when events like these are combined with politics, which in itself has a high news value, it becomes clear that, measured by age-old standards for newsworthiness, acts of terrorism have an intrinsic news value. Add to that the existing order which concerns a large number of readers, it becomes clear why terrorism has a high news value.

19. For [name of Peruvian newspaper] acts of terrorism have no news value. We don't give publicity to terrorists. That's precisely what they want.

20. Dramatic, involving human suffering, focusing on more or less important problems.

Our editors' answers reveal a greater variety of news values than those suggested by Galtung and Ruge's list (which is discussed in more detail in Crelinsten, Chapter 10, this volume). What is absent in the editors' answers is a direct reference to that commercial aspect of violent news that is only alluded to in the answer of editor 6—a contraction of the old journalistic adage "Good news is bad news and bad news is good news and no news is bad news." What is also absent is an explicit admission of a fact acknowledged implicitly in most answers to another question: "Do you accept the suggestion that terrorists manufacture violent events to gain media access and thereby 'status'?" Only 2 respondents out of 20 rejected this suggestion; none chose "don't know." [4]

This is a crucial point. While it is true that everybody tries to use the media, the terrorists do so by spilling other people's blood, including the blood of innocents. The purposeful creation of bad events by means of terroristic violence can assure them free access to the news system. Expressed somewhat cynically: Some people have to perish at the hands of terrorists so that editors will publicize the existence, demands, and goals of terrorists. Where terrorism is predominantly media oriented—and a great deal of it is—editors can become accessories (often unwitting accessories) to murder. Some experts are rather direct about this relationship. Walter Laqueur holds that "the media are the terrorists' best friend," while R. Friedlander even goes so far as to state that "terrorism is a creature of the media" (quoted in Tan, 1989, p. 202).

Are editors fully aware of their complicity? Have they—in the light of this fatal nexus between terrorist event making and editorial news policy—modified their conceptualization of "news"? I asked them, "Has the arrival of terrorism changed your definition of what is to be considered 'newsworthy'?" Of the 20 respondents, 15 answered no, and 3 answered with a simple yes (2 of them were Irish, the third was a Kenyan).[5]

A slightly different distribution of responses was received to the question, "Has the coverage of terrorism in your medium changed in the last decade?" There were 13 editors who answered no, 7 yes. However, when I turned the question on the linkage between violence and media attention upside down, only 5 respondents answered affirmatively, 2 of them with qualifications; 2 more answered that they did not know, while the majority answered in the negative. I asked, "Do you believe that greater media attention to nonviolent forms of waging conflict would reduce the number of terrorist incidents?"

I also asked the editors whether new laws had been introduced in their countries restricting the reporting on/portrayal of terrorist events in the mass media in the last decade. Only 2 answered affirmatively, the rest negatively.

Of the latter group, however, 4 added qualifications such as "What seems to have changed are the internal guidelines of media organizations."

Approaching the problem from another angle, I asked, "Do you feel that the media have a responsibility in combating terrorism?" Here the answer was, surprisingly, overwhelmingly affirmative, with 15 respondents sharing this view. One of those who denied such responsibility nevertheless added that the media "must not willingly make themselves instruments" of terrorists.

Yet in order to be on guard about possible abuse, one must know what terrorists want from the media. There were two questions that touched on this problem, the first of which was, "Do you have concrete evidence of how terrorists think about the news coverage they obtain?" Here only 3 answered affirmatively, while 1 of the 7 who answered negatively underlined "concrete," indicating a general knowledge. The second question was, "Has research on the impact of detailed coverage of acts of terrorism influenced your medium's coverage?" Here 5 answered positively; from the remaining 15 only 1 negative answer was qualified ("not directly"). Those who answered affirmatively did not, however, refer to specific academic research, but vaguely quoted "expert opinion."

The tenor of the answers did not reveal a sharp awareness on the part of the editors that they might be "blood brothers" (as an African respondent put it) of terrorists. Neither did the responses create the impression that editors are sometimes coerced into cooperation with terrorists. Outside the context of the answers to this questionnaire, I was informed of one case in which an editor of a newspaper in India received a letter from an underground organization that was about to launch a terrorist campaign for the independence of Kashmir. In this letter the editor was told how he had to cover the impending campaign of violence. He was instructed "not to call us terrorists." To give weight to this demand, a bullet was included in the letter. Apparently this was not without influence on the subsequent coverage: The paper labeled the terrorists "militants" (personal communication).

## Media-Linked Effects of Terrorist Acts

The question of complicity—in the sense that the media are participants rather than mere observers of the reported events—is obviously linked to the one of the probable social impacts of media-transmitted acts of terrorism. In order to explore these, I asked the editors, "What are, in your view, the main effects of media-portrayed acts of terrorism on society?" There was a great variety in their answers, some contradicting each other. Several of their suggestions are well worth pursuing in further research. For these reasons, the answers are presented here verbatim:

1. [The first respondent referred here approvingly to two quotes I had given the respondents as food for thought. The first was from D. Lopez: "Terrorism is aimed at people watching television. Television declares who is important and who has an identity. Terrorists have found that the world road to identity is to do something violent. This becomes causation and the sole justification for many terrorist activities, giving them exactly what they want, and that's power." The second quote I offered was from Conor Cruise O'Brien: "We in the Irish state regard the appearance of terrorists on television as an incitement to murder. The incitement is addressed not so much to the general public as to other terrorists and potential terrorists."]

2. Revulsion against the terrorist.

3. They *can* cause insecurity and anxiety. Everything depends on how such acts are presented.

4. There is no law that states that acts of violence on TV only cause alarm, frighten and weaken a society/government bodies. It also can have the opposite effect of strengthening the will of a community/country to deal firmly with this threat.

5. Fear.

6. Usually to polarize views but also to shock/horrify peaceful people.

7. Habituation.

8. Insecurity, fear, irritation . . .

9. Generally speaking, they are counterproductive.

10. Again I say, "Yes, but." Newspapers do already go to great trouble to try to explain what is going on in the world. In the Western democracies it is not difficult to know about disputes and problems. There is no need for the IRA, for example, to blow people up to remind us all that Ireland has been an unfortunate country for centuries and that Catholics and Protestants there did monstrous things to one another. The main effect of reading about acts of terrorism is to bore the reader and convince him of the callous nature of terrorists and therefore to oppose whatever they demand. A side effect is to make the public oppose any policy which might express sympathy towards even reasonable grievances. Terrorism hardens the heart.

11. To make the general public tired of conflict and become more willing to examine avenues which could lead to a cessation of the conflict.

12. Increasing fatalism and anger at politicians/governments who seem powerless to prevent terrorism.

13. Their impact on societies is usually mixed and varies according to the ACTS themselves, and to the societies concerned. They may awaken certain societies to certain grievances, hitherto unknown to them. In others, they may create sympathy, or anger or fear. It is very difficult to generalize.

14. Accurate reporting by the media provides information, as opposed to rumour. Rumour can magnify terror.

15. Acts of terrorism, when in the name of freedom, are not accepted by the public. I wouldn't be surprised that the "public," the "mass" doesn't appreciate the struggle for freedom by the have-nots. Egotism and fear for losing their own well-being transform many people into racists and vulgar materialists.

16. A fear which is often exaggerated in comparison with other causes of insecurity (e.g., traffic accidents!). A reaction of rejection with regard to the motives which are perhaps defensible (at least in principle).

17. If they are correctly reported, terrorism acts in the media will not produce any damage. Anyway, it is our right to know what's happening around us, even if it is not giving rise to enthusiasm.

18. Rather a mixed bag:

    (1) Aversion and horror on the side of those who do not condone violence.

    (2) I suspect that frequent media exposure to acts of terrorism might blunt at least part of society: if violence becomes the rule, it might eventually shock less. But aggression against terrorists and more polarization and hardening of attitudes would follow among other members of society.

    (3) I would accept that, among those who support the terrorists' cause, there could be two effects: on the one hand there would be those who support such acts anyhow, and those who might change their minds at the sight of death and violence.

19. The main effect is to present terrorism as a "force" in a country, as a "power."

20. Creating disgust for their methods but curiosity as to their motives.

The effects perceived by editors, then, are manyfold. Many of them can hardly be intended by the terrorists themselves, though some of them might even gain a masochistic satisfaction from "glorious failures." One editor pointed out that "media access is not a guarantee to gain sympathies." Another editor even denied that terrorists are given access: "Terrorists may get media attention but not media access, there is a very significant difference. Any attention they get does not alter their status." Yet another held that

terrorists, and indeed many writers on terrorism, grotesquely overvalue the publicity achieved by the reporting of incidents. They forget how fickle public opinion is. They overestimate the fear their actions create. They are wrong-headed to believe that because their cause is brought to prominence through outrage that people in general will therefore sympathize with that cause. The so-called status they achieve is to become objects of hatred.

Two of the respondents held that there was no damage "if they are correctly reported" (respondent 17) and that everything depends "on how such acts are presented" (respondent 3). If this is true, the editor who selects and composes the terrorist news is indeed a crucial person. He or she can apparently cushion or expand the psychological impact of acts of terrorism.

To some degree editors can also bestow or withhold a degree of legitimacy from terrorists, for instance by labeling them not "terrorists" but "freedom fighters," "members of the armed resistance," or "urban guerrillas." I asked editors whether they agreed with the statement, "One man's terrorist is another man's freedom fighter." Here the views were divided, with 9 answering affirmatively (1 qualifying "not always"), 10 answering in the negative. Of the latter group, 1 qualified: "In an ethical sense this is a totally relativist position unacceptable to me—but from a journalistic position I accept this as a reality of life and international politics."

Some editors, like many other people, are apparently also prone to condone certain means when they agree with the ends sought. Since there is also no agreement with regard to a definition of terrorism among the editors, the question of mediated effects of reporting on terrorism becomes even more complicated.

One effect usually attributed to the media is the contagion effect: One act with special features (e.g., a coercive hijacking followed by an escape by parachute after ransom was obtained) can trigger imitations. However, only 3 of the 20 respondents answered affirmatively to a question asking whether they had any (personal) knowledge of examples where media-reported acts of terrorism led to imitative acts.

A special form of imitation is revenge in kind. In this regard one Irish editor answered:

> Northern Ireland has long suffered from retaliation as one side or the other seeks to maintain the cycle of violence. While the media reports of an incident might not always be enough to spark retaliation, there have been many occasions (too numerous to mention) when written and verbal reports have contributed to the decision by certain groups to take action.

On the other hand, media reports have also stopped revenge acts, as one respondent recalls, reflecting on the aftermath of the Enniskillen bombing by the Provisional IRA that caused many innocent civilian fatalities in November 1987: "This act could have provoked massive retaliation, but a powerful interview with a bereaved father is generally believed to have saved lives."

Media-induced violent contagion can also take place following fictional action programs (sometimes, in turn, modeled on true terrorist events). However, in this regard the editors' awareness (or memory) was not great. Only 4 out of the 20 respondents answered affirmatively to a question asking whether they had any (personal) knowledge of examples where fictional portrayals of violence (in "action" series such as the Rambo movies) led to "copycat" crimes in real life.

Only 3 of the 20 respondents recalled cases where media coverage had significantly influenced the outcome of a terrorist incident. This is, however, hard to evaluate, since we cannot say with certainty what outcome there would have been without the media's presence. Indeed, one of the major complaints about the media with regard to terrorism is that they tend to become part of the story, that they have moved from news gathering to news making. In place of mirroring reality, media reshape reality in their own image, in cooperation with terrorists who are aware of the particular frames designed for news stories. This is especially true for television.

In a small case study of TWA Flight 847 published elsewhere, I have tried to illustrate how the media became participants, affecting and even shaping the course of events rather than merely reporting them (Schmid, 1989). Another observer, Michael J. O'Neill (1986), came to a similar conclusion when he discussed the U.S. television networks' role in this TWA hijacking incident in June 1985:

> They were not just watchers, standing and observing, but card-carrying participants who helped to shape and direct the unfolding drama. They merged with the crisis, became part of it, and action and coverage became so intertwined it was hard to tell one from the other. Reporters were no longer just reporters, journalism no longer just journalism but a unique bonding of newsmaking and news reporting, dictated by television's special nature and lying beyond traditional definitions of news. . . . When a network anchor is making news, he is neither a government official nor a journalist; he is a hybrid. He has no credentials in the first role and loses them in the second. (p. 53)

Among the effects terrorism has on the media there is one that is rather direct; it indicates how important the media are to terrorists. I refer to attacks on media personnel and media premises. Journalists and camera operators have become targets of threats, kneecappings, kidnappings, and assassinations. While only one editor in the sample was confronted with this type of incident in his immediate surrounding, several editors recalled incidents that affected other media in Beirut, Rome, or Belfast. Six editors reported that there had been bomb threats and actual bombings directed against their medium in the last decade. A German editor recalled a threat to kill editors who had written "anti-Iranian" editorials. An Irish editor remembered an occupation of the newspaper office in Belfast by IRA gunmen who wanted to make sure that the staff carried all their statements in future. Not in all cases did the violence come from insurgent terrorists. One Irish editor wrote: "Reporters and photographers for this newspaper have been batoned by police, stoned by demonstrators, threatened by many people in pursuit of their reports and pictures."

The media have become a major battleground in today's struggles for political power because they can manage perceptions of both leaders and masses, thereby making them often more important than the actual state of affairs. Samuel Huntington, the veteran political scientist from Harvard University, put it cogently: "Whichever side can convince the target group that it is winning is, in fact, winning" (quoted in Waugh, 1982, p. 143).

A recent illustration of the importance of television was the power struggle between President Marcos and Corazon Aquino in 1986 in the Philippines. An aide to Marcos later recalled: "When we lost Channel 4, we were in trouble. And when Channel 9 fell, we lost all the initiative" (O'Neill, 1986, p. 16).

Physical control over a television channel is a drastic form of editorial control, but not essentially different from the control of nonviolent editors. Editors can—collectively—frame (though not control) the perceptions of their audiences. A national audience's beliefs are crucial in the political struggle for seats of government as well as for lesser terrorist goals. One of the editors in our sample admitted, "Obviously, if the media do not speak of terrorism it will not have any social relevance."

## Media Control by the Government

Calls for controlling the media with regard to the coverage of terrorist events usually come from the government. Government spokespersons blame the media for being "accomplices to terrorism" (R. Oakley, the former director of the U.S. Office to Combat Terrorism, quoted in Rosie, 1986,

p. 196). Former British Prime Minister Margaret Thatcher insisted that we "must find ways to starve the terrorists and hijackers of the oxygen of publicity on which they depend" (*New York Times*, July 16, 1985). Richard Clutterbuck (1981), a former British military officer and an expert on terrorism, has suggested the establishment of an "Institute for the Mass Media" that would establish an ethical code that would be binding for all editors of major media. Irresponsible or antisocial misuse of the power of the mass media could be punished by withdrawal of the license of a journalist or station editor (p. 162). In many countries government censorship is a direct reaction to terrorist and guerrilla campaigns.[7]

In my questionnaire I asked the editors whether their governments attempted to influence their coverage on terrorism. Five editors from the German Federal Republic, Northern Ireland, Italy, and South Africa answered affirmatively, while a dozen denied such an influence.

The ways a regime exerts influence can be subtle. One editor from South Africa put it this way:

> Firstly, one is subjected to what one could call a system of pre-censorship: Because of the strict emergency regulations—which are applied from time to time—one is very much aware of the fact that certain types of coverage would not be tolerated by the government. In the case of this newspaper, at least, we tailor our stories to this.
>
> Secondly, from time to time editors and senior members of the editorial staff are briefed—with strict confidentiality—by members of the cabinet and members of the various security forces. These background sessions do not only cover terrorism, but all matters concerning security. Overtly they are meant to keep the media informed, but it would be naive not to accept that they are a subtle way of inducing reporting in the vein the authorities would prefer. Their success rate, from the point of the authorities, would vary from editor to editor and from issue to issue. Attempts at direct intervention in stories do happen, but only rarely, mostly by way of a cordial telephone call, asking the editor to keep certain things in mind when the story is written. These calls are not necessarily successful; it depends on how the particular editor sees the particular issue.

While some editors of national media are subjected to "massage" in such "security briefings," one editor in chief of a global news agency noted that he was also sensing some pressure. He said that "various governments would like us to report differently, in particular to describe certain groups as terrorist."

Asked whether there was a special forum in their countries where representatives of the media and the government meet to discuss points of friction with regard to the handling of news on acts of terrorism, none of the respondents answered with an unqualified yes. Some mentioned ad hoc discussions in specific cases. None of the respondents found that such forums, where they exist, work satisfactorily.

There seems to be considerable reluctance to consider suggestions coming from the government's judiciary, executive, or legislative branch. Asked whether former U.S. Senator J. A. Denton's (R-AL) idea that the media should "omit the names of terrorist groups taking credit for violent incidents" was acceptable for their medium, only a single (Swiss) editor answered affirmatively.[8]

An issue that leads to clashes between the authorities and the media is the question of interviews with terrorists. Of the 20 respondents, 11 said that their medium had in the past decade interviewed terrorists in the underground (9 said that their medium had not); 5 editors said that their medium had interviewed terrorists in prison (13 said they had not). However, the most debatable situation—interviews during ongoing incidents—occurred only rarely: only 2 (a Swedish and a Belgian) respondents to this question admitted to it. Asked whether such interviews were forbidden, 4 answered affirmatively (a fifth respondent answered "yes and no, grey zone"); 13 answered in the negative, but 1 of these spoke of "strong moral pressure" being exerted by the (Kenyan) government on him.

In Switzerland, such interviews can be interpreted by the authorities as an act of favoritism (*Begünstigung*). In Northern Ireland, the emergency legislation and the laws on incitement passed by the government of the United Kingdom also make such interviews difficult. In the Irish Republic, such interviews are prohibited on television and radio by the Broadcasting Act, while there are no effective restrictions on the written press. In South Africa, the media were said to be free to interview terrorists (though the government frowns upon it). However, there are constraints when it comes to publishing these interviews. Since many South African "terrorists" were so-called listed persons, they were not allowed to be quoted directly. In the period 1986-1990, when the emergency regulations were operative in South Africa, the media were not free to report on terrorist events without police clearance.

Since the government is usually a party to the conflict, government control of the media is likely to result in misuse of the media by those in power. Depending on the degree of support and legitimacy a government enjoys, such control may not primarily serve the public interest but a partisan interest.

## The Media's Ethical Principles
## and the Content of Guidelines

Over the last century a set of ethical principles of journalism has emerged in the Western democracies among the quality newspapers that includes the following elements:

1. to report truthfully (that is, honestly, accurately, objectively, and reliably)
2. to report comprehensively so that the public gets the best information available in order to develop understanding of conflicting viewpoints and to reduce ignorance of significant issues
3. to report impartially (that is, with fairness to all sides who have a point)
4. to maintain editorial independence against all interest groups
5. to separate news from commentary ("Facts are sacred. Comment is free.") so that one's bias toward a person or institution does not influence a news report[9]

These are marvelous principles, but they are not binding for the whole of the journalistic profession. In fact, such principles live strongly only among the editors of relatively few quality newspapers and radio and television stations. Implicit in them are the assumptions that the media can, if they wish, remain neutral observers of events; that the media do not themselves influence the course of events; and that the media have access to all relevant information to provide a well-rounded portrayal of the situation. However, when the situation is one of local emergency or national crisis, these principles are likely to face hard times.

When it comes to the coverage of terrorism, it is arguably not only the violation of these principles that makes media coverage problematic, but also the issues not covered adequately by these principles. If a terrorist leader instructs his disciples literally—and this is a quote from an Algerian terrorist fighting France in the late 1950s: "We must have blood in the headlines of all the newspapers" (Schmid, 1984, p. 221)—an ethical problem arises for the editor that demands new instruments to cope with such manipulation.

Since the second half of the 1970s, a number of Western news media have developed specific guidelines on the coverage of terrorism. Their range is reflected in the answers I obtained from the editors. Below are some verbatim answers to the question, "What ethical principles should be applicable with regard to the coverage of terrorism?"

- Don't serve as spokesman/accomplice of terrorists.
- Am I being used by the terrorist to promote his ends?
- Caution in order not to endanger lives (hostages).
- Not to portray terror as attractive, romantic, or heroic; honest portrayal of motives of terrorists.
- To prevent (active) cooperation by participating in events that are specially and exclusively organized for the media.
- You may, sometimes, be obliged to hold back news where there is clear and immediate danger to life and limb.
- To avoid, where possible, unchallenged terrorist propaganda.
- To ensure that the human suffering is not overshadowed by the terrorist act.
- Coverage should be restricted to "Facts" but must not imply encouragement, glorification, or condoning of acts of terrorism.
- Portray the cowardice, blindness, and frequent barbarism of the terrorists.
- Not to encourage further use of it if it's against freedom and human rights.
- Accuracy, concern not to endanger lives, caution not to become a player in the game, avoid becoming a messenger of the terrorists.
- Try not to get involved—being there can trigger an action.
- Never try to *solve* a situation.[10]

Only 5 of 20 respondents said that they had no special policy for handling news on terrorism. However, only 3 said that their media had written guidelines. In one case, there were no written guidelines (only oral guidelines) for fear that these might fall into the hands of any of several terrorist organizations who would seek to use them against the paper. The written guidelines were formulated by the editor's medium itself, rather than by a national news council, a mixed media-government commission. In one case (Italy), the author of the guidelines was a parliamentary commission in control of public TV. Some of the guidelines were said to be publicly known, while others were said to be confidential.

In written guidelines, recommendations such as the following are made:

- Reporters should take nothing for granted; everything must be checked as far as humanly possible. No group or individual is allowed to make unsubstantiated accusations.
- No statements are to be carried that could result in the deaths of or injuries to others.
- Avoid identifying potential targets (individual faces, car numbers), sensitive locations, giving advance warning of VIP's presence.

- Don't exaggerate by showing pictures of terrorism causing minor damage or a single casualty.
- Don't show sequences of pictures of massacres and of heavily injured people (this is not censorship; broadcasting horror has nothing to do with information duties). In many cases suggesting a bloodbath has a better and above all a more human effect than showing cruelty. Some pictures—if necessary for complete information—can be reserved for the late news bulletins.

A majority of the respondents who said that their media had no *written* guidelines nevertheless stated that they had "a certain policy for handling news on terrorism." This often included not giving "more publicity to the particular terrorist group than is necessary."

Some of our respondents, such as the editor in chief of an international news agency, pointed out that written guidelines "are useful as a quick reference for consistency of action in a highly decentralized organization." Another respondent qualified that they are only useful "if they are CLEAR, SHORT, and PRECISE." He noted that it takes some time before they become "normal" practice with the editors. Yet another editor from the Benelux, who preferred "dialogue" with his journalists to "administration," found that "written guidelines have only an effect for a small period." He stressed that "the editor in chief has to preview all the pictures before the broadcast." A news and current affairs editor from a British news organization saw the advantage of written guidelines in the fact that ill-conceived programs are sometimes not made and elementary security lapses are usually avoided.

In answer to a question inquiring whether the media have a responsibility for combating terrorism, our editors volunteered some additional suggestions as to what the media should do in the coverage of terrorism:

- Mobilize opinion against violence.
- Promote peace and alternative methods that can be used to effect change if change is necessary/needed/essential.
- Ensure that terrorist frontmen are never given an easy ride and that their support for violence is always questioned.

Such answers seem to imply that some editors at least are prepared to depart from normal reporting routines in a situation when the media are used by terrorists. Answers such as these are also an indication that many of the editors answering the questionnaire are well aware that news is more than a commodity to be sold in the marketplace. Terrorist news is more than ordinary information that is for sale.


## Information for What?

"All the news that's fit to print" is the slogan of the *New York Times*. The editor is, in principle, the one who decides what is fit to print or broadcast. He or she is the filter between a slice of reality and the audience's perception of (a selective slice of) reality. For better or worse, the editor decides what is fit or not fit to have mass impact. Even if an editor does not decide, he or she provides, by the act of omission, free access to terrorists. Both government and terrorist try to create perceptions in an audience that further their political aims. Editors are likely to be subject to efforts at manipulation. At the same time, they have a chance to frame audience perceptions themselves by giving or withholding access and by deciding on the form of presentation each side is allowed to have.

The form of presentation of news can be tailored to address primarily the public's need to know, its demand for clear information to reduce uncertainty about current dangers to its well-being and survival. However, news can also be tailored to the public's desire to be entertained. There is a voyeuristic component that is catered to by many show-businesslike news items on terrorist violence. Since usually only a small sector of the public is terrorized due to a high degree of identification with significant others who are victimized, the rest of the public can receive the terrorist news more relaxedly, even using ongoing real-life dramas conveyed by the media as thrilling recreational entertainment.

News as information can be intimidating, and there is no way of disconnecting intimidation completely from information. The art of responsible news judgment on the part of an editor consists of finding a suitable balance among the public's need to know, its mere desire to know, the terrorists' wish to intimidate and/or to propagandize the public or sectors thereof, and, last but not least, the hostages' and other victims' right to survive.[11]

The actors involved in the event actively try to affect the nature of the coverage. Editors might want to remain neutral in reporting a terrorist event, but their chief sources, as actors in the conflict, are decidedly not neutral; they try to manipulate the coverage in their own favor (e.g., if dramatic coverage leads to panic, this might serve the terrorists' purpose). The editors' integrity is then under assault. In such situations editors have to decide where their priorities lie:

- Is an editor first of all responsible to members of the public, who deserve full and fast information so they can stay out of danger zones?
- Is an editor first of all responsible to hostages and other victims whose lives might be immediately threatened?
- Is it an editor's first duty to be the citizens' watchdog on the actions of the government?
- Is it an editor's first duty to give terrorists sufficient coverage so that the publicity success satisfies them and decreases their felt need to engage in (more) actual violence?
- Is it an editor's duty, as a citizen who can influence the outcome of a terrorist event, to convey, if necessary, false information to the terrorists—and thereby also to the public?

An editor can avoid many problems of negative social impact by delaying transmission of sensitive information until an incident has come to a halt. The likelihood of the media becoming participants in, rather than observers of, a violent situation is thereby greatly reduced. The public's right to know can be satisfied as soon as the potential victims' right to life has been guaranteed and the authorities' attempt to resolve an incident has been effectuated. In practice, however, competition among the media makes delayed coverage difficult to realize. The commercial basis of information also requires that news be sold while it is still fresh. If extra profits can be made by being irresponsible, there will always be irresponsible editors— unless the extra profits obtained in such a way are creamed off and used for a good purpose, such as supporting victims of terrorism.

## Conclusion

Zoe Tan (1989) has observed that "there seems to be little doubt that the central battles of day-to-day politics in democracies are increasingly fought out in the media and through the media" (p. 209). In this game of mobilizing public opinion and managing public perception, a terrible new actor has made an appearance. The terrorist creates a violent reality with a high news value as a means of communication with his constituency and in order to have a shock effect on the public at large.

The editorial news value system fits into the terrorist strategy of obtaining a psychological impact through magnification by mass communication. So far, the division of labor between the terrorist as fear generator and the unwitting editor as fear amplifier and transmitter has not been fully perceived and absorbed by all those responsible for the media. The traditional principles of journalism and even the more recent guidelines on covering terrorist events do not adequately address some of the key problems.

Foremost is the problem that the act of reporting changes the character of the event reported, and that the anticipation of reporting can become a causal element in initiating a violent act. Ideally, the editor should be able to distinguish between original events (which would take place anyway, without the existence of the media) and staged events that are produced to fit the news value system, turning the media into participants in terrorist event making. If such pseudoevents are acts of violence, serious consideration should be given not to pass them on to a mass audience in a form satisfying the intentions of those who spill blood for effect. Yet how can editors differentiate between genuine "natural" violence and terroristic "contrived" violence? Only experience can give an editor a feel as to what is genuine and what is media-oriented violence. While it might not be possible to give the latter no coverage at all, such acts could at least be downplayed. In particular, repetitive showing of the same dramatic film sequences should be avoided.

Another related element hardly addressed in current guidelines is the relative time/space given to terrorist stories vis-à-vis other newsworthy events. Balancing the news stories of the day is often neglected when dramatic visual footage from one or another terrorist story is available. By giving prominence to terrorist stories, editors are in fact setting the public agenda in a way that downplays other issues of at least equal if not greater social importance. This agenda-setting can become self-reinforcing: Reality begins to reflect media representation, rather than the other way around. Content analysis has shown that "images of terrorism in the media do not represent an accurate picture of the nature and extent of terrorism in the real world" (Crelinsten, 1990, p. 167). This, in turn, has two effects: First, it increases general public fear of terrorist victimization; second, it can lead to copycat crimes perpetrated by a lunatic fringe, whether political or pathological. The problem of inspiring contagion is very difficult to measure, but it is sufficiently serious to be taken into account. In the media coverage of terrorism, models of political activism are offered that can waken dormant fantasies of violence, serving as inciting examples for a very small sector of the public.[12]

Editors should always keep in mind that their media stories are somebody else's real-life dramas, and that the decision to go on the air immediately or to delay for postincident reporting can be a matter of life and death. By intervening or not intervening with coverage in a real-life situation susceptible to feedback processes, an editor can not only waste or save lives but also increase or decrease the chances of the occurrence of similar events in the future. A good story is not worth a life, and it can be told better when the event has reached its natural end, without delay or speeding up caused by media interference. The real issue, in many cases, is not one of (self-)censorship versus freedom of the press, but a question of timing, of telling the full story now or a little later. While freedom of the press is a precious good, citizens' lives should not be sacrificed to scoops. The editor is in a crucial position to frame public experiences obtained from the media. When it comes to the coverage of publicity-seeking terrorists, the editor's position should be strengthened against commercial pressures. After all, the professional responsibility of the editor is to edit.

# Appendix:
## Terrorist Uses of the Media

The following lists, which are based on empirical observations and suggestions in the secondary literature, provide some insight into possible misuses of the media by terrorists.

### DIFFUSION AND AMPLIFICATION OF VIOLENT PROPAGANDA

- magnifying impact of fearful events by transporting mass audiences, as it were, to the scene of action of a terrorist episode
- forcing national and international opinion to listen to terrorist demands and put these on the public agenda
- generating disproportionate fear of the opponent by media's exaggeration of their strength, thereby aiding terrorist organization in its mythmaking
- announcing further actions
- inciting public against government
- winning favorable publicity by means of statements expressed by grateful released hostages
- winning publicity by granting exclusive interviews in the underground

- manufacturing violent events for the primary purpose of being reported by the mass media in order to create, through imitation of such acts, a contagion effect
- extending identification offers to like-minded members in the mass audience, thereby instigating replication

## WINNING INFORMATION AND INTELLIGENCE ON THE OUTSIDE WORLD FOR UNDERGROUND ORGANIZATION

- obtaining information about the identity, status, or actions of hostages and utilization of this knowledge for coercive bargaining (e.g., prominent person X, who, according to media reports, is among the hostages, will be killed first when ultimatum expires)
- obtaining sensitive information on countermeasures by security forces
- identifying future targets for terroristic violence on the basis of news clipping archives
- basing tactics and reactions on intelligence obtained from the media
- using media as go-between between underground terrorists and their above-ground support groups and potential constituencies
- learning new terrorist techniques from the media (modeling)
- misleading opponent by spreading false information
- verifying demand compliance by the opponent (e.g., watch release of comrades from prison on TV)
- obtaining information about the reaction of (sectors of the) public to terrorist act

## (RE-)DIRECTING ATTRIBUTION OF RESPONSIBILITY, LEADING TO POSSIBLE LEGITIMATION OF TERRORIST VIOLENCE

- obtaining status through recognition by the media that terrorist group is important enough to be covered
- linking (propagandist) message to victim
- discrediting victim by making parts of his or her "confessions" public
- discrediting opponent by making victim's "confessions" public
- advertising terrorist movement and cause represented
- making converts, attracting new members to terrorist movement
- placing the government, or specific public officials, in a bad light
- providing a basis for the public's justification or rationalization of the terrorist act
- gaining a Robin Hood image

## COERCION AND BLACKMAIL OF A THIRD PARTY

- intimidating media by maiming or killing journalists
- demanding publication of manifesto under threat of harm to victim or target
- occupying broadcasting station to issue message
- using media as conduits for threats, demands, and bargaining
- arousing public concern for victims to pressure government into making concessions
- staging visual violent events for threat emphasis (e.g., hanging one kidnapped person in front of video camera)

## OTHER

- using media presence at site of siege as insurance against "dirty tricks" by security forces
- using journalists as negotiators in bargaining situation
- deflecting public attention from disliked current or forthcoming issue (e.g., democratic election) by "bombing" it from front pages
- polarizing public opinion
- triggering contagious behavior
- obtaining psychological gratification from media exposure, morale boosting

# Notes

1. An example of an editor/anchorman being overruled occurred at CBS during the June 1985 TWA hijacking. Dan Rather, the anchorman, "personally ruled against using tapes of hostages speaking under terrorist control, but they were used anyway" (Shales, 1986; quoted in O'Neill, 1986, p. 41).

2. The sample of editors in chief, executive editors, managing editors, foreign editors, heads of foreign news departments, and chairmen consisted of German, Kenyan, Swiss, Swedish, Dutch, British, Irish, Jordanian, Belgian, Italian, South African, Norwegian, and Peruvian respondents. Of these, 12 worked for daily newspapers, 2 worked for weeklies, 4 worked for TV and radio stations, and 2 were in charge of news agencies (1 national, 1 international). The questionnaire was answered in early 1988.

3. State terrorism, on the other hand, with its incremental process rather than episodic event character, fits less well into the news value system.

4. However, some respondents qualified their yeses, adding remarks such as "sometimes, but not always" or "it is probably ONE of their motivations."

5. The Peruvian respondent answered no, adding: "Because we think that something that tries to destroy our country can't be newsworthy." One respondent thought that this was "a silly question," because "terrorism has existed for centuries." Another acknowledged that the question made sense, but added that this was not new: "Terrorism of one form or another has been present in Ireland throughout my life."

6. Although there is no consensus on a definition of terrorism, there is a good degree of consensus with regard to the labeling of certain acts of political violence as terrorism. The following acts were labeled "terroristic": hijacking for coercive bargaining (14 out of 20 respondents), indiscriminate bombing (15 out of 20), hostage taking (16 out of 20), assassination (15 out of 20). There was less consensus with regard to urban guerrilla warfare; 14 out of 20 labeled it terroristic. The respective figures for three other acts were as follows: sabotage, 13 out of 20; torture, 9 out of 20; hijacking for escape, 7 out of 20.

Here is a verbatim selection of some of the editors' own personal definitions of terrorism:

The policy of violence to obtain political demands.

Use of violence outside the traditional patterns of warfare (i.e., in violation of traditional laws and regulations of war).

Terroristic acts are acts of wanton and unprovoked violence, carried out against innocent and unarmed civilians, in countries that are free from foreign domination and state terrorism.

To spread terror in order to gain publicity and in order to cause an overreaction by state security forces.

The use of violence against nonrelated persons or goods with the purpose to coerce a third party to accede to the activists' demands.

Impossible to define but you recognize it when it happens.

7. At the same time, censorship is one precondition for state terrorism, which depends on secrecy as much as insurgent terrorism appears to depend on publicity.

8. This particular idea does not seem to be fruitful, given that, somewhat paradoxically, the opposite of publicity can also be an asset. One of our respondents put it this way: "I believe that terrorists thrive on mystery rather than on publicity. The more detailed information which can be published about their organizations, their leaders, and tactics the better. Any mystification achieved by hiding true facts serves only to intensify the climate of fear in which these people thrive." One only has to think of the publicity-avoiding Abu Nidal group to see the validity of this point.

9. This list was made on the basis of responses of editors to the question "What are, in your view, the main ethical principles which should guide journalism?" It reflects professional standards as codified, for instance, in the International Code of Honour of the International Federation of Journalists (1954; see Doomen, 1987, p. 323) or the Code of Ethics or Canons of Journalism of the American Society of Newspaper Editors (1923), the American Society of Newspaper Editors (1975), and the Society of Professional Journalists, Sigma Delta Chi (as reproduced in Thomson, 1978, pp. 55-60).

10. The last two items are from a journalist who answered the questionnaire; he was not part of the sample of 20 editors.

11. This problem has been expressed most clearly by Alan H. Protheroe (1990), the chairman of the Association of British Editors: "Part of the difficulty for the media is to determine when a terrorist stunt is just that, a stunt designed for the media. From whom do we take advice? Who is really qualified to advise us that it is just a publicity stunt? Is one letter bomb that actually

explodes and for which responsibility is claimed by a hitherto unknown group merely a stunt, or is it evidence that a new group really is at work? Do we wait for the second bomb, when the publicity for the first might have alerted people to be on the lookout? The responsibility is horrendous, and the judgments cannot be the media's alone" (p. 68).

12. F. S. Andison (1977) has written: "It seems quite clear that according to the findings of the studies collected there is at least a weak positive relationship between watching violence on television and the subsequent aggression displayed by viewers of that violence. . . . Therefore, it seems reasonable to tentatively accept the 'TV violence as a stimulant to aggression' theory and to reject the 'no-difference' and 'cathartic' theories, at least until further, contradictory study is completed concerning this matter" (p. 323). While this refers to televised violence in general, Gabriel Weimann and Hans-Bernard Brosius (1988) write more specifically about nonstate terrorism: "There is accumulating empirical evidence pointing to the contagiousness of terrorism and the media's role in this process" (p. 499).

# References

Andison, F. S. (1977). T.V. violence and viewer aggression: A culmination of study results, 1956-1976. *Public Opinion Quarterly, 41*, 314-331.

Clutterbuck, R. (1981). *The media and political violence.* London: Macmillan.

Cohen, A. A., Adoni, H., & Bantz, C. R. (1990). *Social conflict and television news.* London: Sage.

Crelinsten, R. D. (1990). Images of terrorism in the media: 1966-1985. *Terrorism, 12*, 167-198.

Doomen, J. (1987). *Opinies over journalistiek gedrag.* Arnhem: Gouda Quint.

Galtung, J., & Ruge, M. H. (1965). The structure of foreign news: The presentation of the Congo, Cuba and Cyprus crises in four foreign newspapers. *Journal of Peace Research, 1*, 64-90.

Galtung, J., & Ruge, M. H. (1977). Structuring and selecting news. In J. Tunstall (Ed.), *The media are American: Anglo-American media in the world* (pp. 259-298). London: Constable.

Midgley, S., & Rice, V. (Eds.). (1984). *Terrorism and the media in the 1980s.* Washington, DC: Media Institute.

O'Neill, M. J. (1986). *Terrorist spectaculars: Should TV coverage be curbed?* New York: Priority.

Protheroe, A. H. (1990). Terrorism, journalism, and democracy. In Y. Alexander & R. Latter (Eds.), *Terrorism and the media: Dilemmas for government, journalists and the public.* London: McClean, Brassey's.

Rosie, G. (1986). *The directory of international terrorism.* Edinburgh: Mainstream.

Schmid, A. P. (1984). *Political terrorism: A research guide to concepts, theories, data bases, and literature.* Amsterdam: North-Holland.

Schmid, A. P. (1989). Terrorism and the media: The ethics of publicity. *Journal of Terrorism and Political Violence, 1*, 539-565.

Schmid, A. P., & De Graaf, J. F. A. (1982). *Violence as communication: Insurgent terrorism and the Western news media.* London: Sage.

Shales, T. (1986, June 29). TV's great hostage fest. *Washington Post.*

Tan, Z. W. C. (1989). The role of media in insurgent terrorism: Issues and perspectives. *Gazette, 44*, 191-215.

Thomson, J. C., Jr. (1978). Journalistic ethics: Some probings by a media keeper. In B. Rubin (Ed.), *Questioning media ethics.* New York: Praeger.

Waugh, W. L., Jr. (1982). *International terrorism: How nations respond to terrorists.* Salisbury: Documentary.

Weimann, G., & Brosius, H.-B. (1988). The predictability of international terrorism: A time-series analysis. *Terrorism, 11*(6).

# Reporters' Perspectives

Mark Blaisse

Ever since the days of Hearst, the media have made every effort to discover and reveal the news. Dictatorships may do their best to conceal the news and distort the facts, but the essence of democracy is openness. In a democracy, the media have an obligation to keep the public informed, even if only to emphasize the contrast with the kind of a country where the media are slaves to the powers that be. But as the access to *knowledge* has become simpler and growing numbers of people have become knowledgeable about more and more matters, there has been a reduction in the amount of actual *information*. This has been due not only to the demands of the reading and viewing audience, but also to the economic repositioning of most of the media, particularly those involving electronic communication.

The audience has to be kept entertained. This would seem to be today's main purpose of radio, television, and, to an increasing extent, newspapers and magazines as well. Amusement, diversion, and recreation would seem to have become much more important than information. The tired democrat

Editors' Note: We wish to thank the Arbeiderspers for their permission to use this text, which is based on the book *Abu Nidal bestaat niet*, by Mark Blaisse, copyright 1989, Arbeiderspers, Amsterdam.

who comes home after a hard day's free enterprise wants to be cheered up, not depressed. And the media are only too eager to give that person what he or she wants. After all, they have little choice but to focus on such technicalities as profits, ratings, circulation figures, success, and popularity. The one with the highest score can charge the highest prices for advertisements and commercials. For information, this competition is lethal. And for the integrity of the interaction between the media and their audiences, the effects are dubious as well.

According to Jean-François Revel, the French social critic, the mutual admiration society that tends to flourish within that interaction has turned information into little more than a farce. The media give consumers what they want, and they express their gratitude by paying, advertising, or buying. The media and consumers merely pretend to respect each other; in their hearts they distrust, fear, and look down upon each other. The goal is to score, to beat the enemy, to win. These are the details to pay attention to, rather than the matter of keeping the so highly esteemed consumer informed. The short term prevails, not the in-depth aspect. All too often, it is immediate success that counts.

When viewers watch the news on television, they evaluate the appearance, the charm, and the charisma of the newscasters rather than the information they are presenting. Newscasters are stars, with high or even exorbitant salaries to match. This is the case not only in the United States, where a man like Dan Rather earns a good $3.5 million a year at CBS, but elsewhere as well. In France, for example, in 1987 Christine Ockrent took home 280,000 francs, almost $50,000, a month for presenting the news on her country's Channel One. "It is what the audience wants," the directors say—personalities instead of information; form instead of content (though Ockrent is far from incompetent).

In democratic countries, the media give the impression of being freer than they actually are. In reality, the need to be successful and profitable puts them under stultifying pressure. This in turn has repercussions on the ways reporters and the people in charge of them go about their work.

The phrase *freedom of the press* is open to quite a few interpretations. In August 1988, editor in chief Claude Julien wrote in *Le Monde Diplomatique*: "The press is free. Several mammoths who never tire of expanding their empire are only all too aware of that." He was talking about the freedom to buy the media. The press is free: If you have the money, you can buy all the newspapers and radio and television stations you want. The effect of this freedom to buy, Julien cautioned, is conglomeration, monopoly, and, in the end, the limitation of the freedom of the press democratic nations claim to be so fond of. To a growing extent, media mean money—lots of money.

As long as the reporters score, the media are free. As long they get their scoops, reporters are free. In his masterpiece titled *Scoop*, Evelyn Waugh's approach to this brand of compulsory success is almost too ironic; it cannot really be as bad as all that, the lay reader is apt to think. But it often is that bad, and worse. There is very little the men and women of the press would not do to "score," to be "number one," to get "prime time." Facts are sometimes distorted, sometimes invented. Enormous risks are often involved, and humiliations—begging for a visa, waiting for hours on end in stuffy rooms, cajoling and coaxing just to get an interview. To say nothing of having to submit questions beforehand and then having to make do with written answers. Even on television, it is all part of the game, even in democratic countries. The media are free, but it is frequently someone else who writes the rules.

The media are free, free to be lured this way and that. Relationships tend to play quite a role in the game. The agreements that are made with lobbies, political parties, groups, or individuals might be "gentlemen's agreements," but you rarely get something for nothing. One favor deserves another. A reporter without the right connections is not likely to have much to report. A Christmas card for Yasir Arafat, a dinner for an Israeli diplomat, a crate of good wine for the Soviet embassy—they are all indispensable. In your enthusiasm for the names in your own black book, you might overlook the fact that the other side also has a point to make. But there is very little you can do about that; certain connections are worth their weight in gold. So certain things are better overlooked. Bonn, Washington, Brussels, or the Hague, it is obvious you cannot be a political journalist without the right friends in the right places.

The more powerful the periodical or the program, the freer journalists are to ignore their contacts' wishes. In a certain sense, the man or woman who works for an important American newspaper represents the United States, and compared with a reporter for a Dutch daily, a correspondent for *Le Monde* often has a head start. The less political power you represent, however indirectly, the "trickier" you will have to be.

The media are free to decide how they are to get their information. If they should refuse to reveal their sources, there is ample legislation to protect them. And there are no laws against paying for a scoop. Is it ethical to pay for an interview? Even if the money goes to finance acts of violence?

In the interest of your sales figures, is it ethical to get into a car with two gangsters pointing guns at their hostages? This is something that actually happened in West Germany in August 1988. And what about going on a death trip with these very same gangsters all across the country just to get the scoop? Was it right for the reporter from *Express*, a Cologne paper, and the photographer who just happened to be at the scene of the drama to volunteer their services as intermediaries as they did, becoming part of the story?

Is it all right to provoke violence to get a story? In 1981 the French photographer Alain Mingam won any number of prizes for his account of the execution of an Afghan officer by the Mujahedeen rebels. Mingam was specifically brought to the site to witness the event. "If I had not been there, the man would not have been shot and then ritually beheaded," Mingam says today. For months he could not sleep because he felt like an accomplice. And surely we all remember the BBC affair in Biafra. Two men were executed. The firing squad was ready and was just about to carry out the death sentence when the British crew informed them that something was wrong with the camera, and could they please postpone the execution for just a little while. It was not until the reporters gave them the okay that the men picked up their guns and aimed and fired.

As long as the money keeps coming in, anything goes. Now and then, a professional has to overlook the fact that he or she is dealing with murderers. The media are free to forget and to promote collective amnesia. Whoever wants to keep the audience interested will have to keep putting a new face on old news, without paying much attention to the historical framework. If one works from the assumption that the audience remembers everything, then there is not much point to writing a new article or making a new program, is there? The media are free to forget.

The media are free to choose the kind of partners they can make their "deals" with. In a certain sense, journalism can be compared to the tango. When you think of the tango, you think of total theater, with stage sets, costumes, masks, makeup, directors, producers, and stage managers. In accordance with mysterious rules, the tango sweeps and swirls and then abruptly comes to a standstill. It is a disciplined dance, performed by virtual marionettes who seem to have a love/hate relationship. If one takes a step forward, the other can only step back, no ifs, ands, or buts about it. What do unsuspecting observers understand of this sultry *pas de deux*? They are stirred and impressed by what they see, but they fail to recognize the significance of many of the details. The tango is entertainment, with pride and melancholy, power and sadness intertwining. It is masculine and feminine, intangible. The tango stands for winning and seducing. The tango has to do with scoring and with being number one.

When terrorists are caught, when ideologies are promoted and propaganda spread, when rulers speak to their followers, just exactly who is dancing with whom? Reporters know their editors in chief want to be able to present political leaders to readers or viewers, no matter how little those leaders might have to say. Celebrities sell, and to get them, there are certain concessions that have to be made.

In the following pages, I present a series of vignettes about one journalist's encounters—and missed encounters—with Arab terrorists.

## In Search of Abu Nidal

ALGIERS

*Winter 1983.* In the lobby of the luxurious hotel that served as conference center, the guests were engaged in animated conversation. Pinstriped suits and pleated skirts abounded, instead of battle uniforms and machine guns. It was happy hour for these resistance fighters. In these very civilized circles, *terrorists* would hardly seem to be the appropriate term.

Two gentlemen with neat mustaches were smoking their pipes and nipping at their orange juice. Fine though his shoes might have been, one of them had no socks on. When he turned around, for just a split second the flash of a pistol was visible in his belt.

Cookies were served while Italians, West Germans, Japanese, Libyans, Lebanese, Syrians, and Palestinians from all over shook hands and embraced. It was like a family reunion, this meeting of the Palestinian National Council in Algiers. Some 3,000 delegates, friends, relations, and sponsors had arrived, and the organization could barely cope. Some of the delegates had to make do with rooms 50 kilometers from the Algerian capital. How often did you get to see virtually the entire cast of characters of the international terrorist scene in one place? The security checks were strict, though not overly so, and efficient. After all, one well-placed bomb of the Israeli or American secret service . . .

The conversation was not focused solely on the quality of the couscous. In the coffee shop, an American columnist was chatting with Leila Khaled: big brown eyes and thick hair. In 1970 she was the first lady hijacker in history. Together with Patrick Arguello, she tried to force the pilot of an El Al plane bound for New York to detour to Jordan. After a routine stop in Amsterdam, the two hijackers went into action. On board, however, Israeli

security agents managed to overpower them. Two grenades were found in
Leila Khaled's bra. Today she wasn't wearing anything under her T-shirt. The
man slurping on his cigarette with the German television crew gathered
around him was Muhammad Da'ud Awda, alias Abu Da'ud, one of the men
who organized the murder of 11 Israeli athletes at the Munich Olympics in
1972. Everyone was treating him like a hero.

African and South American freedom movements had also sent delegates
to represent them here. Tactics were being discussed above brimming ash-
trays and pitchers of cool water. Eritreans sporting Palestinian kafias, Nica-
raguans speaking Spanish with men from the disputed Western Sahara,
Libyans who seemed to be informing the Irish of the details of the next arms
shipment—but they might also have been telling them how to get to a really
good restaurant. When I showed my interest, I was told the Libyan arms were
free of charge. Even for the IRA.

There was Suriname's ambassador in the Hague, Henk Herrenberg. He
was on vacation in Algiers and was combining business with pleasure. Only
a few weeks earlier, a leading Dutch daily had called him a cocaine dealer.
"That is typically Dutch, I pay about as much attention to that as I do to your
assumption that I am here to buy machine guns," the ambassador remarked
as he continued on his way, laughing heartily.

Nayef Hawatmeh and George Habash were talking to a French reporter.
Habash was the man behind the spectacular hijackings in Jordan in 1970 and
the hijacking of the Lufthansa plane in Mogadiscio in Somalia. Hawatmeh
was responsible for the Ma'alot massacre on May 15, 1974, where 22 Israeli
children had lost their lives. That was almost 10 years ago. Maybe that was
the reason the reporter could smile and overlook it.

I was introduced to Bassam Abu Sherif, one of the PLO hawks. I shook a
hand with only one whole finger and four halves. An Israeli letter bomb, the
Palestinian explained. We had a cup of tea and talked about the imminent
split within the PLO. The lack of unity among the Palestinians was Israel's
strongest weapon, he said. "I wonder how much of that discord is promoted
from outside. Israel is all over," Abu Sherif added before we followed the
crowds into the main hall, where the PLO leaders were to address the
delegates. He waved to a German. "A man I knew in Beirut."

Yasir Arafat was in top shape. A short, fat actor without any particular
charisma, but an eloquent speaker. He didn't actually speak, though; he
barked. With his wild gestures and war cries, he mesmerized the audience.
A wide grin spread across his face when the majority approved his proposals.
When Arafat laughed, his whole face laughed—except his eyes.

There were rumors that Abu Nidal, the archenemy of Yasir Arafat, had planned an attack and that it was going to take place during the conference. Arafat was guarded more carefully than ever. But he did shake the necessary hands, especially media hands. There were drops of spittle at the corners of his mouth. Arafat was all mouth. Under the kafia he never seemed to remove there were shiny beads of perspiration on his forehead. What ever gave him the idea that a five o'clock shadow looked revolutionary? Arafat was on first-name terms with the correspondents stationed in Cairo, Beirut, Amman, Larnaca, the men who covered the PLO on a day-to-day basis. And anyone who had covered the Beirut battles in 1982 was really in for preferential treatment.

Special visits to Palestinian training camps were organized by Mahmud Labadie, who had been the PLO spokesman for years on end before he decided to go into hiding with dissidents in Damascus. As was so often the case, he was very much in the limelight here. What could he arrange for us? But even more important, how much of our work had he read? Had the PLO representatives done their job and translated all the articles about their organization and sent them to Labadie? He had a photographic memory, spoke fluent German and English, and was the man who decided if and when Arafat could be interviewed. He held all the cards, and this time only the politically interesting countries were to have a turn: the United States, France, and West Germany. We were going to have to make do with second-rank PLO officials, and with the "cowboys" who carried out the orders for violence. An all-feelings-banned interview with a terrorist, take it or leave it.

Labadie was exhausted. At two o'clock in the morning, he was still on the phone. Part of his job was to maintain daily contact with PLO representatives all around the globe. He kept the "money men" behind the PLO informed of the latest developments at the conference. "An awful lot of Palestinians have absolutely no desire to live in Palestine," he remarked with more than a touch of bitterness. "It is not like Israel, a country that attracts talent. A lot of the Palestinians with money and intellect live in the United States or in the Gulf and would not dream of leaving. But they do pay their share." He was so tired he couldn't help being honest.

Three years later I ran into him again, this time in Damascus. Guarded by 13-year-old PLO volunteers who could barely hold up under the weight of the kalashnikovs, he opened the door to his office, half a basement apartment with bullet-proof doors. "Now even the Palestinians who do want to live in Palestine are divided," I said. He grinned, or was it a grimace? He had not forgotten our last conversation in Algiers. He had read the articles that followed. Just before our interview started, he took the pistol off his desk, commenting that he knew what we were like and was sure we were going to focus on the pistol at the start of the television broadcast. "Reporters just think of themselves," he laughed, and poured a torrent of propaganda over our heads.

### TUNIS

*Autumn 1982.* Austrian Chancellor Bruno Kreisky was paying an official visit to Tunisian President Bourguiba, who was old and ill. Then Kreisky hurried to his hotel to keep an appointment with Arafat. After its downfall in Beirut, the PLO had set up headquarters in Tunisia. The fact that Kreisky's talk with Bourguiba was only the alibi for his journey to more interesting horizons had already become crystal clear. The Lear jet Kreisky had become so fond of, with no less than the former race car champion Niki Lauda as the pilot in charge, had made an unexpected stop in Tripoli on the way to Tunis. Kreisky spoke to Colonel Qaddafi for half an hour. What they discussed we will never know, but Kreisky was later to pose arm in arm with the colonel in Vienna. The controversial chancellor had long had his eye on the role of intermediary in the Middle East's conflicts. On one of his "secret" missions, I had the good fortune to be one of the small group of journalists handpicked by Kreisky himself. So it wasn't really as "secret" as all that.

Arafat was not on time for the appointment. He had sent his trusted assistant Salah Khalaf, alias Abu Ijad, to do the preliminaries for the talk with Kreisky. Abu Ijad's beige army shirt was clearly a few sizes too small. From a distance, we observed the two men. What struck me was the contrast between the chancellor's enormous black oxfords and the Palestinian's sandals. The Arafat-Kreisky talk was to take place an hour later, but in private. It was way past midnight by the time the Austrian, slumped content-edly in his armchair, told us "off the record" how deep his understanding was of the PLO standpoint. Despite the recent terrorist attacks that put the PLO back on the world's front pages? I was asked to please refrain from using the word *terrorist* so carelessly. Words are also politics.

Two days later I myself was sitting at a table with Arafat. I had been picked up by a silent man in a Peugeot and taken to Salwa Hotel, about 30 miles outside Tunis. Bordj Cedria was the name of the hamlet where the PLO had put up its tents. It was three o'clock in the morning—Arafat's favorite time of day for interviews, because the journalist was usually too tired to think straight and it was easier for Arafat to take the lead.

Arafat was in top shape. The talk did not lead to much. Menacingly, his pistol remained next to my tape recorder on the table, and I had the urge to pick it up, just to feel it. Behind Arafat, two guards chatted incessantly throughout the interview, which was held half in English and half in Arabic. Arafat was annoyed at the interpreter, who did not seem to be able to translate fast enough. It was more of a monologue than an interview. Arafat said what he wanted to say, rarely gave a straight answer to any of the questions, and obviously viewed us as convenient sounding boards for his propaganda.

As was so often the case, the subject was the definition of *terrorism.* What we in the West called terrorism, he explained, was actually a heroic resistance struggle against the Israeli occupiers of the territory that rightly belonged to the Palestinians. Arafat's favorite topic was how no one could blame him for the fact that Europeans and Americans had a guilt complex when it came to the Jews, and how he was not responsible for what had happened in the Second World War. There was no way to counter his argument. With a simple gesture, he informed me that there was no point in even trying, and I kept silent. The Palestinians had become the victims of the collective guilt complex so prevalent in the West, which as a matter of fact was the only reason the state of Israel had ever been founded in the first place. Arafat suddenly quieted down and explained how the West had been systematically misinformed by its politicians and media about the true history of Israel and the Palestinians. "I am here to help you see the light," he announced, and there were tears in his eyes. Arafat the sentimental historian.

It was not until the tape recorder had been turned off that the interview finally became interesting. Arafat's unofficial answers, which were absolutely off the record, were indicative of the ideological battle being waged within the PLO. If less attention were devoted to the most nonsensical details, maybe the peace process would be more apt to get somewhere. But for his own survival, Arafat apparently had to please whoever his partner might be at any particular moment. What journalist would ever dream of breaking the gentlemen's agreement called "off the record"? It would be the last talk that journalist ever had with Arafat, that was one thing that was sure.

Better than almost anyone else, Arafat knows how to manipulate the media. They have hated him and they have adored him, they have condemned him and flattered him, but there are very few journalists who have ever let a chance go by to get him to say a few words into their microphones.

When he was secretary of state, Henry Kissinger once said that the media "made" Arafat, that without their help no one ever would have known his name. At any rate Arafat, alias Abu Amar, "father of the builder," was quick to realize how important it is to be in the limelight. Is that in fact why the man is still alive? Would even the Mossad, the Israeli secret service, hesitate to eliminate Arafat because, despite his unpredictability, he is nonetheless a *known* factor in the Middle East?

In a sense, demanding and receiving attention has been a form of life insurance, a guarantee for Arafat that the PLO would stay in the news. Especially after 1986, when his organization was apt to disappear from the front pages for lengthening periods of time because of the more serious problems in the region, such as the crisis in the Persian Gulf, Arafat did his utmost to keep from fading into oblivion. The Intifada, the Palestinian rebellion in the territories occupied by Israel that broke out on December 8, 1987, surprising virtually everyone, including the PLO leaders, with its intensity and duration, was just what he needed. For the first time since the mass rebellion against the British mandate in 1936-1939, the Palestinians seemed to be united. For the time being, even the Palestinian factions in Syria, Iraq, and Libya seemed to have buried the hatchet. Youngsters throwing stones and then being brutally "pacified" by Israeli troops—Arafat saw right away that this was the stuff that simply begged to be turned into a media event. Any television crews that arrived were soon treated to "spontaneous" actions.

The initial leaders of the Intifada were local Palestinians who operated underground. They had been influenced by the "Jihad islami," fundamentalists to whose ideas the PLO—except for its Lebanon branch—was not very sympathetic. Nonetheless, Arafat was quick to make sure the rebellion was attributed to the official PLO. Most of the Western media were more than willing to lend him a helping hand in this respect. And the Israeli authorities, in turn, had their reasons to want to keep these media out; the strength of the PLO and the power of Arafat were much too strongly stressed, as were the impotence of Israel and its inability to deal with the situation. The media were blamed for the negative image Israel acquired in the process. What is more, the media were even accused of inciting violence.

Disgruntled about the shift of attention, Arafat turned against the "stupid Western media who never understood anything." In the *Revue d'Etudes Palestiniennes*, he lashed out at journalists who failed to recognize the importance of the PLO and had given the fundamentalists credit for inciting the "rebellion of the stones." The media, in Arafat's opinion, had been influenced by the Israeli and American secret services and propaganda machines. What is more, there were a few specific media that the PLO leader took it upon himself to shower with praise, as if he himself were the editor in chief. In Arafat's opinion, for example, the foreign correspondent of none other than the *Washington Post* was responsible for the fact that the resolutions presented at the Casablanca summit in 1985 were well translated. Mohammed al-Khatib, the Jordanian minister of information, had "forgotten" to mention the PLO in his English text as the one and only rightful representative of the Palestinian people. The Arabic-speaking American had been the one to correct the error.

Up to now, only the improbable dimensions of his suspicious mistrust have allowed Arafat to escape unscathed from the infinite numbers of attacks that have been made on his life. Even his friends are eyed suspiciously. Arafat sleeps at a different spot every night; he has no home of his own, no permanent personal relationships, and he barely sees his relatives. The Palestinian press agency WAFA regularly disseminates rumors about the latest spot where Arafat is supposedly thinking of settling. It has happened regularly that reporters have gone to Tunis to speak to him, while he was in some different country at the time.

After Arafat's second appearance before the General Assembly of the United Nations on November 13, 1988, in Geneva, his prestige was greater than ever. "We want peace," he had said, and rejected terrorism as a political instrument. Had he consulted the inhabitants of the occupied territories about this issue, their answers might have been different. The reality of the refugee camps is not the same reality as at the conference table.

The fact that Yasir Arafat was a symbolic figure long before his international success would never have been true without the efforts of the media. He *is* the PLO and thus, to many people, the sole representative of the Palestinians. Even if fate should catch up with him, Arafat will live on as a myth. His worst enemies are within the Palestinian community itself, but since he often has his most daring words spoken by his trusted assistants, up to now he has remained safe from harm. It is the hawks and doves who have been used by Arafat who have had to pay the dues.

TRIPOLI

*Winter 1986.* Mu'ammar Qaddafi consented to an interview. It was preceded by weeks and weeks of coaxing and cajoling, via the embassy in Brussels, which Libya insisted on calling the People's Bureau. Contradictory reports kept on being communicated, each time by a different "representative of the people" to intensify the confusion, but in the end we were informed that we were welcome. No, the visa was not exactly available yet. But as soon as we got there everything would be arranged, the umpteenth nameless official in Brussels assured us on the phone.

Lo and behold, no problems. The cameraman and I were officially welcomed into the strictly Moslem nation and passed through customs without being searched.

The initial plans were for the talk with Colonel Qaddafi to be recorded live at the studio in Tripoli. Qaddafi was not a naive man, and he wanted to make sure no cutting would be done on his messages. Like Arafat, he viewed us as a mouthpiece, not as independently operating journalists. After some deliberation, we refused to accept the proposal, using the excuse that we could not handle it technically. This way we did not offend the leader and the implication was clear that Libya was more modern than the Netherlands. He was nice to us, we were nice to him.

Four days later, we still had not caught our first glimpse of Qaddafi. "Maybe tomorrow," the grinning men on the lookout in the hall suggested. In the Arab world, waiting is an important component of work. Programs that have to go on the air on time, deadlines when articles are due? They could not care less. Patience is a much-respected virtue, that was lesson one. And as soon as they noticed we were in a hurry, they would do whatever they could to slow matters down. Time as a weapon against imperialism . . .

Of course, the American media had once again been very clever indeed: They sent the prettiest reporters—Qaddafi is a ladies' man. They arrived in their dainty sandals, stylish blouses, and glamorous sunglasses. Suntanned, clutching important-looking papers under their arms, they rushed through the lobby, hurrying from telephone to telephone. A top priority seemed to be to make the competition nervous. The truth was that they too would have to do their share of waiting.

The news that we were about to leave the hotel caught everyone unawares. Destination unknown. A bus was ready and waiting, and eight of us were hustled into it. In Libya, every media event is veiled in secrecy. Without the mystery, there is no myth.

We stopped at an open field half an hour's drive from Tripoli and were requested to please line up. With the exception of the two gentlemen from the Netherlands, it was quite a colorful harem. The show could start. Garbed as a peasant on a tractor, the colonel made his grand entrance. Look at me, I am just a simple man, you could see him projecting. From atop the tractor, he invited the ladies to have a cup of tea. The Reuters correspondent thought he looked very exciting, dressed in precisely the color of the desert sand. Without answering any of the questions we fired at him, our voices literally crying out into the wilderness, Qaddafi turned and disappeared. A few days earlier, he had put on the same show for another group of reporters, but then it was on board a frigate. Pointing to the horizon, where part of the American

Sixth Fleet was anchored, he had informed them he was not afraid of anyone or anything and was prepared for whatever confrontation might be in store for him. Several weeks later, the Americans were to bomb Tripoli and Bengazi.

Not much of any significance had been said at the tea party, Judy Miller of the *New York Times* had to admit. But there was an article in it. Months later, it was to appear in the Sunday edition of the *New York Times* under the headline "My Nights with Qaddafi." Miller did indeed spend a couple of weeks in Tripoli, be it playing tennis with the British consul, who secretly brewed his own beer in the ramshackle cellar of his consulate. Miller saw Qaddafi a couple of times and repeatedly interviewed him at night. At most, the American mouthpiece and the officer/terrorist had arrived at a mutual agreement about undesirable but nonetheless necessary cooperation—about the "tango." But the editor in chief in New York apparently thought Miller's experience was interesting enough to give it the eye-catching headline that might logically have been expected to compromise the position of the newspaper—outspokenly pro-Israel and equally outspokenly anti-Qaddafi—and the reputation of a very serious lady journalist. That was barely the case. Instead, "My Nights with Qaddafi" made quite a hit and skyrocketed Miller's fame far faster than all her in-depth Middle East analyses put together.

By the time I was finally admitted to the fort, I knew all about Qaddafi's satin shirts and the dark spots under his armpits. He was indeed a tense man. There was an intent look on his face when he received us in his office and not in the symbolic Bedouin tent featured in so many photographs—a tent set up next to the main building, not in the middle of the desert, as unsuspecting readers and viewers were led to believe. Apparently no one had ever felt the need to shatter the illusion.

Even inside, Mu'ammar Qaddafi preferred not to take off his bullet-proof vest. He seemed to be just as scared of the rest of the world as the world was of him. "The United States and Israel are one and the same state," he shouted, and banged his fist on the desk. Qaddafi might not be totally insane, but he certainly did exhibit all the symptoms of megalomania. And then there was that look in his eyes.

The colonel's bodyguards were short and ugly, but I for one would never underestimate them again. When the cameraman lifted his Betacam to his shoulder and crossed the courtyard where tanks covered by camouflage nets were guarding the Libyan power center, they very resolutely jumped him. Why was the red light on, he had been told that filming was forbidden, hadn't he? Because the red light is always on, was his answer, which was obviously taken to be an outright lie. That was the end of the film, the end of our whole item, the end of "My Days with Qaddafi." By the next day we were on the plane back to Amsterdam, tails between our legs, a laughingstock.

*Spring 1986.* Today there wasn't anything left of the volleyball field in front of Qaddafi's office. The American bombs, it was immediately clear, had been dropped on Libya to put an end to the colonel's life, and not just to scare him. Qaddafi had survived the attack only because of the bomb-proof shelter that had been constructed by Italians a couple of yards away from the main building. One of Qaddafi's adopted children, a girl, had perished under the wreckage before he could get to her. In the course of the years the Qaddafi family had had quite a bit of publicity, but no one had ever even heard of 15-month-old Hanna. Did Qaddafi really think the death of a—fictitious— child would sour the attitude of the Western non-American media toward Washington? He was not above manipulations of this kind, and we did tend to go for sentimental details hook, line, and sinker.

Ever since the bombings, Qaddafi's main means of transportation had been a yellow Daimler-Benz bus. Behind the armored steel (Where did he get a bus like that?) there was a conference room, a telephone switchboard, and a luxurious bathroom. Like Arafat, Qaddafi believed in the security of perma- nent mobility. Anyone who wanted to talk to him inevitably wound up inside or outside that bus. Via the weirdest detours in planes and jeeps, somewhere in Libya you did finally encounter Qaddafi, often surrounded by heavily armed young women, the Green Nuns. The Jamahirya, the "State of the Masses," as Libya under Qaddafi is called, was not just another slogan, for men and women are indeed treated as equals, at least when it comes to working.

The media had spread rumors that Qaddafi was wounded, slightly wounded, that is, on his left arm. In order to illustrate, however, that he was still in fine shape and in good spirits, no matter who claimed otherwise, the colonel invited reporters from the British Sunday paper the *Observer* to come to Libya. The delegation was then instructed to photograph a volleyball game somewhere in the desert, with Qaddafi engaging in the wildest of athletic shenanigans just to demonstrate the fine shape he was in. In the tent that materialized here as well, no one was allowed to photograph the leader in his volleyball attire. Before any pictures could be taken, he donned his traditional cape and hood and was seated in a leather armchair: a Bedouin answering serious questions with dignity, ridiculing everything British in the process. In the objective Sunday paper, Qaddafi informed the readers of his intention to avenge the American bombings. His targets were to be in various countries . . . including England. He also stated that he was actively supporting the Irish Republican Army with funds and arms, and that in his opinion, Americans and Englishmen bore a closer resemblance to apes than to human beings. None of this was to prevent the highly respected reporters, Colin Smith and Donald Trelford, from referring to Qaddafi as "serene" and even "charming." They failed to see even the slightest sign of the "wild dog" in him. Several days prior to this interview, Qaddafi had ordered seven of his regime's opponents hanged in public without bothering to put them on trial. The execution was broadcast live on Libyan television. And yet today very few journalists who got the chance to visit the yellow bus would be likely to refuse.

It was only if they were lucky that they would get a glimpse of the real Qaddafi, since lately there seemed to be a Qaddafi stand-in who took over whenever the colonel scented danger.

## DAMASCUS

*Winter 1984.* The regime of President Hafez al-Assad was increasingly becoming the driving power behind Palestinian extremism. Syria was an enthusiastic sponsor of any and every organization out to promote turmoil in the region.

I had rarely been so cordially welcomed without actually being welcome at all. The first four days of my stay in Syria were spent waiting at the office of Dr. Zaboub, a man with a Ph.D. in the science of keeping reporters occupied. Dripping with perspiration, he constantly conferred on two telephones simultaneously, in the meantime shouting orders at a chubby secretary hurrying to and fro with her files. And would I like a cup of coffee? And did I still want to speak to the president? Or would the minister of propaganda do? Dr. Zaboub persisted in referring to him as the minister of information. It was too much for him, he seemed to be nearing the breaking point, but then that broad grin broke across his face, he stood up, patted me on the shoulder, and assured me that tomorrow would be the day. Then I'd be able to go all the way to the edge of the Golan Heights and see the Israeli occupying forces ("Did you know the Israelis set up a ski lift, just to be able to relax during the occupation? They must think they are going to be able to stay there forever. No way.") and see the Presidential Palace and a training camp for women commandos. Tomorrow, tomorrow. Really.

And the next day it was the same story all over again. Perspiration, coffee, a lot of screaming and gesturing and telephoning and promising. Dr. Zaboub wouldn't even let me film the streets; every bridge and every road was a strategic spot and consequently top secret. On the fourth day, accompanied by a bespectacled spy in a dilapidated American jalopy, we could finally start on our assignment. As soon as the camera was poised to shoot, our spy had to look through the lens for himself just to make sure nothing compromising was being focused on. Reports, notices, forms, stamps, permission, confirmation of permission—it all took hours. And hardly anything received the final approval. We drove for hundreds of miles just to come up against a fanatic officer who had not been properly informed and sent us packing. What a welcome.

We were scrutinized day and night, even though it was sometimes a purely symbolic matter. The new Presidential Palace in the hills to the west of the capital bore a particularly strong resemblance to a big concrete eye, a strategically situated eagle's nest up above the junction of roads leading to Lebanon and the Israeli-occupied Golan Heights, and alongside the route used by armored cars and troops whenever the tension rose in the countries next door. Albert Speer could not have come up with a better design.

In Syria, you can go out alone only at night. In the daytime, the 150,000 or more secret agents and informers President Assad has working for him are much too alert. Syria is a dictatorship, supervised by the vigilant minority tribe of Alavites, who manage to stay in power only by way of the strictest Stalinist methods. It is a country where Abu Nidal felt right at home. He was the only man we wanted to talk to whom we had not put on our official list; he was one of the numerous guests of President Assad, for whom the Palestinian could be a pawn on the region's vast chessboard. Syria dreamed of a Greater Syria, extending to include Lebanon. Abu Nidal's group could help promote the confusion Assad needed, making it unnecessary for Assad to compromise himself.

Even more secretive than the Venezuelan terrorist Carlos, alias Ilich Ramirez Sanchez, Abu Nidal is the most elusive of all the "superterrorists." Obsessed by a desire for revenge, Abu Nidal, "the father of the struggle," has devoted his life to the destruction of the state of Israel. Together with his commandos operating in tiny cells, he has put permanent fear into the hearts of everyone who refuses to declare him- or herself an enemy of the state of Israel. The name Abu Nidal has become synonymous with blind hatred. Whenever the authorities are at a loss to account for some act of terror, his name is brought up.

At the end of 1980, when President Saddam Hussein of Iraq was for a while no longer extending his hospitality to Abu Nidal, Assad had invited him to come and stay. In the Bekaa Valley, under Syrian influence, Abu Nidal's men and women were free to prepare their actions undisturbed.

The Bekaa Valley is sizable and virtually inaccessible as soon as you want to leave the large Damascus-Beirut road. Checkpoints, troops, and unspecified commando units refuse to let anyone or anything pass them by. How did one go about finding Abu Nidal here? It eventually meant going after him in Damascus, the city of secret diplomacy, of tea and silence.

No one was ever where they ought to be, invisible strings led to improbable addresses and the people in power took refuge behind the marble walls of their palaces. Since everyone was suspicious of everyone else and there were ultraviolent feuds, even within the president's own family, even Syrians usually met in public places. If they met at a hotel, it wasn't in one of the rooms, which were systematically equipped with microphones, but in the lobby or the restaurant. Via Eric Rouleau, the Middle East expert at *Le Monde*, I secured the name of a dissident said to be well informed about Abu Nidal's latest activities. The only problem was that I didn't have his address. It was to be given to me one evening at the coffee shop of Cham Palace, the spot where the Damascus upper 10 met and mingled. On white leather sofas, carefully made-up women were waiting for their lovers and greasy-haired officers fingered their chains of beads, whispering as they drank whisky before going downstairs to the club to watch the belly dancers. Children in English clothes played near the fountains in the lobby.

Outside, poverty and chaos reigned supreme, but inside Cham Palace the members of the Assad clique were enjoying the good life. I bought a censored, cut-up copy of the *International Herald Tribune*, which I had agreed to be recognizably sitting there reading. But no one came to meet me. Without my asking for it, a waiter brought me a glass of water—and instructions scribbled on a little piece of paper.

Twice I entered a courtyard strewn with garbage. And there was the inevitable dog barking. I couldn't help smirking—the poor little Dutch boy lost in nocturnal Damascus, wasn't it going a bit too far? I couldn't even read the Arabic street signs. Finally I did somehow arrive at the address of the doctor with whom I apparently had an appointment. It was 9:30 and pitch black outside. The staircase insight was only dimly lit.

On the third floor I rang the bell and a nurse showed me inside. Following an old Ian Fleming example, I invented a sore throat and 10 minutes later I was face to face with a gray-haired gentlemen: the doctor. I immediately began to explain the purpose of my visit, but with a frightened grimace he pointed to the ceiling and put a finger to his lips. In loud, clear voices we discussed the condition of my tonsils, all the while whispering about Assad and international terrorism. "Terrorism is part and parcel of this regime," he explained. "We suffer from it all the time. There are many more political prisoners in the Damascus jails than the 10,000 referred to by Amnesty International. If you are in the opposition here, you are not likely to live very long." The doctor was visibly agitated. He told me the Bekaa Valley was a zone deliberately used by Assad to destabilize the entire region. The fact that Abu Nidal had set up his tents there was not unknown to the doctor. But where? According to him, Abu Nidal was an occasional guest at Assad's home, but that was all he knew. Oh yes, wasn't he seriously ill?

That was obviously all he had to say. I paid and left. Dr. Osman Ayedi, the director of Cham Palace, watched me enter the hotel. He took me aside and asked me to please never go out alone again. "If you disappear, there won't be anything I can do for you," he informed me. In my room, there was a tray with tomato juice and soda water. Between the two glasses, there was a note: "Welcome, my friend." This wasn't paranoia, mere claustrophobia, this was real. Everyone knew everything here. In my dream that night, a nice doctor was being beaten up in a dungeon.

Damascus, the unofficial capital of Lebanon, also housed the leading personality of the Lebanese National Liberation Front, Walid Jumblatt. President Assad had given him a nice bungalow of his own—a small price to pay for the unrest Jumblatt could be credited with in Lebanon, with Syria as the managing director. As a Lebanese, Jumblatt himself would also prefer to see a Greater Syria emerge rather then a Lebanon under Israeli influence, which was what made him the perfect vassal. Clad in a black leather suit, he spent his days speeding about town on a motorcycle. Toward the end of the day, he usually attended a meeting at the Sheraton Hotel. He had aged visibly in the last few years. But despite the beer and the pep pills, the bulging eyes were still alert. As he came out of the elevator with his bodyguards, I went up to him and introduced myself.

Together with my cameraman and sound technician, I was picked up the next evening. We were pushed into a dark Mercedes and sped to a suburb. Overarmed Druses were standing guard, encircling the house at a distance of a few hundred yards. In the car, our feet were propped against sturdy machine guns. There was a grenade launcher in the trunk. In Damascus, you could take your own arms wherever you liked. By now we had no idea where we were. The cameraman did not trust the whole thing. "If you disappear," the words echoed in my mind, "there won't be anything I can do for you." We waited in silence outside the dark house. Then the gate opened and we were led through a garage into a sparsely furnished living room. Half an hour later, dressed in jeans a couple of sizes too large for him and a checked shirt, Jumblatt came in. The energy had gone out of his handshake. He was tired.

One of the bodyguards took a cigarette out of the pack he had in his sock. I saw a stiletto and could only hope the cameraman had not noticed it. The conversation was held in French: Violence was surely disastrous, but how else could Lebanon ever be liberated from the foreign yoke? Syria was a friend, not an imperialist state out to hurt Lebanon.

These were the kind of answers you could fill in yourself beforehand—platitudes and propaganda. So I went ahead and posed the question: Where is Abu Nidal? Jumblatt was not fazed. I tried to feign interest in Jumblatt's radio station in the Shouf Mountains above Beirut. It was from this transmitting station that his political messages were broadcast to Lebanon, which was how he kept his troops motivated.

In order to get to the Shouf Mountains, first you had to cross the Bekaa Valley. He had taken journalists this way before. Yet this time, Jumblatt was not interested. We were obviously not going to be informed of Abu Nidal's whereabouts, and for the first time I began to doubt his very existence. Why would he be so reluctant to meet the press? On the few occasions when he did speak to reporters, it did not do him any harm. Abu Nidal was the opposite of Arafat in this respect, however, and avoided publicity at all costs. Was it a matter of tactics, or was there something else involved here?

A year after my trip to Syria, the first reports started circulating about Abu Nidal's illness. His response consisted of the interviews he gave the Kuwait paper *Al Qabas* and *Der Spiegel* from Hamburg. He used them to refute the "unfounded rumors" that had been printed in an "imperialist" periodical called *Newsweek.* The two *Der Spiegel* correspondents were not only ambitious, they also had good intuition. In order to make sure it was Abu Nidal himself they were dealing with, they asked for proof. Abu Nidal lifted his shirt and showed them the scars of his open-heart surgery. Was that enough proof?

BEIRUT

"You want to understand what terrorism is?" the Palestinian Edward Saïd asked in fluent English, and showed us a transcript of an interview by an Israeli reporter with a terrorist in a South Lebanese jail:

*Reporter:* What was your mission in South Lebanon?
*Answer:* To scare people out of their wits. . . . in other words to go into villages and commit acts of terrorism. And wherever we saw women and children, we would start to terrorize them.
*Reporter:* And do you terrorize people for money or is it a matter of conviction?

*Answer:* No, my God, only for money! What kind of conviction do you think there is? Is there still any kind of conviction at all? For ages now, we have been selling our services to the highest bidder.

This was Israeli radio propaganda, but, cynical as it may sound, it did have a ring of truth to it. It is only one of the many examples illustrating how the motivation of some terrorists bears no relation at all to either politics or religion. You don't have to be a fanatic Moslem or a vehement nationalist to resort to violence as your last chance. It is enough to have been born in a refugee camp, in a slum, or in an isolated, forgotten village. This holds just as true for Lebanon as it does for Northern Ireland and the Basque provinces: Poverty and social and economic isolation are flames easily stirred by political and religious arguments, sparks that can burst into terrorism on a moment's notice.

He who is no one must see to it that he gets something, Jean-Paul Sartre wrote in his biography of Jean Genet—getting by way of violence, becoming someone with guns. A gold Rolex as the primary aim and at the end of the tunnel, power, cars, and women. It sounds primitive, but terrorism is also partly glamour.

Beirut, the urban arena where battles are fought in the name of Allah, Christ, Syria, the ayatollahs, Jordan, the United States, and Israel, has reached the point of exhaustion. Ideals have made way for opportunism. Beirut is now referred to only in strategic terms, except when one more Western reporter, delegate, or businessman is kidnapped. Beirut, where hope and optimism have made way for random violence and fatigue. Beirut is just as dead as the looks in the eyes of the children, even today still keeping up some vague front, although the children seem to be the ones who have the least trouble adjusting to the chaos in this city, where violence and terrorism have become salable commodities. Death is worth money.

Who dares to venture into Beirut nowadays? Better yet, who wants to? The Lebanese pound is worth so little that business is hardly worth doing. The real estate business is the only one that is booming; as soon as a bombing or explosion creates some new ruins, the plot of land is sold and perhaps even resold. But this is the job of the local mafia. The offices are closed; even the media have opted for safer places—Amman, Larnaca, Cairo. The diehard who insists on an appointment arranges to meet outside the city. And even then you still cannot be sure you will be able to outsmart prospective kidnappers.

A great deal has been written about the kidnappings in Beirut. I was not really aware of the full meaning of this form of terrorism until I read the accounts written by French reporter Jean-Paul Kauffmann. He was kept hostage for more than three years before he was released in May 1988, prior to the presidential elections in France. Just before the eight o'clock evening news, day after day, Antenne-2, a French television channel, called its viewers' attention to his plight in order to remind the authorities to exert whatever pressure they could. Kauffmann's wife, Joëlle, had also done all she could, traveling repeatedly to Beirut to try to get the kidnappers to reconsider, giving interviews, constantly addressing reminders to the ministries and in general managing to keep her husband in the news. In a way, the media can help you into jail as well as out of it.

Kauffmann's account made it clear that during those three years when he was tortured, humiliated, and harassed, the kidnappers considered it a game. Torture for fun. One of Kauffmann's three French cellmates died of hepatitis; he had not received medical care. His life could easily have been saved, if only the "rules of the game" had been different in Beirut. But the last of the rules had long since lost their validity.

Kauffmann described how he was kept in chains and how executions were repeatedly simulated, much to the hilarity of his guards. Details of this kind might cause a storm of indignation in the West, but for the people of Beirut, so accustomed to the rituals of kidnapping, they were an everyday matter.

In Beirut you are at the mercy of gangs—gangsters with no other ideology than take the money and run, gangsters who have made kidnapping as routine a pastime as shooting. Is there something about your face they don't like? Is there something funny about your identity card? Do you look rich? There are hundreds of reasons to be kidnapped. Insiders estimate that there are anywhere from 2,000 to 3,000 kidnap victims throughout the city, and no one seems to be doing anything about it.

One day Alfred Yaghobzadeh, a French photographer of Iranian descent, described to me how a kidnapping usually works:

I was told to stop for a routine check and they arrested me and accused me of espionage. Someone, I didn't know who, had seen a picture of me in *Newsweek* and that is what made them think I worked for the CIA. I was locked up in a cell, two yards by half a yard, where I could not stand up and where I couldn't move around. On one side I heard a child crying and on the other side I heard constant screaming, as if someone was being beaten up. It was all psychological warfare, I realized later. But at the time it petrified me and I was willing to admit anything. But no one asked me any questions. Now and then they would give me something to eat. I heard prayers from one of the loudspeakers of a mosque, so I knew I was in West Beirut. But for two weeks on end, that was the only thing I knew for sure. Finally the masked guard let me go to the toilet. One day they simply said: You can go now. But I was afraid to go out into the streets, I thought they were going to shoot me in the back. The guards just laughed and locked the door again. It went on like that for almost a month, constant torment and harassment, until they realized no one was about to pay any ransom for me and it was more expensive to feed me than to let me go. They pushed me into the backseat of a car and threw me out somewhere alongside the road.

There are streets in Beirut where people are killed every day. And yet pedestrians continue to stroll down these streets, like voluntary sacrifices on the altar of the Minotaur. Death as a magnet.

Survival in Beirut can depend on how fast you move. Every man, woman, and child has the instincts of a Marine. Hunched over, they dash from one car to another, hoping to escape the stray bullet, hoping the car they take shelter behind is not going to explode.

Ever since 1975, Beirut has been on its deathbed. On December 6, the Christian Phalangists killed more than 200 Moslems, who were then identified by way of the passports in their pockets. The day went down in history as "Black Saturday." It marked the beginning of the war that lasted into the 1990s. Since then, the age-old custom of kidnapping has come back into use in Beirut. Every self-respecting faction or splinter group has one or more "Kidnap & Co." to its name, and they do what they were set up to do. "It just preserves the equilibrium," as Antoine Basbous of Forces Libanaises, the "official" army of ex-Prime Minister Gemayel, put it.

The less important the hostage, the greater the concern on the part of friends and relatives. It happens all too often that "useless" hostages, in other words, hostages for whom no ransom is expected, are murdered. In a death-oriented Beirut atmosphere of which apparently no one is ashamed, the executions are like ceremonious rituals. Observers are free to stand and watch as members of one clan are dragged down the street, tied to the backs of cars, by members of some other clan. The slow beating to death is also part of the tradition. On occasions like these, the audience crowds round and applauds—a medieval spectacle. Watching the torture helps the spectators blow off steam. In the agitation and excitement of these public executions, children sometimes come forward and urinate on the victims, cheered on by their parents.

Maybe the details do not really matter. And yet it is surprising how little has been written about the day-to-day life in a city where terrorism is rampant. Apparently there has to be some link between the events in Beirut and "normal" life in the rest of the world, otherwise no one is interested. At most, Beirut is relevant if and when international politics is involved, but local woes and distress are not really anyone else's concern. If the people of Beirut kill each other, that is their business.

The massacres at the Palestinian refugee camps Sabra and Chatila in September 1982 are a good example of how local news becomes international as soon as there is the slightest suspicion that a country is involved that we in the West are interested in. The link between Israel and the events in the two Palestinian camps was immediately clear. The political implications and the underlying causes have already been the subject of numerous debates and articles. Most editors in chief were reluctant to allow reporters to write about just exactly what had happened. The details seemed to come from such a completely different world that it was difficult to believe them. Very few people were aware that what happened at Sabra and Chatila had long been the daily routine throughout Lebanon, be it on a smaller scale.

Just after the discovery of the massacre, Jewish reporter Amnon Kapeliouk spoke to a 13-year-old girl who had lost both her parents, her sisters, and her brother:

> The women were screaming and begging them to stop and I ran away and hid in the bathtub. When I came out I saw that everyone had been murdered. They threw me onto the pile of bodies and asked whether I was Palestinian and I said yes. Right next to me, my nine-month-old nephew was crying. It irritated one of the soldiers, so he shot him in the shoulder. Then I started crying too and I told him the baby was the only relative I had left. But that irritated the militiaman even more and he picked up the baby and tore him to pieces.

There is no solution to the dilemma some critics feel reporters ought to be in: Is it ethical to approach the people who throw bombs into school buses? Isn't news just news? The question is how to deal with the actors. A tango is undeniably being danced. But this does not warrant citing the media as the only dancers. Governments, police departments, secret services, even judges, lawyers, and relatives join in the dance. In the first instance, Walter Laqueur's notion that without media coverage there would be no terrorism does seem to ring true. But what about the role played by governments?

Governments do negotiate, promise, pay, and thus play an active role in the whole process of terrorism. By way of their agreements, often highly secret ones, democratic governments make it clear that they take terrorist organizations seriously. In itself this is stimulating enough, since recognition means influence and esteem. In this way, there are governments actually responsible for keeping terrorist organizations alive, and they do so without the media as intermediaries, since the media are not even informed of the agreements being made. Without secrecy, it is hard to make a deal.

Some Western governments, especially the British, have favored various forms of censorship. Yet with censorship alone you cannot put a stop to terrorism. Anyone who lives in a democracy, and wishes to continue doing so, will have to realize that he or she lives in a paradise for terrorists: open borders, easily accessible airports and means of communication, relatively small-scale police departments, and humane legislation are just a few of the features that make democracies so livable and at the same time so vulnerable. According to a Rand Corporation poll, 79% of the terrorists arrested in the West are not apt be sentenced to capital punishment or even life imprisonment. It is the system, not the media, that plays such an important role in instigating acts of terrorism.

In democratic nations, the police, secret services, judges, lawyers, and relatives of victims also play a role in affecting the attitudes of terrorists. Whether working through official or private channels, these agencies and individuals are all in a position to make their own agreements with terrorists. If the authorities say national security is involved, what are we likely ever to know of the deals made between a judge and a ministry? In France, a highly respected judge gave permission to exchange a terrorist for hostages, thus making kidnapping "pay." Jean-Paul Kauffmann's wife, Joëlle, took individual action, turning terrorists into her own personal negotiation partners. Secret services collaborate with ministers. And all this is done for the good of the public—but preferably in private.

ARNHEM

*Autumn 1986.* There was a Kurd with a snack bar in the Dutch town of Arnhem who spent most of his free time phoning television reporters. He had good contacts in the Middle East, he said. He knew people who knew people who could help us get in touch with Qaddafi. I invited him for a little chat. M gave me a couple of telephone numbers that did indeed prove very useful, so when I got a chance to go to Libya, I returned the favor by taking M along as interpreter. M had learned Arabic in Iraq and he had friends in Tripoli. It meant he would have to close the snack bar for a while, so I promised to compensate him for his trouble—just so that it was clear it wasn't the names of his friends I was paying for.

In the plane, M told me that if the whole thing worked out with Qaddafi, he would be hailed as a "friend of the people's revolution" in Libya. The colonel had personally announced his interest in contacting a representative of the Western media; there were a couple of things he wanted to tell the world. For a change, he did not want an American television network. So, in a manner of speaking, we were indirectly arriving upon request.

M, who was apparently very familiar with the workings of the "People's Bureau" representing the cause in the Benelux, admitted that the embassy in Brussels had also been asked to suggest an anchorman from the appropriate media. Appropriate media? Well, actually, television was the only appropriate one. Is that right? M confessed he was also helping another Dutch television reporter get into Libya with his whole crew. M expected to be generously rewarded for arranging for the "appropriate" media, and then he in turn would be in a position to reward me for my trouble. How? He alluded to Abu Nidal, who had found a safe haven for himself in Libya after President Assad expelled him from Syria in 1984. Assad had decided the Palestinian was becoming too much of a bother and was doing a lot of harm to the image of Syria.

As soon as we arrived in Tripoli, M discovered that Abu Nidal was in Teheran. This confirmed the comments made by Ahmed Jibril of the People's Front for the Liberation of Palestine in *Corriere della Sera*. Qaddafi had been anxious to get rid of Abu Nidal for some time, certainly after the superterrorist gave some interviews in Tripoli suggesting that he and Qaddafi were on even friendlier terms than had been hitherto assumed. Qaddafi was not happy with this, and he made no secret of it. The colonel, apparently aware of the existence of "public relations," realized they were something even a revolutionary leader had to worry about. The Teheran option was all the more plausible since members of the Abu Nidal group had been given training facilities in Iran. The ayatollahs couldn't care less whom they supported, as long as Israel and the United States suffered in the end. One advantage of Iran was that media access was so limited.

M was proud of his contacts. I immediately assumed there was a link between his Iraqi descent and the connections he claimed would soon lead us to Abu Nidal. For quite a lengthy period of time, the Palestinian had operated from Iraq, so it was only logical.

At night M regularly disappeared, only to reappear the next morning at the breakfast table in the hotel, smiling mysteriously, and tell me that everything was going "fine." It wasn't until we were back in the Netherlands that I went ahead and asked him to please be more specific. By then we had indirectly paid for our Libyan visa. We had run into an unknown henchman of the Libyan government and treated him to as much as he could eat and drink, just so he would act as our interpreter. We weren't sure whether M was doing his best to translate or was perhaps mainly paying attention to the impression he was making. And we didn't know whether the money for M would wind up funding Libyan or Kurdish terrorism. The fact that we were not the only people around who were not exactly obeying the rules was not much of a consolation.

A few weeks after I came back to Amsterdam, Willem Oltmans, a political wheeler-dealer who likes to pose as a journalist, offered to organize an interview for us with Qaddafi for "a small fee"; I think it was something like $2,500 he was asking for, so there was obviously a lively market in Qaddafi interviews. The Dutch broadcasting network I was free-lancing for at the time was not about to pay that kind of money, though a couple of months later they did agree to have Oltmans arrange for an interview with Desi Bouterse, the military strongman in Suriname.

But what about people who are still in official positions of power, what about the active leaders of political parties or organizations? Especially if and when they are heading a particularly controversial nation or movement? Of course, they themselves are never going to be the ones who ask for the money. It goes by way of intermediaries or organizations. And should you rightly hesitate to pay if you don't know what is going to be done with the check and there is a chance it will be used to finance someone's very violent death? In the course of this discussion, someone once commented that this is how the media finance their own news.

These were the questions that came to mind on the day the Kurd from Arnhem informed me that he had finally arranged for me to interview Abu Nidal—not in Iran, but in East Germany. Further details were to be revealed later, and the price was to be $5,000. I told him I would get the money—without asking him any questions about how it was going to be used, and without asking the people who were going to pay any questions about their motives. Abu Nidal, at long last; I wasn't about to let ethical considerations get in my way.

More than ever, Abu Nidal was big game, sought after by all the media. Violence was hot news. Bitterlin, the chairman of the French-Arab Solidarity Union, had interviewed Abu Nidal in Tripoli. He had taken photographs to prove it, though they were never actually published. Why not? When I asked him this question on the phone, he said that was the agreement he had made with Abu Nidal. He said he was sure he had interviewed Abu Nidal himself, and not an impostor.

Just after the publication of this interview, with Bitterlin's relatively friendly comments on Abu Nidal, there was an interview with Qaddafi in *Profil*, an Austrian magazine. One of the topics of discussion was Abu Nidal, and the Libyan leader's comments were far less friendly. He was contemptuous in fact, and even went so far as to call Abu Nidal a profiteer. In exchange for the interview, the lady author, Renate Posaring, had spent the night with Qaddafi, or so Lingens, the *Profil* editor in chief, claimed a week after the article was published. The magazine itself even added that Posaring had converted to Islam just to make an impression. What was the world coming to?

According to my trusty Kurd, the meeting with Abu Nidal was to take place in Karl Marx Stadt. The Palestinian was in the intensive care ward of a hospital there, or so I was told. "He has cancer," M said, "and he already went into a coma once." Time was obviously running out. In the rush that followed, I initially forgot to ask the most important question: How will I know if it is really Abu Nidal I am talking to? Why should a Dutch reporter of all people be the one to interview the world's most wanted terrorist? Will the interview only serve to embellish the myth? Does it really matter if it is the real Abu Nidal or not? Are we being used to keep a myth alive without asking too many questions? After all, we are not Americans. One day I presented all these questions to my Kurd, who was too offended to go any further with our delicate negotiations. I have not heard from him since. The snack bar isn't there any more; an explosion caused by a gas leak was the end of it. Perhaps it is a bit farfetched to conclude that M was punished for failing to convince us to play the game. He certainly did come close.

One thing was becoming clearer by the day. If it did not matter whether or not our camera was focused on the real Abu Nidal, then what in the world were we doing? As soon as any act of seemingly random terrorism took place, the police would automatically assume Abu Nidal was involved. The media were unlikely to disagree, and their readers and viewers had little choice but to swallow the "information." Now and then, just to break the silence, some Abu Nidal group would publicize a denial. In July 1988, for example, there was little reason to hold Abu Nidal responsible for the attack on the Greek cruiser *City of Poros*, with a death toll of nine, though this did not stop anyone from doing so. A statement made by Atef Abu Bakr, the spokesman of the Fatah Revolutionary Council, one of the pseudonyms for Abu Nidal's group, made it clear that it was the work of a completely different group of terrorists.

Here and there I suggested: "Maybe Abu Nidal is dead." Usually the only reaction was laughter. So what were the arguments to back the assumption that, despite the lack of tangible evidence, Abu Nidal was still the man behind certain acts of terrorism? First, there was the fact that as soon as the rumors about Abu Nidal's disappearance increased, there was also a rise in the activities of the group. This led experts to conclude that the leader was still active after all. Of course, a temporary "disappearance" could sometimes be very much in a terrorist's interest, and the rumors might be spread by the group itself. In this line of reasoning, the whole thing would then be nothing but a meaningless game. So what was *not* meaningless? The fact that texts were being published in what was said to be the style of Abu Nidal? As if there was a style in existence that could not be imitated.

No, it was the *myth* of Abu Nidal that was being kept alive, and for reasons that did not have that much to do with the man himself. The important thing was that extremist Palestinians were able to operate under one name, a name respected by victims and authorities alike. And even though Abu Nidal had perhaps long since retired, the remaining leaders weren't going to tell anyone. And a wise move it was. But keeping the myth alive could be useful for the other side as well, for instance, for the Mossad, the Israeli secret service, one of the best of its kind in the world. Even the Mossad had been unable to get anywhere in the vicinity of Abu Nidal. If the Mossad could refer to all its "uncatchable" enemies under one and the same name, this meant it was embarrassed only once. So why not attribute all the unsolved crimes of terrorism to Abu Nidal, and that's that.

In the meantime, the media continued to take their nourishment wherever they could find it—either from the remaining members of the group who, for whatever reason, wanted to see Abu Nidal declared dead or alive, depending on their mood, or from the authorities, who were perhaps curious to see how the elusive Sabri al-Banna was going to react to "disclosures" in the media.

The only objective reason to doubt the role of Abu Nidal was his physical condition. After two open-heart operations, a man who was under permanent pressure did not have an easy time of it. The answer to the crucial question— Abu Nidal, myth or reality?—came from one of his sworn opponents in Paris.

PARIS, TUNIS, ALGIERS

*Autumn 1988.* Ibrahim Souss, the permanent PLO representative in Paris, wrote a book explaining the peaceful intentions of the PLO in an uncommonly moderate manner. In the course of a discussion we had in Paris, he elaborated upon what he claimed Arafat himself could just as well have said: The PLO rejects terrorism, extends its hand to peace-loving Israeli and recognizes—in so many words—the existence of Israel. The main idea of the book was that the Western world had misconstrued the ideas of the PLO and had unjustly been willing to give only Israel the benefit of the doubt.

In his book, Souss acted as if he were speaking to a Jewish friend, but in reality he was addressing the French intellectuals he expected to pass the word. He hoped he would also convince the rest of Western Europe to adopt an independent standpoint toward the Palestinians—independent of the United States, that is.

Souss could not have chosen a better moment to present his message of peace to the world: The Intifada had been raging for a good year, causing what seemed to be irreversible damage to Israel's positive image. The PLO had been able to confine Palestinian terrorism to within the borders of the occupied territories. The organization wanted to live up to its new reputation as idealists who had finally reached maturity. Souss was ordered to exploit the Intifada politically, starting with a book.

No one seemed to be very concerned about the opposition of extremist groups among the Palestinians themselves. Souss assured me that the prospect of sharing the fate of other Palestinian doves was not something that scared him. Saïd Hammami, the moderate PLO representative in London, had been assassinated in 1976, as had Souss's predecessor Ezzedine Qalaq in 1978 and Dr. Issam Sartawi in 1983—all victims of acts of revenge inspired by Abu Nidal.

I wanted to know why Souss was not afraid, but all I got was a very vague reply. Unlike Sartawi, Souss did not believe in a guardian angel or in the magic hand of Allah. Nothing could shake his conviction that the extremists would not bother him. Because Abu Nidal was no longer around? "I am guarded day and night by four French policemen because they fear for my life. The French are not only thinking of Abu Nidal, they are also thinking of the Palestinians supported by Syria, people like Abu Musa. I myself am not so worried, certainly not about Abu Nidal. I can't explain why. I can only assure you that he is alive; a few months ago Abu Ijad pinched him in the arm. And it hurt."

He could not stop laughing. His friend Sartawi, I ventured, had doubted the existence of Abu Nidal. He had said on various occasions that Abu Nidal was an invention of the Israelis, who had made him up just to harm the reputation of the PLO. Souss was suddenly totally serious. "Come back next week. Then we will talk about it," he said in a tone of urgency.

The reviews of Souss's book, which was written in French, were glowing, and at the Frankfurt Book Fair, Dutch publishers expressed their interest in a translation. It was going to be translated. Souss sounded very satisfied when he called me. "You understand," he said, "that the Netherlands is important. Thanks to you, the people of your country can read that the Palestinians are not just a gang of bandits. I will arrange for you to have an interview on the very highest level. You want to talk to Abu Ijad? I'll call him right now." I was being duly rewarded for services rendered. You do me a favor, I'll do you a favor. Souss was convinced I had written a glowing review of his book, even though he hadn't been able to read it and it hadn't been translated. He called me by my first name. I was one of the boys. It was a matter of intuition. That was the way it worked.

As it turned out, all Souss was willing to do was comment on Abu Nidal on the phone. "The theory is good," he said.

> Maybe he does not exist in the way that other people exist. In any case, he has departed from his physical reality. Sartawi's theory has been adopted by a number of Palestinians. I do not believe in it. If you say that the PLO does not have to be afraid of Abu Nidal any more, does that mean he is dead? In a certain sense, it does. The old Abu Nidal no longer exists. . . . If the PLO leaders talk to the new Abu Nidal, then it is about the Palestinian cause. In his own way, he serves the cause. I do not always approve. But as long as he keeps his hands off the Palestinian brothers, we continue to talk to him. Or to his organization. Because of course he is not alone. In a certain sense, he is a myth, a collection of myths. Who knows who might be hiding behind him . . . lurking behind him? Abu Ijad will be able to tell you all about it.

When I showed up for the interview with Abu Ijad, which was supposed to take place at the PLO office on Rue Mérimer in Paris, he was not there. Here again, there was the old waiting ritual: a cup of tea, magazines in Arabic, yawning bodyguards lounging about and watching television. It was surprising how similar the atmosphere of the whole scene was to the one in Beirut or Tunis. Waiting. In vain. The rules of the game remained the same, friend or no friend. Maybe tomorrow. In Tunisia.

While the ballot boxes were being set up in Israel for the parliamentary elections, the PLO leaders were conferring in Tunis to prepare for the coming conference of the Palestinian National Council in Algiers. There was an out-of-the-ordinary hustle and bustle at the headquarters. The Tunisian authorities, who had announced two years earlier that they had extended their "hospitality" to the Palestinians for long enough, had recently begun once again allowing unrestricted numbers of Palestinians to enter the country. They ignored the regulation about no more than four Palestinians a day being allowed entry just as totally as they ignored whatever arrangements had been made about the security of the PLO leaders. Heavily armed Palestinian patrols were, however, no longer restricted to within the gates of the PLO buildings.

By the time I was finally shown in to see Abu Ijad at one o'clock in the morning, my briefcase had already been turned inside out three times. "Just doing our job," the red-headed bodyguard said with a grin. That was when George Habash and Nayef Hawatmeh, Arafat's leading Palestinian critics, came out the door. They were in Tunis to try to come to terms with Arafat's and Abu Ijad's Fatah before the conference in Algiers. The PLO did not want to be trapped in a mire of details for the umpteenth time. In Algiers, they were going to have to come up with some real decisions. Even for the most headstrong of the rebels, the time had come to reconsider; if they wanted to profit from the negative image of Israel and the other benefits of the Intifada, it was now or never.

The windows of Abu Ijad's office were wide open. "I can't afford to live in fear," he told me. "It must be difficult for a European to imagine how we have learned to live with death and just to trust to our instincts. I ought to be more scared of the Mossad than you are of the Palestinian extremists."

He confirmed that Arafat and the PLO were about to adopt a peace policy, even though factions remained that did not agree. "You cannot expect me to have Abu Musa or Abu Nidal eliminated. We are a democratic organization. Even if I do not back the tactics of some people, there is not anything I can do about it. All I can do is dissociate myself from them. We have to be especially cautious when it comes to the factions supported by Syria."

And Abu Nidal? "Ibrahim Souss told me you think he does not exist. You are almost right: he is alive, but he has ceased his terrorist activities. He solemnly promised me that in Algiers in April 1987. So all the activities that have since been attributed to him were actually carried out by others. Abu Nidal has retired." No one can blame the PLO for failing to keep a stray renegade under control. After all, there is not much you can do to discipline a myth. (Abu Ijad was shot by his own bodyguard in 1991.)

U.S. Secretary of State George Schultz never trusted Arafat. The decision not to give the PLO leader a visa for the United States, thus making it impossible for him to address the U.N. General Assembly, was entirely Schultz's responsibility. Schultz against Arafat and 99% of the rest of the world. Why? Because at a National Council meeting, there had been an extremely painful reminder of the recent *Achille Lauro* affair in Algiers. Thanks to the Italian legal system, Abu Abbas, the man who had led the ship's 1985 hijacking (on Arafat's orders, or at any rate with his approval, the U.S. secretary of state was convinced), was still a free man. He had since become one of Arafat's most important advisers. As a member of the Executive Council, Abu Abbas told a reporter in Algiers that it wasn't his fault that Leon Klinghoffer, an old man in a wheelchair, had gone overboard and drowned. "Maybe he was trying to swim away," Abu Abbas said, and grinned.

Schultz was indignant and made a decision that was to cost the virtually bankrupt United Nations an extra $50 million: Arafat and his friends would have to say whatever they had to say somewhere else. Thus delegates were transported to Geneva to hear the PLO standpoint. With the exception of Israel and Great Britain, who supported Schultz (be it reluctantly on Mrs. Thatcher's part), the United States stood alone on this issue.

Did Schultz know what else Abu Abbas had said? Had Schultz heard that he had said:

> You want us to apologize for what you call acts of terrorism, but has Israel ever apologized for the massacres in Sabra and Chatila? Did the United States say it was sorry about the people who lost their lives in Grenada? I wish the names of our martyrs were as well known as Klinghoffer's. Can you name ten Palestinians who were killed by Israeli gas, or ten pregnant Palestinian women who were shot and mutilated?

Walter Ruby, the New York correspondent of the *Jerusalem Post* who was interviewing Abu Abbas, did not have an answer to any of these questions. The way Abu Abbas saw it, the death of one American was more important to the media—and to their audience—than the death of hundreds of Palestinians. So, from his point of view, the media didn't confine themselves to the PLO's game, they also played the opponent's game.

## Conclusion

The nice thing about Ruby was that in one of his articles, this Israeli reporter cautioned against emotional bias and asked his American readers to try looking at things from the other side for once. Partly due to the overreacting media, Americans had a distorted picture of Palestinians—and vice versa. It was not the articles about terrorism—and counterterrorism—that were dangerous in themselves, Ruby felt, but simply the tone and the style in which they were written. This message is different from the calls for censuring news on terrorism in general. Effective media censorship means that the authorities can initiate whatever measures they like with impunity.

If for no other reason, the media have an obligation to fulfill their critical function because they not only keep people informed, they also serve as an obstacle to excesses of all kinds. Without truly free media, there can be no democracy. In this day and age of media conglomerates, frequent takeovers, centralization, and commercialism, assuring the media's independence is no simple matter. But at least let the media decide for themselves what they want to present as news, and how they want to do it, even though they might find making deals an indispensable part of the process.

The fascination with the subject of terrorism—in the widest sense of the word—has nothing to do with perverse curiosity. It is a logical side effect of the fascination with the subject of power. Violence and power—aren't they the engines that keep history going? And aren't they therefore precisely what the media ought to be interested in?

Terrorism and power cannot be separated from each other. Terrorism is power and power is all too often terrorizing. Who is commanding whom? Who is obeying whom? Who is using whom?

# 9

# Public's Perspectives

## Christopher Hewitt

The familiar concept of "terrorism as theater" obviously presupposes that the public constitutes an audience for terrorists, and that acts of terrorism are intended to produce certain responses from that audience (Jenkins, 1975). However, the public constitutes a number of different audiences. Furthermore, there are important differences between terrorist groups in the strategies they use to affect public opinion.

### Constituencies, Enemies, and Bystanders: A Classification of Public Opinion Audiences

For terrorists, the public contains two significant audiences: their constituencies of actual and potential supporters and their enemies. Since the two types of insurgent terrorists, nationalists and revolutionaries, define their

Author's Note: The research for this article was partially funded by the United States Institute of Peace. The opinions, findings, and conclusions are those of the author, and do not necessarily reflect the views of the United States Institute of Peace.

**Table 9.1** Audiences for Nationalist Terrorists

| Group | Constituency | Enemy |
| --- | --- | --- |
| IRA | Irish Catholics | British/Ulster Protestants |
| ETA | Basques | Spaniards |
| PLO | Palestinians | Jews |
| FLQ | French Quebecois | English Canadians |

situations differently and have very different strategies, we have four significant audiences, plus a residual category (the bystanders).

Nationalists see their land as being occupied and their people as being oppressed by foreigners; thus their conceptual map takes the form of an ethnic dichotomy, as shown in Table 9.1.

The ethnic diaspora may be important as a source of financial aid or weapons. Irish Americans, for example, have smuggled weapons to and provided considerable sums for the IRA, and the Provisionals have cultivated their support assiduously (McGuire, 1973). Some nationalist terrorists are largely dependent upon émigré communities (e.g., the Croatians, South Moluccans, Armenians).

Given that many contemporary nationalist groups profess to be socialists or seek support from liberal public opinion, this ethnocentrism is often muted or disguised. The PLO claims to be struggling against Zionism, not against Jews. Irish Republicans argue that Ulster Protestants are really members of the Irish nation (who mistakenly think of themselves as British). Protestants per se are not the enemy, only those who are agents of British imperialism.

Revolutionary terrorists see society as divided between a ruling class and an exploited class. To orthodox Marxists (such as the Red Brigades) the exploited class is the proletariat, but revolutionary terrorists frequently extend the concept to include almost everybody except for the very rich and their agents. The Tupamaros, for example, saw the struggle as one between the "oligarchy" and the "Uruguayan people," and considered the latter to include civil servants, bank clerks, and students. At the other extreme, some groups inspired by the New Left had such a surrealistic ideology that it is difficult to define their real constituency in any meaningful way. The Weather Underground in the United States and the German Red Army Faction rejected the domestic working class as too corrupted by consumerism and claimed to be fighting for the Third World oppressed. According to one German terrorist:

The analysis of imperialism tells us that the struggle no longer starts in the metropolis, that it's no longer a matter of the working class, but . . . what's needed is a vanguard in the metropolis that declares its solidarity with the liberation movements of the Third World. Since it lives in the head of the monster, it can do the greatest damage there. Even if the masses in the European metropolis don't put themselves on the side of the revolution—the working class among us is privileged and takes part in the exploitation of the Third World—the only possibility for those who build the Vanguard here, who take part in the struggle here, is to destroy the infra-structure of imperialism, destroy the apparatus. (quoted in Rapoport, 1988, p. 44)

One American terrorist thought of herself as a member of the "Ameri-Cong," and at crucial moments would ask herself "whether or not the Vietcong would approve of this or that behavior" (Rapoport, 1988, p. 43).

The rest of the world—those uninvolved in the struggle because they are neither enemies nor supporters of the terrorists—can be classified as bystanders. Many acts of transnational terrorism, such as the 1972 Munich Olympics massacre or the killings of Turkish diplomats by ASALA in Canada, are played out before bystanders. In such cases the terrorists usually try to avoid alienating those who are uninvolved. After an attack on a British Army base in West Germany, the IRA hastened to "assure the German people that none of our attacks are aimed at them, but solely at the British forces who are oppressing our people" (*Keesing's Contemporary Archives*, June 1980, p. 30293). The distinction between bystanders and sympathizers or between bystanders and enemies is not always clear-cut. For example, terrorist groups may try to convert neutral bystanders into sympathizers. Thus "world public opinion" is sometimes an important audience for terrorists who hope to mobilize pressure against their enemies. The EOKA campaign in Cyprus was intended "to arouse international public opinion . . . by deeds of heroism and self-sacrifice" (Grivas, 1965, p. 204).

Although much has been written about what terrorists *hope* to achieve, little research has been done on the actual effects of terrorism on public opinion. Furthermore, such studies as we do have tend to be case studies of particular countries, and cross-national comparisons are rarely made.

In this chapter I describe and attempt to explain public attitudes toward terrorism by analyzing a large number of public opinion polls.[1] The available survey data are unfortunately, but not surprisingly, short of being ideal. On some topics we lack any information at all. It is difficult to make some comparisons among countries, because questions are rarely asked in the same form. Although we are interested in whether terrorism changes public attitudes, on several matters data exist for only one point in time.

For six cases there is a reasonable amount of material. As might be expected, these are all countries where terrorism has been sustained and politically significant (Northern Ireland/Great Britain, Basque provinces/ Spain, Israel and the occupied territories, Italy, Germany, and Uruguay). Fragmentary information is available for some other countries, including Canada, France, South Africa, and the Netherlands. In these latter cases, terrorism has been intermittent and far less deadly. Therefore, the analysis will concentrate on the six cases where terrorism has been most significant and the data are most complete. Three topics will be examined: terrorism as a means of attracting public attention, public opinion and nationalist terrorism, and public opinion and revolutionary terrorism.

By focusing on insurgent terrorism, I am, of course, ignoring right-wing terrorism and state-sponsored terrorism. These are important omissions, given that such violence is usually far more deadly than insurgent violence. In Latin America, the death squads (often linked to the security services) have killed thousands, far more than the victims claimed by revolutionary terrorism. In Italy, Spain, and Germany, neo-Fascist bombs in public places, such as the Bologna railway station or the Oktoberfest in Munich, have killed and wounded large numbers of ordinary civilians. Herman (1982) contends that such violence is largely ignored by the media, and this claim may be justified with regard to Latin America. However, in Italy and Spain, neo-Fascist violence has received significant media coverage—all of it negative. No public opinion polls on right-wing terrorism could be found.

## How the Media Portray Terrorism

The role played by the media in forming public opinion is problematic. We need to know, first, how the media present news about terrorism and, second, what other sources of information are available to the public.

How the news is presented depends upon two sets of factors. First, there are technical considerations, such as the availability of sources, news formats, and time constraints. Second, there are the political values of the media controllers and the extent of government censorship. Furthermore, the media are not monolithic: Television coverage is different from newspaper coverage, and newspapers differ in their politics.

Very few studies have examined systematically how the media portray terrorism. Paletz, Fozzard, and Ayanian (1982, 1983) carried out a content analysis of how the *New York Times* and U.S. television covered the IRA,

Red Brigades, and FALN; Altheide (1987) examined British and American coverage of two IRA bombings; and Knight and Dean (1982) looked at Canadian coverage of a terrorist takeover of the Iranian embassy in London. They found that terrorist motives and goals were largely ignored, that official perspectives were reinforced, and that governmental repression was legitimated. Paletz et al. (1983) note, however, that there were "dramatic differences in the coverage" of the three groups they examined. The IRA position was often "presented eloquently" by sympathizers, whereas the goals of the Red Brigades were ignored. The FALN was described as a group of "fanatics" who wanted to make Puerto Rico independent "whether Puerto Rico likes it or not." To see whether similar patterns could be found in the cases for which I have public opinion data, I examined published accounts and interviewed a small number of journalists and academics.

In Uruguay during 1968-1969, the media disseminated the ideas of the Tupamaros by publishing their communiqués and interviewing their leaders. Tupamaro activities were reported sympathetically, and this helped to create the group's Robin Hood image. Beginning in late 1969, however, the government imposed strict censorship. The press was forbidden to use such words as *cell, commando, terrorist, extremist, subversive,* or *Tupamaro.* In April 1971, a presidential decree prohibited all news about guerrilla activities except that supplied by the government. Newspapers were frequently closed down for publishing "subversive" stories, but throughout the emergency the press attacked antiterrorist policies as a denial of civil liberties and criticized security force abuses (Moss, 1972; Porzecanski, 1973).

The German media, by contrast, were hostile to revolutionary ideology, exaggerated the dangers of terrorism, and supported government countermeasures wholeheartedly. "The picture presented by the media, especially the press, was often one of unmitigated hysteria. This impression could be gained by following the detailed reporting and sometimes obsessive editorials of the German newspapers, both popular and quality ones" (Lodge, 1981, p. 42).

In Italy, coverage changed significantly throughout the period. Initially, the media

> were slow to take an unambiguous stand against terrorism. The black *stragi* were of course universally condemned. But at the time of the kidnapping of Sossi in 1974, the then still mysterious red brigadiers were widely regarded as proletarian Robin Hoods. . . . Attitudes began to change with the assassination of Coco in 1976 and the Robin Hoods became inhuman monsters. During 1976 and 1977 what little was left of press sympathy was destroyed by a series of

assaults on journalists, notably the deputy editor of *La Stampa*, Carlo Casa-
lengo, who died of his wounds. . . . By 1979 condemnation of terrorism had
become virtually unanimous. Unanimity was harder to reach on the controversial issue of how much publicity terrorists should be permitted. During the
Moro crisis all the BR's communiques, and many of Moro's letters from his
"prison," were published in the press. But gradually it came to be seen that
publicity was their very life-blood, without which they would find it hard to
survive. During the D'Urso crisis most of the press observed a blackout, though
even then it was not complete. (Lodge, 1988, p. 107)

Weinberg and Eubank (1987) point out:

The media repeatedly communicated vivid descriptions and pictures of terrorism's victims. These portrayals included not only accounts of political
leaders, Aldo Moro most conspicuously, but of ordinary people who were
killed or maimed as the result of terrorist atrocities. There was also an
increasing tendency to depict their acts as ones of senseless bestiality devoid
of serious political content. (p. 138)

Despite the growing hostility of the mainline media, radical views were
advocated in the "movement press"—*Avanguardia Operaia, Il Manifesto,*
and *Lotta Continua.* Such papers were a major channel of communication
and an independent outlet for the diffusion of revolutionary ideology (Tarrow, 1989, p. 230).

Cleavages within the media are even more obvious in the case of nationalist terrorism. In Northern Ireland, the *Irish News*, whose readership is 93%
Catholic, advocates the nationalist position, while the *News-Letter* is read
mainly by Protestants (87%) and takes a unionist stance (Rose, 1971,
pp. 343-344). The two papers also differ in that the *Irish News* is likely to
highlight abuses by the security forces, and the *News-Letter* to claim that
they are not doing enough. The *Belfast Telegraph*, TV, and radio have mixed
audiences, and consequently present a spectrum of political views. Terrorism
is certainly not portrayed as senseless. Indeed, there is constant discussion
of the terrorists' strategy and motives.

Terrorist violence is condemned not only in editorials and commentaries
but also in how the news is presented. One Ulster informant commented that
"it has become a ritual—so routinized that it may no longer have any effect
on the public. TV will show the scene of the incident, the body covered by
a sheet, and interviews with spokesmen from both communities condemning
the atrocity. Then a few days later the funerals with pictures of the wife and
kids." He went on to say that "the recent Armagh bombing (in which two

policemen and a nun were killed) was a perfect opportunity for editorializing to the Catholic community. The police were run of the mill, but it was the first time a nun had been killed. They all played up the fact that the nun's relatives went to the policeman's funeral." Condemnation of IRA terrorism is not universal, however. *An Phoblacht*, published by Sinn Fein and distributed in working-class Catholic areas, vigorously defends and justifies IRA attacks. Its weekly circulation is about 12,000, although at times it has reached 30,000 or more. Perhaps 10-15% of Catholic households read it fairly regularly.

British media coverage of Northern Ireland is examined by Curtis (1984). She argues that the Irish nationalist perspective is ignored, and that there is an almost total reliance upon official sources, with the result that the IRA is often blamed for killings it did not do. The British army is shown in a highly favorable light:

> Soldiers were photographed chatting up children, doing their bit in Santa Claus outfits, and, as in one picture published in London's *Evening News* in 1972, accepting a cup of tea in "a friendly Protestant neighbourhood." The army appeared as almost above the fray—brave, tormented, but largely inactive except as a rather superior kind of Boy Scout Troop. There were several stories of soldiers coming to the aid of the local population on foot, in boats or in helicopters.

Curtis details numerous cases in which allegations of army brutality or torture of internees were ignored or censored by editors and the BBC. "The media worked in tandem with the army's public relations staff" (p. 83).

In the Basque provinces the situation is very similar to that found in Ulster. Since freedom of the press was guaranteed in 1978, the local media have reflected the main political tendencies in the region. *El Correo Español* (read by ethnic Spaniards) is anti-ETA and opposed to Basque autonomy and independence. During the 1979 election campaign, the paper "published front-page stories everyday detailing acts of terrorism and violence in the region and elsewhere. Reports on strikes and terrorism filled more than half the news columns in the issues published during the months before the elections" (Penniman, 1985, p. 270). *El Diario Vasco* and *Deia* (linked to the PNV) advocate a moderate version of Basque nationalism, and tend to be critical of both ETA terrorism and Spanish security policies. *Egin* is militantly nationalist, justifies and supports ETA terrorism, and is hostile to the security forces. There is a rough correspondence between the readership of these papers and the vote for each political tendency.

The Spanish press, outside the Basque provinces, portrays ETA violence as reprehensible, as do the state-controlled radio and television networks. Terrorism receives extensive coverage. For example, "all newspapers and magazines stressed terrorism as an issue in the 1979 campaign. Several papers seized on the problem of terrorism as a reason to criticize the government, parliamentary democracy, the political parties, and even as a basis for defending the need for a military coup" (Penniman, 1985, p. 263). On the other hand, many left-wing and liberal newspapers claimed that terrorist groups described by the government as "extreme leftists" were, in fact, connected to the extreme right or the police (pp. 263, 269-270). The most widely read and influential paper, *El Pais*, takes a strong civil liberties stance, and is often critical of government repression.

Although there is considerable variation in how terrorism is portrayed by the media, certain patterns can be discerned. First, terrorism usually receives extensive media coverage, with the results of terrorist violence depicted in gruesome detail on TV screens and in newspaper photos—dead bodies, funerals, grieving relatives, and physical destruction. This phenomenon is presumably related to the media's appetite for dramatic visual images (Paletz et al., 1983, p. 160). This negative view of terrorist violence is reinforced by editorials and interviews with community leaders condemning violence. Justifications of violence are exceptional and to be found only in newspapers such as *Egin* and *An Phoblacht*, which are linked to terrorist groups. In both Uruguay and Italy, an initial tendency to romanticize terrorist exploits ceased once the campaigns became more deadly.

Second, the tendency in the United States, Canada, and Great Britain for the media to ignore the social causes of terrorism and its goals and objectives is not found in the other cases. Where terrorism is carried out by indigenous groups their political goals are noted and often analyzed in detail. The extent to which the cause is sympathetically portrayed depends upon the political situation in each society. In West Germany, where revolutionary attitudes are uncommon, the ideology of the RAF was presented unfavorably. In Italy and Uruguay, however, where Marxism was a significant ideology, at both mass and elite levels, the media were, at least initially, sympathetic. The editor of *Il Manifesto*, for example, remarked that "reading the BR's communiques was like turning the pages of an old family photograph album" (Lodge, 1988, p. 106). The goals of nationalist terrorist groups are strongly supported by their ethnic communities and by the ethnic media.

Third, the media do not invariably reflect the official perspective. In explaining why the U.S. media emphasize government positions, Paletz et al. (1983) are probably correct: "The authorities arrive first and are there to provide details, explanations and their interpretations to the press" (p. 158). However, in other societies important sections of the press are skeptical of government explanations and critical of government policies. This adversarial stance seems to be a product of political ideology and historical circumstances. The Irish Catholic and Basque press are normally hostile to the government perspective. In Spain many influential publications such as *El Pais* or *Cambio* emerged during the transition to democracy, and see their role, therefore, as advocates of civil liberties against government repression (Giner, 1983; Sanchez-Gijon, 1983). In Italy and Uruguay, partisan politics explain such antigovernment sentiments. Many leftist Italian newspapers accused the secret police of fomenting terrorism to justify a rightist coup, and until the mid-1970s were strongly opposed to the security measures that were imposed (Silj, 1979; Weinberg & Eubank, 1987). The peculiarities of the Uruguayan electoral system meant that President Pacheco was elected with only a minority of votes. Thus not only the left-wing press but many bourgeois newspapers took a critical stance toward the repressive policies he adopted.

## Terrorism and Public Concern

The argument that terrorism is an attempt to draw attention to a grievance that would otherwise be ignored is plausible in several cases; however, such public attention is usually short-lived and the political results fall short of what the terrorists want. Schmid and De Graaf (1980) point out that the South Moluccans "sought and received publicity and attention . . . but publicity without the ability to turn attention into political results leads to nothing" (p. 306). Dutch public opinion became less sympathetic toward the South Moluccans and their cause after they engaged in terrorism. Violence forced the Northern Ireland issue to the attention of the British public for a brief period in 1971-1972, but thereafter public interest almost disappeared. Similarly, within Spain the issue of regional autonomy was seen as one of the most important issues by 7% in 1978 (Esteban, 1979), but after 1980 it was never cited by more than 1% of the population.

The primary motive behind Palestinian terrorism over the last 20 years has been "to put the Palestinian issue on the agenda of world and regional politics and to keep the issue on that agenda" (Stohl, 1988, p. 531). In this aim the terrorists have been highly successful. The world in general has become aware of the Palestinian problem, and in 1974 the PLO was recognized by

**Table 9.2** Terrorism as a Problem

|  | Most Important Problem | (%) | Deaths from Terrorism |
|---|---|---|---|
| Northern Ireland 1982 | terrorism | 34 | 2,269 |
| Spain 1979-1982 | terrorism/public order | 22 | 455 |
| Italy 1972-1979 | public order | 16 | 227 |
| Israel 1977 | security | 29 | 196 |
| Great Britain 1971-1972 | Northern Ireland | 13 | 155 |
| France 1985-1987 | terrorism | 5 | 124 |
| Germany 1976 | public order | 8 | 25 |
| Uruguay 1968-1969 | disorder/subversion | 4 | 14 |

SOURCE: Data compiled by the author from BBC (1982); public opinion polls published in various issues of *Revista Española de Investigaciones Sociologicas* (1979-1982); Fabris (1977); Penniman (1979); Rose, McAllister, and Mair (1978); *Index to International Public Opinion* (1985-1987); Cerny (1978); and the *Indice Gallup de Opinion Publica* (1968-1969), provided by Gallup Uruguay.

the United Nations as "the sole legitimate representative of the Palestinian people." The aspiration for a Palestinian homeland, however, is still no closer to fulfillment than it ever was.

Insofar as terrorists seek to attract attention, they target the enemy public or uncommitted bystanders. Most terrorist campaigns take place in societies where the issue for which the terrorists are fighting is well known. Such issues as Irish unity, Basque independence, and Quebec nationalism do not require terrorism to publicize them. As Pinard and Hamilton (1977) comment, "It is difficult to argue that many French Canadians would be unaware of the [independence] issue after more than fifteen years of intense debate on the subject within Quebec." Similarly, the revolutionary Marxism of the Red Brigades has been a theme of Italian politics for decades.

Usually it is terrorist violence itself that becomes the issue for the public, rather than the terrorists' cause. One standard survey question asks respondents what they feel is the most important problem facing the country. Table 9.2 shows the percentages selecting terrorism or a related topic.

These answers are obviously affected by the list of topics suggested and by the question wording. Insofar as the question forces a single choice on respondents, it does not take account of those who see terrorism as a significant problem but not the most important one. In Spain, for example, if those who selected terrorism as the second most important problem are included, the number is much higher. Furthermore, for certain groups terrorism may be more important. In Northern Ireland, Protestants were more likely than Catholics to see terrorism as the most serious issue (41% and 24%, respectively).

The simplest explanation for the degree of public concern is that it is directly linked to the amount of terrorism: The more terrorism, the more concern. This interpretation is supported by two pieces of evidence. First, in a crude way, cross-national differences in the proportion saying that terrorism is the most important problem do correspond to variations in the level of terrorism. If we consider terrorism-related deaths for the period prior to when the polls were taken, the rank order is generally correct. Northern Ireland had the most deaths, followed by Spain and then Italy, with the other countries having far fewer, and this corresponds to the concern expressed. In Israel, "security" obviously includes the threat of military invasion by the Arab states, so the statistic somewhat exaggerates public concern over terrorism.

Second, within Spain, the changing level of concern is closely linked to the monthly death totals. Indeed, it is striking how quickly public attitudes change in respect to short-term fluctuations in the numbers killed (see Figure 9.1). Unfortunately, none of the other countries has a sufficient number of observations to make possible an examination of changes over time.

Clearly, however, the amount of violence is not the only factor operating on public opinion. In the case of Spain, we can also examine regional differences to see whether there is more concern where terrorist violence is highest (see Table 9.3). Contrary to expectations, it is those areas with the highest levels of violence that are the *least* likely to see terrorism as a significant problem. This can be explained by considering the role of ethnicity in Barcelona and the Basque provinces, where most violence has taken place. Basques and Catalans have strong regional and ethnic identities, and sizable minorities support separatist parties.[2] Terrorism is directed primarily not against fellow ethnics but against the Guardia Civil, who are—as a deliberate policy—drawn from other regions of Spain.[3]

A similar explanation can be offered for the Northern Irish situation, where Catholics feel much less concern about terrorism than do Protestants. By 1982 (when the survey was taken) the victims of terrorism were disproportionately Protestant.[4] On the other hand, the Catholic rate of unemployment was much higher than the Protestant rate. Not surprisingly, Protestants rated terrorism the main problem facing Northern Ireland, with unemployment ranked second, while Catholics reversed the order.

The importance of Northern Ireland to the British public can also be explained by considering *who* was being killed. During 1971-1972 British

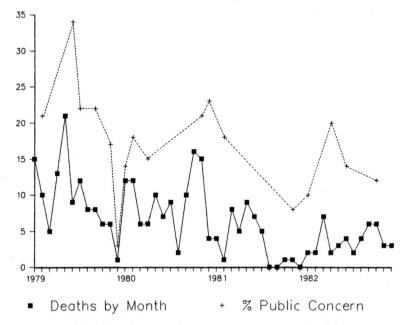

**Deaths by Month       +   % Public Concern**

**Figure 9.1.** Terrorism and the Level of Public Concern in Spain (1979-1982)

SOURCE: Data from opinion polls published in various issues of *Revista Española de Investigaciones Sociologicas* (1979-1982).

concern reached a peak, with 13% on average saying it was the most important problem for the country. The salience of the Northern Ireland issue was lower than would have been predicted given the total number of deaths during the period (679). However, if we focus on the number of *British* soldiers and English civilians killed (155), the concern expressed is at about the expected level. Since the early 1970s British interest in Northern Ireland has diminished considerably, paralleling the decline in the number of British soldiers killed.

Only IRA violence *within* England now arouses English concern. "In December, 1974, 23 per cent of respondents thought Ulster the first or second most important problem. . . . The question was asked shortly after an IRA bombing in Birmingham cost 24 lives" (Rose, McAllister, & Mair 1978, p. 26). A similar response followed a bombing of Harrods department store that killed 6 and injured 94. The next month (January 1983), 14% thought Northern Ireland was an important problem.

**Table 9.3**  Public Concern in Spain Over Terrorism, by Province and Death Rate

|  | Terrorist Killings per Million Population | Terrorism Main Problem (%) |
|---|---|---|
| Basque provinces | 191.9 | 10.5 |
| Madrid | 18.1 | 14.2 |
| Barcelona | 7.0 | 10.1 |
| Galicia | 1.8 | 16.5 |
| Catalonia | 0.8 | 15.7 |
| Andalucia | 0.8 | 18.4 |
| Canaries | 0.7 | 19.9 |
| All other provinces | 1.4 | 21.9 |

SOURCE: Data compiled by the author from public opinion polls published in various issues of *Revista Española de Investigaciones Sociológicas* (1979-1982).

## Public Opinion and the Nationalist Scenario

Nationalists see their land as occupied by foreigners. These foreign imperialists and settlers are the enemy, who must be driven out. The basic strategy is to raise the costs to the enemy occupiers until they withdraw. One ETA leader argues that "nationalistic struggles always try to make the price of loss of life unacceptably high so the enemy will give up its oppression. There comes a time when a nation says 'Too much—we have to leave' " (Segaller, 1986, p. 97). Following the IRA attack in England, the organization issued a statement that said, "We have a message for the British Government who rule our country against the will of the Irish people. While your soldiers occupy Ireland, we are prepared to extract from you both in England and Ireland and beyond a cost which in the end will prove too expensive" (*Keesing's Contemporary Archives*, 1981, p. 30867).

These costs can be economic. In Northern Ireland the IRA bombing campaign was intended to increase the financial burden to the British government, who paid compensation to the victims. The purpose of ETA's "vacation war" was to damage the Spanish tourist industry. The usual way of raising costs, however, is to kill members of the security forces. Soldiers and police are easy targets: They symbolize foreign domination, and their deaths, it is assumed, will lead the enemy public to favor withdrawal. IRA leaders believe that history shows the validity of this logic. According to McGuire (1973), the original aim of the IRA

**Table 9.4**  Israeli Attitudes Toward Palestinians

|  | *January 1974* | *July 1974* | *February 1975* | *January 1978* | *October 1979* | *August 1982* | *July 1983* | *February 1984* |
|---|---|---|---|---|---|---|---|---|
| No negotiation with PLO | 67 | 71 | | 87 | 63 | 61 | | |
| For Palestinian state on West Bank and Gaza Strip | 18 | 20 | 9 | 9 | 22 | 5 | 8 | 7 |

SOURCE: Data from Asi (1986).

> was to kill thirty six British soldiers—the same number who died in Aden. The target was reached in early November 1971. But this, the Army Council felt, was not enough: I remember Dave, amongst others, saying: "We've got to get eighty." Once eighty had been killed, the pressure on the British to negotiate would be immense. I remember the feeling of satisfaction we had at hearing another one had died. As it happened, the total killed by the time of the truce in June 1972 was 102. (p. 75)

Similarly, PLO terrorism within the occupied territories "is consistent with the assessment that under pressure Israel will show greater willingness to return these territories as part of a political settlement" (Kurz, 1987, pp. 27-28).

As a strategy for breaking the will of the enemy, nationalist terrorism has had mixed results. The IRA's campaign has been greatly successful in affecting public opinion in Great Britain. Since 1974, the proportion favoring troop withdrawal has remained stable, with a clear majority favoring withdrawal, and a plurality a United Ireland.[5] The metropolitan Spaniards have been far more resistant; the most recent poll reveals that only 14% favor giving in to terrorist demands, or negotiating with the terrorists.[6] Israeli public opinion similarly shows little sign of weakening as a result of PLO attacks. Throughout the period since the 1967 war, and by overwhelming majorities, Israelis have rejected negotiations with the PLO and the creation of a Palestinian state (see Table 9.4).

The greater resolve of the Spaniards and Israelis compared with the British is explained by the relative salience of the issue. For the Israelis, Palestinian terrorism is seen as a threat to their very existence as a nation and to their physical survival. If the Spaniards conceded independence to the Basques,

**Table 9.5** Attitudes Within Nationalist Constituency

|  | Agree With Goals | Positive Image of Terrorists | Approve Violence |
|---|---|---|---|
| PLO and Palestinians | 95 | 86-95 | 61 |
| ETA and Basques | 46 | 66 | 3-8 |
| IRA and Northern Irish Catholics | 40 | 46 | 6 |
| FLQ and Quebecois | 11 | — | 1 |
| ANC and South African blacks | — | 38 | 28 |

SOURCE: Data compiled by the author from Shadid and Seltzer (1988), Clark (1984), BBC (1982), Moxon-Browne (1981), *Index to International Public Opinion* (1981-1982, 1986-1987), Pinard and Hamilton (1977), and Morris (1981).

other separatist movements would be strengthened, leading to the disintegration of the Spanish state.

As regards their constituency, nationalist terrorists must maintain a high level of at least passive support in order to run an effective campaign. Support can be defined in several ways: as agreement with nationalist goals, as having a positive image of the terrorists, and as approval of political violence. Table 9.5 shows the amount of support that different nationalist groups have, measured in these three ways. The statistics indicate that the PLO, ETA, and IRA have a high degree of support within their respective ethnic constituencies.

Nationalist aspirations are strong in all three groups and appear to be relatively stable over time and unaffected by the level of terrorist violence. The overwhelming majority of Palestinians, both in the occupied territories and in Israel itself, want an independent Palestinian state (see Table 9.6). They disagree only as to the boundaries of this entity: whether it should include all of historic Palestine, follow the 1947 U.N. partition plan, or be limited to the pre-1967 boundaries. Using somewhat procrustean procedures on the available data, it seems that the Palestinians in the occupied territories support the most extreme option, while those in Israel are more moderate.

The people of Northern Ireland have been asked repeatedly for their views on "the best solution to the Northern Irish problem" or their "long-term constitutional preference." Despite the fact that the options and the form of the question vary somewhat among the different polls, the answers can be compared over time. (Only a handful of respondents refuse to answer or have no opinion.) There is no sign that attitudes toward Irish unity have changed

**Table 9.6** Palestinian Preferences for a Political Settlement

|  | Within Israel | | Within Occupied Territories | | | |
|---|---|---|---|---|---|---|
|  | 1980 | 1982 | 1982 | 1982 | 1983 | 1986 |
| Historic Palestine | 11.8 | 24.6 | 56.7 | 60.0 | 58.5 | 77.9 |
| 1947 U.N. partition borders | 25.7 | 19.9 | 3.8 | | | |
| Pre-1967 borders | 48.9 | 48.9 | 22.1 | 27.0 | 32.9 | 16.9 |
| No Palestinian state | 12.6 | 4.9 | 4.6 | 2.0 | 6.1 | 4.9 |

SOURCE: Data compiled by the author from Asi (1986) and Shadid and Seltzer (1988).

within either the Catholic or the Protestant community since the troubles began. Among Catholics, a united Ireland is usually favored by a plurality but not a majority, and there is no clear trend in the level of support. (The low point in nationalist sentiment coincides with the attempt at "power sharing" during 1973-1974.) Of equal significance is the fact that Protestants show no sign of accepting the desirability of Irish unity and continue overwhelmingly to support the British connection.

For the Basque provinces, Clark (1984, pp. 168-178) presents data from a large number of surveys on support for Basque independence. Unfortunately, as he notes, many respondents "simply refuse to answer questions about ETA, terrorism or politics in general." There is no consistent trend in the proportion that wants full independence, although the proportion seems to have declined after the granting of autonomy in 1979.

Public perceptions of the PLO, ETA, and IRA are very positive. In the Basque provinces, surveys have asked whether terrorists are patriots, idealists, madmen, criminals, or individuals manipulated by outside forces. In Northern Ireland, respondents were asked whether they agreed or disagreed that the IRA were "basically patriots and idealists." The Palestinians have been asked repeatedly whether they "consider the PLO their sole legitimate representative," or some variant of this question.

With the obvious exception of the Palestinians, explicit approval of political violence is usually low. Among the Palestinians 60.7% approved "armed struggle" as the best strategy. There was even considerable support for terrorist attacks on civilians. A fifth (20.7%) justified putting a bomb on a civilian airliner, and an even higher proportion (36.9%) approved the attacks on Rome and Vienna airports in December 1985 (Shadid & Seltzer, 1988). In Northern Ireland, however, only 6% of Catholics approved of violence to achieve political objectives (*Index to International Public*

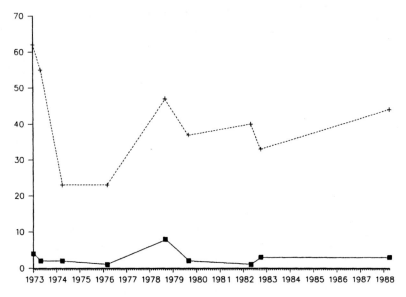

■  Protestant Support                    +  Catholic Support

**Figure 9.2.** Support for Irish Unity in Northern Ireland, by Religion
SOURCE: Data from "What Ulster Thinks" (1973), Carrick James Market Research (n.d.), "Seven Out of Ten" (1974), Moxon-Browne (1981), "What the People of Ulster Think" (1979), "Public Reaction in N. Ireland" (1982), *Fortnight* (July-August 1982), BBC (1982), Market Observation Research Institute (1984), and a June 5, 1974, public opinion poll provided to the author by the Opinion Research Center.

*Opinion*, 1981-1982). Within the Basque provinces the proportion supporting armed struggle has fluctuated between 3% and 8% (Clark, 1984, pp. 170-
172). In Quebec only 1% gave "total approval" to the FLQ kidnappings
(*Canadian Annual Review*, 1970, p. 61). Although these percentages are low
compared to the Palestinian statistics, they still imply that a large *number* of
people see political violence as legitimate. In Quebec, for instance, 1% of 6
million people is 60,000—a pool large enough to provide a steady stream of
recruits to groups such as the FLQ. Furthermore, survey responses presumably underreport support for violence.

Not everybody who is a nationalist has a favorable image of national
terrorists or approves of political violence. However, there is a tendency for
the categories to overlap and to include the same kind of people. Ethnicity
is the most obvious predictor. Few non-Basques support Basque indepen-

dence or hold a favorable view of ETA. Only a handful of Protestants want a united Ireland, and a minority see the IRA as patriots. Israeli Jews have a very hostile image of the PLO, and almost none wish to live in a Palestinian state.[7] Within the ethnic constituency, class is not an important factor in affecting attitudes. What class differences exist can be explained by the class composition of the different ethnic groups. Thus Northern Irish Catholics are disproportionately working-class, so Irish nationalists are more likely to be working-class; ethnic Basques are disproportionately middle-class, so Basque nationalists are more likely to be middle-class.[8]

The high level of support for militant nationalism requires an explanation. Nationalist terrorists kill more people than do revolutionary terrorists, and are undoubtedly guilty of atrocities against civilians. Yet such atrocities do not discredit the cause for which they fight; neither do they tarnish their patriotic image.[9]

One popular interpretation of militant nationalism sees it as a result of discrimination and deprivation. The difficulty with this argument is that most deprived minorities are not militant nationalists. Why should Palestinians be more supportive of violence than black South Africans?[10] Why did French Canadians not support the FLQ to the extent that Irish Catholics support the IRA?

The crucial factor seems to be political socialization. Militant nationalism is strong where people are taught to be militant nationalists. McCann (1974) provides a personal account of the process in his autobiography. Clark (1984, pp. 143-165) gives an excellent description of how young Basques become ETA members. Young Palestinians in the refugee camps are indoctrinated with an ideology of radicalism and violence (Stohl, 1988, p. 529).

Given the existence of a militant nationalist ideology transmitted within the ethnic community, nationalist violence is legitimated. In their campaigns the IRA, PLO, and ETA usually behave like patriots fighting a national liberation struggle. Their targets are predominantly military, and (at least in the case of ETA and the IRA) they rarely kill innocent civilians deliberately.[11]

Insurgent violence provokes repressive violence. Confronting an ethnic insurgency, the authorities adopt policies that have an impact upon all members of the ethnic community. In Northern Ireland, those arrested, interned, or shot by the security forces have been predominantly and disproportionately Catholic. Within Catholic areas, routine identity checks and house searches affect all the inhabitants, regardless of their politics or involvement in political violence. A similar situation obtains in Spain, where Basque provinces have experienced the full rigors of Spanish counter-insurgency policies. The result is widespread alienation among Catholics

**Table 9.7** Support for Security Measures, by Country and Ethnic Group

| Northern Ireland | Catholics | Protestants |
|---|---|---|
| British government should take a tougher line with IRA | 55 | 95 |
| Agree with internment | 5 | 52 |
| Person gets fair trial in Northern Ireland | 12 | 73 |
| No concessions to hunger strikers | 38 | 97 |
| Reintroduce death penalty for all terrorist murderers | 20 | 69 |
| Shoot to kill terrorists | 7 | 61 |
| Approve plastic bullets | 13 | 86 |
| Hang terrorists | 29 | 74 |

| Spain | Basques | Rest of Spain |
|---|---|---|
| ETA are terrorists who should be pursued and eliminated | 17 | 50 |
| Don't accept demands or negotiate with terrorists | 43 | 85 |

| Quebec | French | English |
|---|---|---|
| Favor War Measures Act | 51 | 73 |

SOURCE: Data compiled by the author from Moxon-Browne (1981); "Public Attitudes to Internment" (1974); *Index to International Public Opinion* (1981-1982); "Opinion Poll" (1985); *Belfast Telegraph* (February 6, 1985); Clark (1984); Gunther et al. (1986); Bourne and Eisenberg (1972).

and Basques, and a polarization of attitudes toward security policy between Catholics and Protestants, Basques and non-Basques (see Table 9.7). This in turn maintains support for the insurgents.

In the Quebec case, the victims of FLQ terrorism were predominantly French Canadians, the security measures were enacted by a French Canadian premier, and the security forces deployed were French Canadian. Thus ethnic polarization and support for the FLQ were minimized.[12]

## Public Opinion and
## the Revolutionary Scenario

Revolutionary terrorists employ very different strategies from those used by nationalist insurgents. Their goal is to make a revolution, and they believe that terrorism can be a catalyst in creating a revolutionary situation. Two processes supposedly produce revolutionary consciousness. In the nine-

**Table 9.8** Public Attitudes Toward Revolution

|  | Support Revolution | Positive Image | Approve Violence |
|---|---|---|---|
| Uruguay | 12 | 34 | — |
| Italy | 13 | 28 | 2 |
| Germany | 2 | 18 | 1 |

SOURCE: Data compiled by the author from *Indice Gallup de Opinion Publica* (1968), provided by Gallup Uruguay; *Index to International Public Opinion* (1981-1982); *L'Espresso* (January 10, 1982); Weinberg and Eubank (1987); Lodge (1988); and data provided by the Allensbach Institut fur Demoskopie.

teenth century, many anarchists and social revolutionaries believed that the masses would be inspired by the "propaganda of the deed" to rise up against oppression. The Narodnaya Volya's manifesto claimed that "terrorist activity . . . aims to undermine the prestige of the government, to demonstrate the possibility of struggle against the government [and] to arouse in this manner the revolutionary spirit of the people and their confidence in the success of their cause." Kropotkin said that one terrorist act could "make more propaganda than a thousand pamphlets. Above all, it awakens the spirit of revolt" (quoted in Schmid & De Graaf, 1982). This view was echoed a century later by Latin American revolutionaries. Regis Debray (1967) wrote that "the destruction of one troop transport truck is more effective propaganda for the local population than a thousand speeches." According to the Tupamaros, "revolutionary action in itself . . . generates revolutionary consciousness, organization and conditions" (Moss, 1972).

An alternative view of how to create a revolutionary situation is the "provocation-repression" theory. By attacking the establishment and the security forces, the insurgents provoke the state into mass repression, which alienates the general public and increases support for the rebels. Brazilian revolutionary Carlos Marighella is one of the best-known advocates of this tactic.

In addition to mobilizing and radicalizing their own potential supporters, revolutionary terrorists seek to destroy the morale of their enemies. For the Tupamaros, "intimidation and reprisals constituted an essential guerrilla tactic in that they can lead to the moral defeat of key components of the security forces or the government machine" (Porzecanski, 1973, pp. 45-46).

As Table 9.8 shows, revolutionary terrorists typically start off with a much smaller degree of popular support than do nationalist terrorists. Only a small proportion of the population favors revolutionary change.

Survey data are available for Uruguay, Italy, Germany, and Spain on general ideological orientations and their changes over time. In Uruguay the population was asked whether they believed the solution to the country's problems lay in "armed revolution" or "law and order." In Germany and Italy the options were "radical change by revolutionary action," "gradual improvement by reforms," and "valiant defense against all subversive forces."

The public perception of revolutionary terrorists is less favorable than the public perception of nationalist terrorists. In Uruguay, respondents were asked whether the Tupamaros were well-intentioned revolutionaries or common delinquents. In Italy, the public was asked to choose one or two phrases that best applied to the Red Brigade members. Three phrases were negative (instruments controlled from on high, dangerous assassins, or crazy) but the others were ambivalent (pursuing a just end with the wrong means) or very positive (fighting for a better society). In Germany the question was whether the Baader-Meinof gang "acted out of political convictions or if they had now become true criminals."

Revolutionary terrorists lack clearly defined constituencies. Their Marxist rhetoric suggests that their support should be concentrated in the working class and among the poor. In fact, the Tupamaros and Baader-Meinoff were viewed most sympathetically by those of higher socioeconomic status, although the differences were small. Demography rather than class was a differentiating factor, with men somewhat more sympathetic then women, and the young noticeably more so than the old. A similar pattern was found in support for revolution.

The low level of support for revolution and revolutionary terrorists is easily explained. Modern Western societies are generally prosperous, with rising standards of living and well-developed systems of social welfare. Politically, they are free and democratic. For the great mass of citizens, therefore, demands for a revolutionary transformation of society are incomprehensible. In Uruguay and Italy, revolutionary attitudes were more prevalent than elsewhere because of economic decline and political instability. The Tupamaros emerged in a society with the highest rate of inflation and the lowest rate of growth in Latin America. Of all EEC countries, Italy had the highest percentage of those dissatisfied with "the way that democracy is working in my country." Germans, on the other hand, had the highest degree of satisfaction with democracy, and the lowest percentage advocating revolution.

The only group in modern Western society for whom millennial movements have a strong appeal are the university educated in general, and students in particular.[13] Several explanations are offered for this phenomenon. Halperin (1976) argues that universities produce an oversupply of liberal arts and social science graduates who are unable to find suitable employment. Revolutionary movements

> express the despair of young members of the administrative class radicalized and alienated from society by the deterioration of their prospects in countries of stagnant economy. . . . In case of success the movements offer political power and a new role for the administrative class. (p. 52)

Other writers emphasize specific problems faced by Italian and German students: "Inadequate classroom and living facilities and a poor student-teacher ratio were the result of overcrowding. A more fundamental set of problems centered around the archaic nature of the university system" (Stohl, 1988, p. 418). Some students became revolutionaries because they took their professors' radical ideologies seriously. As Adorno plaintively remarked, "I presented a theoretical model,—how could I suspect that people would want to put it into effect with Molotov cocktails?" [14]

Terrorist attacks clearly failed to generate a revolutionary mood in the general population. In Uruguay and Italy, where major left-wing campaigns were mounted, the number favoring revolution declined steadily throughout the period of terrorist activity. In Uruguay, the figure dropped from 12% in July 1968 to 1% in July 1972, while in Italy the decline was from 13% in November 1976 to 6% in October 1981. In Germany, where leftist terrorism was conducted at a much lower level, the proportion of revolutionaries remained virtually unchanged at a trivial level.

Instead, terrorism generated a backlash, with increased support for tough law-and-order measures. In Uruguay, Germany, and Italy there is clear evidence of such a relationship. In Uruguay, the number of terrorist acts rose each year during 1968-1972, and this is matched by a steady increase in the law-and-order category. The worst years for terrorism in Germany were 1977 and 1980, and in Italy 1978 and 1980, and during these years the percentage of the population favoring a "valiant defense of society" reached a maximum.

These shifts in Italy and Germany can be compared with those found in the EEC bloc as a whole, to see whether the trend is due to a general change in political climate in the 1970s. In fact, the trend in the other EEC countries is different. From November 1976 to April 1981, the average of the other EEC countries (excluding Germany and Italy) shows a slight increase in the proportion of revolutionaries (6% to 7%) and no change in the proportion favoring a valiant defense against subversion (27% at both dates).

Attacks on public places produce fear and anger in the public. After the bombing of a Frankfurt department store, one German radical was exultant. "A burning department store with burning people transmits for the first time in a major European city that stirring Vietnam feeling" (Stohl, 1988, p. 421). Ordinary Germans are unlikely to have shared such feelings. When nationalist terrorists kill soldiers their victims are foreigners, but in Italy and Germany when revolutionary terrorists killed policemen the working class identified with their victims (Clutterbuck, 1978, p. 38).

The Uruguayan situation is ambiguous, however, in that Tupamaro violence does not appear to have affected public perceptions of them. Since this assessment differs from the conventional wisdom, and since the data are exceptionally good, the Uruguayan case will be examined in more detail.

In the early stages of their campaign, the Tupamaros carefully avoided unnecessary violence, and attacked only the rich and elite. During Christmas they hijacked a food truck and distributed the groceries in the slums of Montevideo. They robbed the casino, but returned the share that would have gone to the employees. They broke into a financial institution and publicized its corrupt and illegal practices (thus implicating a cabinet minister). When one of their kidnap victims had a heart attack, they kidnapped a specialist to treat him, and then released their prisoner when his condition worsened.

Such tactics created a favorable image for the Tupamaros, but the public supposedly turned against them once they began to murder people. "They lost their original Robin Hood image as imaginative student pranksters who pilfered from the rich to give to the poor, by systematically murdering policemen as well as an American hostage, Dan Mitrione" (Moss, 1972, p. 223). This is a common view, usually supported by citing polls that show a dramatic decline in those thinking the Tupamaros were "motivated by a concern for social justice" from 59% in 1971 to 4% in 1972.[15]

However, an analysis of the polls of Gallup Uruguay suggests a different conclusion. Three questions were asked repeatedly: whether a specific action was a legitimate revolutionary act or a crime; whether the Tupamaros were well-intentioned revolutionaries or common delinquents; and whether there was any justification for the Tupamaros "under the political conditions of our country."

Some evidence does suggest that a soft-line campaign helps maintain a more favorable terrorist image. For example, the proportion of respondents who believed kidnappings to be legitimate revolutionary acts increased *after* the victims were returned unharmed, as happened in the cases of Claude Fly and Geoffrey Jackson.[16] When Fly was first kidnapped, only 18% of the individuals surveyed thought it a legitimate revolutionary act, but 32% saw

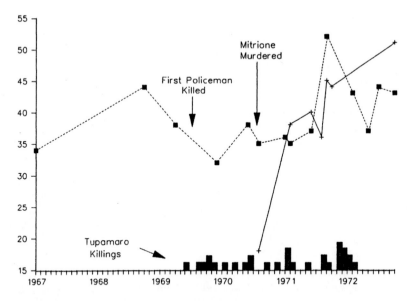

**Figure 9.3.** Attitudes Toward the Tupamaros

SOURCE: Data from the *Indice Gallup de Opinion Publica* (1967-1972), provided to the author by Gallup Uruguay.

it as such after he was released. In the case of Jackson the figure rose from 30% to 36%. On the other hand, the killing of Mitrione brought about a dramatic decline in those thinking his abduction was justified. The week before his death, the public was evenly divided between those who thought it a legitimate revolutionary act (34%) and those who considered it a crime (34%). After his murder the respective figures became 18% and 44%.

However, terrorist violence clearly has only a temporary effect. Figure 9.3, showing the proportion considering the Tupamaros "well-intentioned revolutionaries" and their actions "justified under the political conditions of the country," does not suggest any deterioration of their public image. The first killings of policemen were not until July 1969, but the public perception of them as well-intentioned revolutionaries averaged 38.7% before that date, compared with 38.9% afterward. Mitrione's murder had no discernible impact on public opinion either. Nor does the actual number of killings appear to be a negative factor. The percentage of respondents thinking the

Tupamaros' actions justified under the political conditions of the country increased substantially during the period when terrorist killings were highest.

Why the public perceptions of the Tupamaros remained favorable, even though the proportion favoring revolution was declining, is difficult to explain. Perhaps public attitudes were affected by government counter-measures against the guerrillas.

The hope that terrorism would provoke the authorities into massive and indiscriminate repression that would turn the public against the government was not realized in any of the three cases. In all three countries governments did respond with repression to the outbreak of political violence. They declared a state of emergency, reduced civil liberties, and gave special powers to the security forces. Large numbers were arrested or interned. People were stopped and questioned on the street, and their houses searched. Several, including some innocent of any participation in violence, were killed or wounded. However, for the most part the public approved of these tough measures.

The crucial determinant of public attitudes toward government security policies seems to be who is affected by them (see Table 9.9). In Italy and Germany, security measures affected the general public only temporarily and during clearly defined crises (such as the Moro and Schleyer kidnappings). At other times, "since the terrorists proclaim themselves to be revolutionary leftists, radical left-wing groups are naturally suspect and become targets of intensive investigation and sometimes harassment by the security forces" (Mack, 1981). In Uruguay from mid-1970 onward, mass searches and roadblocks affected the public at large, but most of those arrested and brutally interrogated were members of the left-wing party, Frente Amplio.

In Italy and Germany, political leftists opposed government security policies, but they constituted only a small percentage of the population and were already radicalized. Working-class supporters of the German SDP and the Italian PCI approved the policies to almost the same degree as those supporting the conservative parties.

In the case of Uruguay, opposition seems to have been more widespread. Moss (1972) claims that "emergency measures alienated public opinion" (p. 217). Porzecanski (1973) says that the police "became well known among the population for extensive and routine use of torture, as well as for heavy-handed citywide search operations" (pp. 55-56). These massive searches "conducted clumsily at all hours of the night . . . created great resentment among Montevideo's population." Labrousse (1973) describes how "the population was incensed by the continual police controls" (p. 130). The fact that antiterrorist measures had more of an impact on the general

**Table 9.9** Support for Security Measures, by Country and Party

| Uruguay | Colorados | Blancos | Frente Amplio | Total |
|---|---|---|---|---|
| Favor hard line with terrorists | 35 | 23 | 7 | 22 |
| Approve military courts for terrorists | 64 | 55 | 20 | 48 |
| Severe penalties justified | 49 | 57 | 29 | 43 |
| Suspension of individual guarantees justified | 70 | 57 | 23 | 50 |
| Approve emergency measures | 74 | 53 | 15 | 43 |
| Approve declaration of state of internal war | 84 | 55 | 33 | 55 |
| Detention well handled and justified | 68 | 59 | 16 | 48 |
| Identity checks and street searches necessary | 87 | 80 | 39 | 70 |

| Germany | SPD | FPD | CDU | Total |
|---|---|---|---|---|
| Stricter antiterrorism laws needed | 64 | 85 | 60 | 71 |
| More severe penalties for acts of terrorism | — | — | — | 86 |
| Death penalty for terrorists | 52 | 43 | 60 | 55 |
| Approve shoot-to-kill policy | — | — | — | 49 |
| Terrorists received fair trial at Stammheim | 60 | 66 | 68 | 60 |
| No blame to authorities in hunger strikers' death | 75 | 77 | 85 | 77 |
| Willing to give up personal freedoms to fight terrorism | 55 | 53 | 66 | 60 |
| Accept house searches to fight terrorism | 62 | 40 | 72 | 69 |

| Italy | DP | PCI | PSI | DC | Total |
|---|---|---|---|---|---|
| More severe penalties for acts of terrorism | — | — | — | — | 87 |
| Police should act with force and decision | 11 | 45 | 58 | 78 | 65 |

SOURCE: Data from Indice Gallup de Opinion Publica (1967-1972) provided to the author by Gallup Uruguay, *Index to International Public Opinion* (1979-1983), Fabris (1977), and data for 1968-1978 provided by the Allensbach Institut fur Demoskopie.

public in Uruguay than elsewhere probably accounts for the noticeably lower degree of support for such measures. It may also explain why the public continued to regard the terrorists as "well-intentioned revolutionaries" and "justified under the political conditions of the country."

## The Media and
## Public Attitudes Toward Terrorism

To be convincing, those who claim that the media significantly affect public attitudes toward terrorism must show first that there is a correspondence between how the media portray terrorism and public opinion, and second that public attitudes are not more easily explained by other factors.

### AGENDA-SETTING

One can make a plausible case that the media play an important agenda-setting role. Weimann (1982) cites studies that find "that public rankings of the importance of various issues coincide . . . closely with media rankings" (p. 214). He suggests that the high attention paid to terrorism by the media "determines a consequent priority in the public's perception of priority of issues."

Several writers argue that the media exaggerate the dangers of terrorism and thus magnify public fears. Merari and Friedland (1985) claim that

> the printed space and broadcast time devoted to terrorism and terrorist incidents turn terrorism into an ever present threat in individuals' consciousness. The media's technical capabilities, which allow them to convey information in real time, by word, sound, and image, force millions to experience vicariously the horrors of terrorism. (p. 200)

One account of the German public's response refers to "fears stoked by the media that terrorism could hit anybody at any time" (Lodge, 1988, p. 81). Certainly public concern over terrorism is much greater than one would expect from any realistic evaluation of the risks that it poses (Hewitt, 1988).

Furthermore, by emphasizing terrorist *violence* rather than the terrorists' cause, the media determine *how* the public will perceive the issue. As noted earlier in this chapter, the public sees terrorist violence as the issue, and this corresponds to the pattern of media coverage. Exposure to vivid and horri-

**Table 9.10** Classification of Public Audiences

|  | *Constituency* | *Bystanders* | *Enemy* |
|---|---|---|---|
| Sophisticated awareness | IRA (Northern Ireland Catholics) |  | IRA (Northern Ireland Protestants) |
|  | RB (Italian workers) |  | RB (Italian bourgeois) |
| Some knowledge |  | IRA (United States) | IRA (Great Britain) |
| Ignorance |  | RB (United States) | FALN (United States) |

fying pictures of the carnage produced by terrorism explains why the public sees the issue in this way.

CHANGING PUBLIC ATTITUDES

The effects of the media are different for enemies, constituencies, and bystanders. The effects also vary according to the knowledge that the public already has of the terrorist group. Table 9.10 suggests classification of different publics along these two dimensions. There are two empty spaces on the table indicating implausible situations. Thus it is unlikely that the public would have much knowledge of terrorist groups that do not affect them, or that a terrorists' constituency would know little about them.

In most societies where there is sustained terrorism by indigenous groups the public is usually aware of the political goals and ideology of the terrorists. Such would be the case in Northern Ireland, the Basque provinces, Israel and the occupied territories, and—to a somewhat lesser extent—Italy and Uruguay.

Curtis (1984) explains why the media have very little effect on Catholic and Protestant attitudes within Northern Ireland:

> The national media do not have a monopoly on news or analysis of the conflict. The unionist and nationalist communities each have their own papers, and their own political, educational and cultural institutions, and in an area with a population of only one-and-a-half million—news travels fast by word of mouth. While people in the North consume a relatively large amount of news and current affairs coverage, they are also very critical. Using mutually exclusive standards, nationalists and unionists evaluate the output of the

national media according to how it reflects their own experiences and the perceptions shared by their respective communities. (pp. 1-2)

The public is likely to have a similar degree of sophistication in other societies with deep-rooted ethnic-nationalist conflicts, or revolutionary traditions. In such societies the role of the media in affecting public attitudes toward terrorism is a relatively minor one. Most basic social and political attitudes concerning social inequality, national identity, and regime legitimacy are formed by socialization. The primary agencies in this process are family, school, and church, with the media usually reflecting and reinforcing such values. These basic ideologies determine whether political violence is understood and justified or dismissed as crazy and criminal behavior.

Furthermore, where political violence is a chronic feature of society many individuals are directly acquainted with the results of terrorism, and even more have firsthand experience of government repression (roadblocks, house searches, security force brutality, and so on). In Northern Ireland, a 1979 survey found that 2% had been injured and another 20% had had someone close to them, such as friends or family members, harmed. Some 15% had had someone close to them killed, 10% had changed their residences, and 3% had changed their jobs as a direct result of the violence ("What the People of Ulster Think," 1979). In such cases attitudes toward the security forces and government policies are explained most simply by such personal experiences, and it seems unnecessary to postulate any significant media effect.

The media certainly reflect and reinforce public attitudes. Their ability to do this derives from the fact that readers of different newspapers vary in their social characteristics and political opinions. Different newspapers offer alternative interpretations of the violence, the government's response, and so on, and such interpretations usually correspond to those of their readers, who in turn have their opinions reinforced by what they read. Rose (1971, p. 344) found that in 1968 Catholics who read the nationalist *Irish News* were somewhat more likely to support illegal demonstrations than those who read other newspapers. Similarly, Protestants who read the *News-Letter* were slightly more likely than other Protestants to take a hard-line position. Rose concludes that "the absence of stronger correlations is evidence that those who take political news from the press evaluate what they read in terms of outlooks formed independently of their newspaper" (p. 344), but his data suggest some tendency for opinions to be reinforced. Although no survey data exist on the political opinions of its readership, the areas where *An Phoblacht* are sold are the same areas that vote Sinn Fein and where most

IRA violence occurs. In the Basque provinces, the circulation of *Egin* corresponds to the areas of ETA violence.

A similar link can be suggested between revolutionary ideology and the readership of the "alternative" or "movement" press in Italy and Germany. Tarrow (1989) points out that in Italy this press emerged simultaneously with the wave of left-wing protest in 1968:

> The movement newspapers were a major innovation that accelerated the diffusion of social protest. For example, *Il Manifesto*, which appealed to left-wing communists as well as anti-communist leftists, had a circulation well beyond the size of the groups' own membership. It thus helped to set the political agenda of the social movement sector, and was able to alert people to protests occurring in another part of the country, to the themes and forms of action used in those protests, and to the probable responses of elites if they were copied. For a time, walking around with a copy of one of these newspapers in one's back pocket was a symbol of membership in the movement. (p. 230)

A study of the alternative press in West Germany described readers as "the radical young in the big cities especially Berlin." On occasion these papers were raided by the police and their equipment confiscated. "The pretext for such action has been alleged subversion, in particular the accusation that certain publications have been guilty of incitement to violence and terrorism" (Humphreys, 1990, pp. 120-121).

It would be an exaggeration to claim that these newspapers created revolutionary attitudes or support for terrorism. Indeed, their editorials often condemned terrorism as counterproductive. However, their coverage was at least ambiguously sympathetic to the terrorist perspective and may have served to maintain favorable attitudes toward the Red Brigades and Red Army Faction among youthful radicals.

Negative sentiments toward revolutionary terrorism among the general public may be linked to media coverage. Clutterbuck (1978) claims that in Italy and Germany, when policemen were murdered "television pictures of their fearful working-class families created widespread anger" (p. 38). This argument receives some support from the Uruguayan case, where the government censored news about terrorist attacks. Perhaps the *lack* of media coverage explains why public attitudes toward the Tupamaros remained favorable even after they began to kill policemen.

There is another way in which the media may affect support for political violence. One school of thought holds that television violence stimulates aggression. After reviewing 67 studies, Andison (1977) concludes that "viewing television violence can in fact lead to aggressive behavior" (p. 318). Since political violence is not correlated with other forms of violence, it is unlikely that watching television violence in general has much to do with support for political violence. However, it is possible that broadcasting scenes of *political* violence may stimulate more political violence. For a terrorist campaign to continue, militants must believe that ultimately they will be victorious. As the graffiti in Northern Ireland proclaim, "Tiocfaidh ar la" (Our day will come). Such sentiments can be maintained only if terrorist attacks are seen to continue. Thus one Irish journalist has suggested that the main purpose of IRA bombings in London was to maintain morale among Republican militants:

> You have to remember that the Provisionals look at things in a very different way from the way you and I would. One big factor for them is that when they set off a bomb like this in London whatever the damage it might do, as we would see it, to their cause, the fact is that it is tremendous for the morale of their volunteers, the low down guys back home. They see it as a blow struck at the soft underbelly of the enemy. (quoted in Altheide, 1987, p. 108)

Reporting violence by one side may provoke violence from the other side. In the mid-1970s, the Northern Irish media debated whether reporting the religious identity of those killed led to tit-for-tat sectarian reprisals. Weinberg and Eubank (1987) point out that in Italy "the provocative role played by neo-fascism in stimulating leftist terrorism was heightened by the abundance of press accounts of neo-fascist violence, para-military camps and conspiracies published in the late 1960s and early 1970s" (pp. 17-18).

The media's role is most significant in situations where the public has very little direct experience with terrorism or knowledge about the terrorists' cause. Thus the media are most likely to influence public opinion in the case of bystanders or enemies. The American and English cases exemplify this type of situation. More than 90% of terrorist attacks against Americans have occurred outside the United States. Terrorism by domestic groups has been a rare phenomenon, and terrorist attacks within each country have usually come from outsiders, such as the FALN in the United States or the IRA in England. Consequently there is general ignorance about terrorist groups, their goals, and their sociopolitical backgrounds. According to Curtis (1984):

> People in Britain receive only a dribble of news from the North, except when a crisis hijacks the headlines. They have no direct experience of the conflict, save for intermittent bombings in British cities, and Ireland is conspicuously

**Table 9.11** Favorable Image of Terrorists (in percentages)

| | | |
|---|---|---|
| IRA in Great Britain | (1983) | 3 |
| IRA in Canada | (1979) | 10 |
| PLO in Great Britain | (1983) | 12 |
| PLO in Canada | (1979) | 14 |

SOURCE: Data from the *Index to International Public Opinion* (1979-1984).
NOTE: Statistic refers to those considering group "freedom fighters."

> absent from educational curricula. Groups trying to circulate alternative infor-
> mation about events in the North are small and impoverished. British people
> are, therefore, almost entirely dependent on the mass media for news and
> interpretations of events in Ireland. (p. 2)

McDougall (1986), in an article on North American media coverage of
Puerto Rico, says:

> On peripheral issues—issues in which neither the public nor the media take
> any intense or compelling interest—the media are likely to reflect the attitudes
> of the general public. The public has little knowledge about or interest in Puerto
> Rico. This combination of ignorance and apathy tends to be reflected in most
> media coverage of Puerto Rico. Data go unverified, stereotypes are reinforced,
> and reports from on-the-scene correspondents tend to follow safe, predictable
> patterns, so as not to raise any eyebrows among the editors back homes. (p. 56)

Public opinion therefore constitutes a virtual *tabula rasa* upon which the
media may work their will. We would predict, therefore, that public perceptions of terrorism will correspond closely to media portrayals.

As already noted, research in the United States, Canada, and England has
shown that the media usually follow the official perspective and portray
terrorists in a negative fashion. We would expect, therefore, that, in general,
the public will have a negative view of terrorists, and this is the case in
Canada and Great Britain. The especially negative view of the IRA in Great
Britain can be explained, presumably, as a result of their bombing campaign
against civilian targets in England (see Table 9.11).

There is almost complete absence of relevant polls for the United States.
A 1986 Gallup survey on public attitudes toward the news media asked about
the coverage of international terrorism. Three-fourths of the public rated the
coverage as "good" or "excellent." However, slightly more than half thought

**Table 9.12**  Attitudes Toward Insurgent Groups Among Maryland Student Sample
(in percentages)

|  | Could Identify Group | Group Are Freedom Fighters |
|---|---|---|
| PLO | 64 | 11 |
| IRA | 45 | 27 |
| ANC | 32 | 65 |
| Weathermen | 14 | 18 |
| Red Brigades | 11 | 11 |
| FALN | 4 | 0 |

NOTE: Freedom fighter percentage calculated only for those who could identify the group.

that news organizations devoted too much attention to terrorist incidents, and
that terrorists were given "too much opportunity to promote their cause."

Another study examined the effect of televised presidential addresses on
public opinion toward Middle East terrorism (Gilboa, 1990). By comparing
public attitudes before and after President Reagan's speeches during two
crises (the 1983 bombing of the U.S. Marine headquarters in Beirut and the
1985 TWA hijacking), Gilboa (1990) shows that support for government
policies increased, as did approval of Reagan's handling of the crises. He
concludes:

> The mass media played an important role in the process that started with the
> presidential addresses and ended with changes in public opinion. In the two
> cases reported here and in many other cases the media set the agenda—the
> reservations and the questions that the president had to answer. This role is
> clearly evident in the context, contents and structure of specific questions and
> answers that appear in the media's sponsored polls. In his televised addresses
> Reagan mainly dealt with questions raised by the media, both in reports and
> public opinion polls. (p. 52)

A survey of a sample of University of Maryland students found a high
degree of ignorance about specific insurgent/terrorist groups, and a general
tendency to label the groups as "terrorists" rather than "freedom fighters." [17]
Very few students knew what the goals of the groups were. Some interesting
differences and perceptions of the various groups are apparent, with the PLO
the best-known group and the Puerto Rican FALN virtually unknown. Only
the ANC was regarded as a group of freedom fighters (see Table 9.12).

**Table 9.13**  Disapproval of Terrorism

| | |
|---|---|
| Northern Ireland | –82 |
| Great Britain | –72 |
| Spain | –69 |
| Denmark | –64 |
| Italy | –63 |
| West Germany | –61 |
| Japan | –55 |
| Irish Republic | –53 |
| France | –53 |
| Belgium | –43 |
| Netherlands | –38 |
| Argentina | –51 |
| Chile | –37 |
| Uruguay | –32 |
| Ecuador | –22 |
| Brazil | –19 |
| Peru | + 1 |
| Venezuela | + 9 |
| Colombia | +31 |

SOURCE: Data from *Index to International Public Opinion* (1980-1983).
NOTE: Statistic shows percentage approving minus percentage disapproving.

Two cross-national surveys reveal a similar pattern of general disapproval (see Table 9.13). When asked if "there may be certain circumstances where terrorism is justified" or if "terrorism must always be condemned," in all the countries in the survey the second statement was chosen by a clear majority. Latin Americans were slightly more sympathetic when asked whether a specific terrorist act, by the Colombian M19 group, was a "legitimate revolutionary act" or not. In the eight-country sample, negative judgments exceeded positive evaluations in all but three countries.

The cross-national variation in public attitudes is suggestive. To what extent does it reflect experience with terrorism and to what extent is it a result of differences in how the media portray terrorism? Disapproval tends to be strongest in those countries where terrorism has claimed the most victims. Also, the relatively tolerant attitudes of the Dutch and Belgian publics may be explained by more liberal press coverage in those countries. More research is needed on both public attitudes toward terrorism and how the media in different countries portray terrorism.

# Notes

1. Since the media commission a high proportion of the polls, they may be said to create public opinion in a very literal sense. About half of the polls used in this article were published in newspapers or magazines; the remainder were a result of academic research. However, editors rarely involve themselves in the details of the polls.

2. A statewide survey by Jimenez-Blanco (1977) on regional consciousness found that Barcelona and the Basque country expressed the most acute grievances over administrative centralization, were most likely to support independence, and were the most likely to vote for separatist parties.

3. On the basis of their names, only 30 out of 403 victims of terrorism in the Basque provinces appear to have been ethnic Basques.

4. In the five years before the survey (1978-1983), 61 Catholics and 199 Protestants were victims of terrorism. Thus Protestants, who make up 63% of the population, suffered 76% of the deaths.

5. From 1974 through 1977 those favoring troop withdrawal averaged 57%, and from 1978-1981 those wanting to withdraw the troops immediately or within five years also averaged 57%. See Rose et al. (1978) for figures before 1977; for later figures, see the *Index to International Public Opinion.*

6. See Gunther, Sani, and Shabad (1986, p. 362). Earlier polls by Linz in 1978 and 1979 show a decline in those supporting negotiation or acceptance of terrorist demands, from 24% to 17% (Gordenker, 1980, p. 48).

7. About 3% of English-speaking Quebecois support independence, and 3% of Ulster Protestants a united Ireland (Pinard & Hamilton, 1978; Moxon-Browne, 1981); 3% of Israeli Jews saw a "united secular Palestinian state" as the most acceptable solution to the Middle Eastern conflict (Asi, 1986).

8. For details on the characteristics of nationalists and revolutionaries, see Hewitt (1990).

9. A 1984 poll found 48% of Catholics agreeing that the IRA were patriots and idealists, virtually the same as in Moxon-Browne's 1978 survey (Market Observation Research Institute, 1984). Even the bombing of a Remembrance Day memorial ceremony at Enniskillen produced only a 5% decline in those saying they sympathized with the IRA (*Fortnight*, April 1988).

10. In South Africa, only 28% of blacks believed that "violence is justified to change the apartheid system" (*Index to International Public Opinion*, 1986-1987), and when asked about a group of ANC guerrillas who took over a bank, only 38% of a Soweto sample thought they were "heroes" (Morris, 1981).

11. Military or political targets constitute 80% of ETA's victims and 65% of the IRA's victims. The IRA kneecaps petty criminals and ETA "executes" drug dealers (Hewitt, 1984).

12. There are accounts of support among the youth: "An alarming groundswell of support for the terrorists was meanwhile rising within the French speaking youth of Montreal. At several junior colleges in the city there were teach-ins and even student strikes in sympathy with FLQ" (Radwanski, 1971, pp. 57-58).

13. On the political alienation and radicalism of German and Italian students, see Alexander and Gleason (1981, pp. 256-282) and Weinberg and Eubank (1987, p. 36).

14. This is quoted in Pridham's chapter in Lodge (1981). On the ambivalent relationship between leftist intellectuals and terrorists, see that essay and the one by Furlong in the same volume.

15. The often-cited poll showing a decline in public support for the Tupamaros can be accounted for by errors committed by both Crozier and Clutterbuck. See Hewitt (1990) for details.

16. Fly, an American agricultural expert, was kidnapped in 1970, and Jackson, the British consul, in 1971.

17. The survey included 19 graduate students and 62 seniors and sophomores in my class on terrorism. The question asked was, "Can you identify any of the following groups (e.g., which country are they from and what do they want)? Do you consider them to be terrorists or freedom fighters?"

# References

Alexander, Y., & Gleason, J. (Eds.). (1981). *Behavioral and quantitative perspectives on terrorism.* New York: Pergamon.

Altheide, D. L. (1987). Format and symbols in TV coverage of terrorism in the United States and Great Britain. *International Studies Quarterly, 31,* 161-176.

Andison, F. S. (1977). T.V. violence and viewer aggression: A culmination of study results, 1956-1976. *Public Opinion Quarterly, 41,* 314-331.

Asi, M. (1986). *Israeli and Palestinian public opinion.* Washington, DC: International Center for Research and Public Policy.

BBC. (1982, October). *Attitudes to the Northern Ireland Assembly.* London: Author.

Bourne, P., & Eisenberg, J. A. (1972). *The law and the police.* Ontario: Don Mills.

*Canadian annual review.* (annual). Toronto: University of Toronto Press.

Carrick James Market Research. (n.d.). Ulster 1973. *Fortnight/Sunday Times.*

Cerny, K. H. (1978). *Germany at the polls.* Washington, DC: American Enterprise Institute.

Clark, R. (1984). *The Basque insurgents: ETA 1952-80.* Madison: University of Wisconsin Press.

Clutterbuck, R. (1978). *Kidnap and ransom: The response.* London: Faber.

Curtis, L. (1984). *Ireland: The propaganda war.* London: Pluto.

Debray, R. (1967). *Revolution in the revolution?* Westport, CT: Greenwood.

Esteban, J. de. (1979). *Las elecciones legislativas.* Madrid: Centro de Investigaciones Sociologicas.

Fabris, G. (1977). *Il comportamento politico degli italiani.* Milano: Franco Angeli.

Gilboa, E. (1990). Effects of televised presidential addresses on public opinion: President Reagan and terrorism in the Middle East. *Presidential Studies Quarterly, 20,* 43-54.

Giner, J. (1983). Journalists, mass media and public opinion in Spain 1938-82. In K. Maxwell (Ed.), *The press and the rebirth of Iberian democracy.* Westport, CT: Greenwood.

Gordenker, L. (Ed.). (1980). *Resolving nationality conflicts: The role of public opinion research.* New York: Praeger.

Grivas, G. (1965). *Memoirs.* New York: Praeger.

Gunther, R., Sani, G., & Shabad, G. (1986). *Spain after Franco.* Berkeley: University of California Press.

Halperin, E. (1976). *Terrorism in Latin America.* Beverly Hills, CA: Sage.

Herman, E. S. (1985). *The real terror network: Terrorism in fact and propaganda.* Montreal: Black Rose.

Hewitt, C. (1984). *The effectiveness of anti-terrorist policies.* Lanham, MD: University Press of America.

Hewitt, C. (1988). The costs of terrorism: A cross-national study of six countries. *Terrorism, 11,* 169-180.

Hewitt, C. (1990). Terrorism and public opinion: A five country comparison. *Terrorism and Political Violence, 2,* 145-170.

Humphreys, P. (1990). *Media and media policy in West Germany.* New York: St. Martin's.

*Index to international public opinion.* (annual). Westport, CT: Greenwood.

Jenkins, B. (1975). *International terrorism.* Santa Monica, CA: RAND Corporation.

Jimenez-Blanco, J. (1977). La conciencia regional en España. Madrid: Editorial Cuadernos.

Knight, G., & Dean, T. (1982). Myth and the structure of news. *Journal of Communication, 32*(2), 144-161.

Kurz, A. (Ed.). (1987). *Contemporary trends in world terrorism.* New York: Praeger.

Labrousse, A. (1973). *The Tupamaros.* Harmondsworth: Penguin.

Lodge, J. (Ed.). (1981). *Terrorism: A challenge to the state.* New York: St. Martin's.

Lodge, J. (Ed.). (1988). *The threat of terrorism.* Boulder, CO: Westview.

Mack, A. (1981). The utility of terrorism. *Australian and New Zealand Journal of Criminology, 14,* 197-224.

Market Observation Research Institute. (1984). *From the shadow of the gun.* London: Author.

McCann, E. (1974). *War and an Irish town.* Harmondsworth: Penguin.

McDougall, G. (1986). Mainland news media coverage of Puerto Rico. In P. Falk (Ed.), *The political status of Puerto Rico.* Lexington, MA: D. C. Heath.

McGuire, M. (1973). *To take arms: A year with the Provisional IRA.* London: Macmillan.

Merari, A., & Friedland, N. (1985). *Social psychological aspects of political terrorism.* Tel Aviv: Tel Aviv University.

Morris, M. (1981). *South African security: Some considerations for the '80s.* Capetown: Terrorism Research Centre.

Moss, R. (1972). *Urban guerrillas.* London: Temple Smith.

Moxon-Browne, E. (1981). The water and the fish: Public opinion and the Provisional IRA in Northern Ireland. *Terrorism, 5,* 41-72.

Opinion poll. (1985, May). *BBC Spotlight.*

Paletz, D. L., Fozzard, P. A., & Ayanian, J. Z. (1982). The I.R.A., the Red Brigades, and the F.A.L.N. in the "New York Times." *Journal of Communication, 32*(2), 162-171.

Paletz, D. L., Fozzard, P. A., & Ayanian, J. Z. (1983). Terrorism on TV news: The IRA, the FALN, and the Red Brigades. In W. C. Adams (Ed.), *Television coverage of international affairs* (pp. 143-165). Norwood, NJ: Ablex.

Penniman, H. (Ed.). (1979). *Israel at the polls.* Washington, DC: American Enterprise Institute.

Penniman, H. (Ed.). (1985). *Spain at the polls.* Durham, NC: Duke University Press.

Pinard, M., & Hamilton, R. (1977). The independence issue and the polarization of the electorate in the 1973 Quebec election. *Canadian Journal of Political Science, 10,* 215-260.

Porzecanski, A. (1973). *Uruguay's Tupamaros.* New York: Praeger.

Public attitudes to internment. (1974, September 6). *Fortnight.*

Public reaction in N. Ireland to aspects of the prior proposals. (1982, May). *MRBI (Irish Times).*

Radwanski, G. (1971). *No mandate but terror.* Richmond Hill, Ontario: Simon & Schuster.

Rapoport, D. (Ed.). (1988). *Inside terrorist organizations.* New York: Columbia University Press.

Rose, R. (1971). *Governing without consensus.* Boston: Beacon.

Rose, R., McAllister, I., & Mair, P. (1978). *Is there a concurring majority about Northern Ireland?* Glasgow: University of Strathclyde, Centre for the Study of Public Policy.

Sanchez-Gijon, A. (1983). The Spanish press in the transition period. In R. P. Clark (Ed.), *Spain in the 1980's.* New York: Ballinger.

Schmid, A. P., & De Graaf, J. F. A. (1980). *Insurgent terrorism and the Western news media.* Leiden: COMT.

Schmid, A. P., & De Graaf, J. F. A. (1982). *Violence as communication: Insurgent terrorism and the Western news media.* Beverly Hills, CA: Sage.

Segaller, S. (1986). *Invisible armies.* London: Michael Joseph.

Seven out of ten back power sharing. (1974, April 19). *Belfast Telegraph.*

Shadid, M., & Seltzer, R. (1988, Winter). Political attitudes of Palestinians in the West Bank and Gaza Strip. *Middle East Journal,* pp. 16-32.

Silj, A. (1979). *Never again without a rifle.* New York: Karz.

Stohl, M. (1988). *The politics of terrorism.* New York: Marcel Dekker.

Tarrow, S. (1989). *Democracy and disorder.* Oxford: Clarendon.

Weimann, G. (1982). The theater of terror: Effects of press coverage. *Journal of Communication, 33,* 38-45.

Weinberg, L., & Eubank, W. (1987). *The rise and fall of Italian terrorism.* Boulder, CO: Westview.

What the people of Ulster think. (1979, September 6). *New Society.*

What Ulster thinks. (1973, February 19). *Belfast Telegraph.*

# 10

## Victims' Perspectives

Ronald D. Crelinsten

On April 22, 1990, Robert Polhill was released after more than three years of captivity in Beirut, Lebanon. He was the first American hostage released in several years. The next day, I was asked by a Canadian television network, CTV, to appear on their morning news program, *Canada AM*, to talk about the "psychological suffering endured by hostages," particularly after their release. I was to appear with Jeremy Levin, who had been one of the first Americans kidnapped in Lebanon and had escaped almost one year later, in February 1985. The person who invited me to appear was the story editor, and when I asked her how she had come up with the idea, she replied simply, "Curiosity." When she had heard Polhill's frail, hoarse voice during his initial television interview, she had wondered what it would be like for him now that he was free.

Victims of terrorism, like victims of other forms of violence, fascinate us. We wonder how they cope and we wonder how we would cope if we were in their shoes. Political kidnapping has many ramifications, and the release of a hostage in Lebanon could be approached from many potentially fascinating angles. Yet the first question usually concerns the physical and psychological state of the hostage. In a survey of 61 victims of terrorism and their families, Louise Montgomery (1988) found that some victims "survived

208

a harrowing ordeal as hostages, only to be met at the end of a long trip home by demanding, rude journalists inquiring, 'How do you feel?' Of all responses to an open-ended question about how journalists should change the way they cover incidents of international terrorism, the most common was a suggestion that the 'how do you feel?' question be eliminated." The *Canada AM* interview "story" was simply another version of this basic news angle, and the opening moments of the actual interview highlighted this even further.

The first question in the live interview was addressed to Jeremy Levin: "What do you think will be the most difficult part of [Polhill's] transition to being a free man?" Levin replied:

> Deciding how much time he wants to spend explaining what happened to him over the next two or three weeks to the public via television. . . . there'll be a tremendous amount of demand for him to be on the air almost all the time and pacing himself I think is extremely important. Most hostages in recent years have gone through that.

When I, in turn, was asked what kinds of problems ex-hostages encounter after their release, I underscored Levin's remarks by speaking of the "double victimization" that victims of terrorism and other forms of violence suffer, once at the hands of their attackers and then at the hands of the media and those who are curious to know "how they feel."

Families and friends can experience the same kind of thing, whether or not the case specifically involves terrorism. Several days after the massacre of 14 women at a school of engineering in Montreal in December 1989, "escaping from journalists [had] become a prime concern of many students of the school" (Aubin, 1989, p. A2). One psychologist noted that "many feel dispossessed of their own life and alienated by the intense public probing of their sentiments and emotions" (p. A2). While many celebrities and public figures can become used to this intense scrutiny even in times of personal tragedy, this is not always the case. When Andrei Sakharov died in December 1989, crowds gathered outside his Moscow apartment. According to one news report:

> Sakharov's widow, Yelena Bonner, suddenly stepped outside . . . and glared teary-eyed at waiting journalists. "You worked hard to see that Andrei died sooner by calling us from morning to night, and never leaving us to our life and work," she shouted. "Be human beings. Leave us." (Pinder, 1989, p. 8)

Yet not all victims of terrorism resent this media attention, and even the sample of respondents surveyed by Montgomery (1988), by an overwhelming majority, "said they would be interviewed again if they were in a newsworthy event" (p. 1). The *Canada AM* interview with Jerry Levin highlighted this as well when he was asked: "How did you cope with that barrage of attention? Did you feel like you wanted to tell your story or did you feel like you just wanted to be left alone?" Levin replied at some length:

> In my case I felt an obligation to try and tell as much as I knew for as long as people wanted to hear about it. For this reason: I was the first in and I was the first out. There was a tremendous mystery concerning what was happening to Americans who were disappearing in Lebanon and I knew things that the American public didn't know and one thing that I knew when I got back was that *the story had been deliberately downplayed by our own people for reasons with which I didn't agree and I felt that that was inimical to the survival of the hostages.* And so I felt a very compelling desire to . . . and a duty . . . to try to inform the American people and give them as much an idea what was going on and why as I possibly could because *I felt that an informed public would be one of the most important measures needed in order to get those hostages out.* And in view of Iran-Contra and some of the other stupid scandals that erupted after I got home I think I was right. So mine was perhaps a special case. I just simply had to do it. (emphasis added)

Clearly, the annoyance of intense media scrutiny was worth it to counter what Levin correctly saw as a deliberate attempt by the U.S. government to play down the hostages in Lebanon. Five years previously, during the 1985 TWA hostage crisis, in which the TWA hostages received saturation coverage, it was Levin who countered criticisms that television coverage had prolonged the crisis by pointing out "that the longest-running hostage crisis was the least covered crisis—the Americans who had disappeared almost without a trace from the streets of Beirut" (Martin & Walcott, 1988, p. 191).

This ambivalent attitude toward the media was also experienced by families of the TWA hostages, who "resented the intrusions but welcomed the coverage which made it impossible for the White House to ignore the hostages' plight" (Martin & Walcott, 1988, p. 192). In fact, it was the families of the "forgotten hostages" referred to by Levin, and so dubbed by the media, who managed briefly, via intense lobbying and emotional meetings with government leaders, to have them included in U.S. negotiations for the release of the TWA hostages: "Almost from the beginning of the crisis, relatives of the seven [forgotten hostages] had been clamoring for equal time" (p. 197). David C. Martin and John Walcott (1988), in their detailed account of the Reagan administration's struggle to combat international terrorism, make a convincing case that it was "the emergence of the seven from the limbo to which the administration had so assiduously assigned them [that] would prove to be one of the more lasting effects of the TWA hijacking" (p. 197). In other words, the increasing frustration and impotence about the hostages in Lebanon, coupled with the intense emotional pressure placed on the administration by the hostage families, led Oliver North and John Poindexter to embark on arms deals with Iran in an attempt to get the hostages out of Lebanon and free President Reagan from the emotional strain created by the hostages' plight.

> The pressure to do something—anything—to end the cruel drama of Americans held hostage overwhelmed the defiant, never-again policy of the Reagan administration as surely as it had the sweet reason of the Carter administration. . . . The Reagan administration was, if anything, even more vulnerable than its predecessor to the violence and theater of terrorism. Reagan played to emotion, not intellect, and the terrorists beat him at his own game. . . . *Magnified by television*, the drama of lives in the balance made people—President Reagan, in particular—feel more strongly about terrorism than they did about other pressing issues. *It was easy to confuse the emotional intensity of terrorism with its significance.* (Martin & Walcott, 1988, p. 364; emphasis added)

Clearly, the media can play a major role in the complex communication process that underlies terrorism. It was Alex Schmid and Janny De Graaf (1982) who first showed systematically how the media use terrorists and their terrorism as much as terrorists use the media. Governments and crisis managers also use the media as much as the terrorists do, and the media are often caught between the two (Crelinsten, 1989). What becomes clear from the preceding discussion is that hostages and their families can also make use of the media and, in doing so, have participated in and contributed to the three-way communication process connecting terrorists to governments via the media. In his congressional testimony concerning media coverage of the TWA hostage crisis in July of 1985, Fred W. Friendly of the Columbia Graduate School of Journalism highlighted the conflict between media and government:

> The press . . . is in the human interest business, and the Government, particularly the President, is in the national interest business. When these two powerful forces collide, the results can be dangerous, sometimes even bizarre. (U.S. House of Representatives, 1985, p. 10)

In his own description of the TWA hostage crisis, Alex Schmid (1989) extends this even further:

> The media were not just neutral observers but simply *one of the four principal actors in a co-production*. Each principal actor was in a different "business": the terrorists in the blackmail business, the hostages in the survival business, the media in the human interest business, and the American President in the national security business. (p. 553; emphasis added)

This chapter will demonstrate how the victims of terrorism and their families try to further their own particular business of survival or getting on with their lives even as terrorists, governments, and the media make use of these same victims to further their own particular business.

## The Nature of Terrorist Victimization

Terrorism is the combined threat and use of violence, planned in secret and executed without warning, that is directed against one set of targets (the direct victims) in order to coerce compliance or to compel allegiance from a second set of targets (targets of demands) and to intimidate or to impress a wider audience (target of terror or target of attention). The act of victimizing captures the attention of particular audiences and allows the terrorist to communicate more specific messages tailored to each one. As Alex Schmid points out in his most recent definition of terrorism, this could entail intimidation for a target of terror, coercion for a target of specific demands, or propaganda for a target of attention (Schmid, Jongman, et al., 1988, p. 28). A fourth message could be compelling allegiance from supporters (targets of demands) or impressing sympathizers (targets of attention). Here, the victimization serves to show supporters or sympathizers that the terrorist is a powerful and effective actor in the political struggle.

In all these cases, the victim of terrorism functions as a message generator. It was Schmid and De Graaf (1982) who first used this term in describing the victims of the 1972 Lydda Airport massacre: "The Japanese terrorists had no relation whatsoever with the victims who only served as message generators" (p. 29). Schmid et al. incorporated the term into their 1988 definition of terrorism: "The immediate human victims of violence . . . serve as message generators" (p. 28). In terrorism, the use of threat and violence against victims—the kidnappings, the bombings, the assassinations, the killings—

serves to transmit specific demands to certain targets and different messages to other targets. The particular message and the particular audience to which that message is addressed will depend on the nature of the victim. Terrorist victimization can have one of three different communicative functions, alone or in combination. The first is an attention-getting function. Here the selection of victims is designed to shock: the innocent civilian, the tourist, the noncombatant. These "targets of opportunity" (Schmid et al., 1988, p. 28) are usually selected at random, and it is the haphazard nature of their victimization and their lack of any kind of affiliation with parties to the conflict that maximize the horror of the message conveyed. This is propaganda of the deed in its purest form, or what has been called the politics of atrocity (Rapoport, 1977). Such victimization is most commonly used to capture mass targets of attention and to create targets of terror within as wide a population as possible—for instance, among tourists, international travelers, average citizens of a particular nation, or nationals of a particular country living abroad.

The second function of terrorist victimization is symbolic. Here the selection of victims is designed to instruct or to warn. Victims who, because of their profession, political affiliation, or ethnic identity, belong to a specific, identifiable population are selected because they represent that population. Here, the victimization instructs targets of attention about the status of such representatives and the populations they represent, implying that they have done something to deserve being targeted. For those who identify with the victim because of something the two hold in common, the function of victimization is to warn them that they might be next. This can create targets of terror among particular populations, such as those whose careers identify them with the targets of violence (e.g., diplomats, businessmen, military personnel, state officials, criminal justice officials, journalists, human rights activists).

The third function of terrorist victimization is an instrumental one. Targets of terror, those who identify most strongly with the victims, can be intimidated into weakening their professional allegiance or their commitment to their jobs. Targeting military personnel, peacekeepers, government leaders, or businessmen can have the effect of deterring others from assuming such positions or from cooperating with the institutions that employ them. Tourists can be scared away from certain regions, air travelers from certain airlines or national carriers. The IRA has tried to deter people from doing business with the British Army by victimizing individuals who sell meat or who provide laundry services or other such everyday services to British soldiers. Certain victims can be selected merely to eliminate them, as in some political assassinations. This is clearly instrumental; however, it is not terroristic unless it is intended to intimidate or deter others. The victimization must be designed to generate messages to others about the possibility of future victimization, or it is not terrorism. Victims can also be selected in order to exert pressure on governments to yield to specific demands. Here the instrumental function is a coercive one similar in many respects to blackmail. Kidnapping and hostage taking are the most common tactics. Kidnapping can be most easily distinguished from hostage taking in terms of the site of sequestration. In kidnapping, the site is usually unknown; in hostage taking it is usually known. For this reason, hostage takings are often called hostage sieges. Skyjackings and seizures of other transport vehicles, such as trains and cruise ships, are merely variations on hostage taking. Clearly, the identity of the victim is important in such cases in the sense that no coercion is possible if the target of demands has no interest in saving the victim.

In sum, then, it is the identity of the victims (targets) and the manner in which they are victimized (tactics) that determine whether the terrorist will be able to generate any messages at all and, if so, what particular messages he or she will be able to convey to what particular audiences.

## Media Coverage of Terrorist Victimization

### IMPACT ON TERRORIST GOALS

Given that terrorist victimization constitutes the central element in a strategy of political communication, it is clear that media coverage of victimization can aid in the generation of messages from terrorists to their various target audiences. One way this could be accomplished is by accentuating the kinds of identification processes inherent in the terrorist's creation of audiences by means of victimization.

> Much of the power of the terrorist statement lies in its symbolic aspects. Often unknown by their killers, the terrorist victims are meant to symbolically represent a nation, a religion, an institution. The terror—as opposed to disgust over the slaughter, or grief over the loss—resides in the personal realization that the victim is a symbol of the self as member of a nation or institution. Only coincidence, fate, timing, or happenstance places that particular member in the hands of the terrorist at that time. It could have been my-self [sic], the symbol says. (Lule, 1987, p. 13)

By focusing on the victims of terrorism, the media can facilitate the process of fear generation and its transmission to targets of terror who identify with the victim. By treating the subject of victimization in a dramatic or sensationalistic way, media coverage can also create wider audiences (targets of attention) than the terrorist might otherwise have been able to achieve merely through the medium of rumor, gossip, and word of mouth. Finally, by emphasizing the fact that the victim could have been anyone, media coverage can reinforce and amplify the symbolic function of terrorist victimization, the terrorist's invitation to identify with the victim (Lule, 1988, pp. 28-29; Schmid, 1989, p. 545). By inviting the media consumer to identify with the victim and to participate in the tragedy, the media thereby allow "real communication between the terrorist and his audience" (Lule, 1988, p. 29).

IMPACT ON GOVERNMENT GOALS

By stimulating and exacerbating public reaction to victim suffering and family tragedy, it is clear that media coverage can also increase pressure on targets of demands. This can seriously limit the range of options open to crisis managers and policymakers, as it did in both the Iranian hostage crisis of 1979-1980 and the TWA hostage crisis of 1985. Martin and Walcott (1988) describe how this happened in the latter case, after some of the airplane passengers had been released by their captors: "Once the television networks reached the passengers who had been released and the relatives of those still being held, the administration's no-concessions stance began drowning in a wave of human emotion" (p. 188).

The media's exclusive focus on the plight of the victims precluded any balance between the short-term needs of the hostages and long-term policy concerns. The impact on decision making was such that decisions concerning media-driven issues—namely, the fate of the hostages— were accelerated at the expense of those issues ignored by the media. *Time* correspondent Peter Stoler (1986) makes a similar point in discussing the effects of television coverage of the hostages and their families:

> The effect of this attention was obvious; it personalized the hostages and their families and turned them from mere names to people with real families who were suffering real emotional crises. But the attention may not have helped the Administration in its efforts to attain their freedom, for the coverage tended to make the hostages' safety the major, if not the only consideration, and effectively forced the Administration, to the extent that it had ever thought

seriously of doing so, to drop any idea of using force to free the captive Americans. (pp. 110-111)

On the other hand, media coverage of victimization can also work to the advantage of governments and crisis managers. For example, media focus on the victims and their suffering can aid in official attempts to depict the terrorist as criminal: The politics of atrocity becomes the atrocity of crime. When media reports accentuate the violence and destruction of terrorist acts, the innocence of their victims, and the human suffering of the victims' families, they draw attention to the extranormality of terrorism. The victim is a means to an end, a mere vehicle for generating messages to other targets and audiences. The medium for transmitting those messages is the victimization of innocents, noncombatants or symbolic targets who usually have no control over whether they are victimized or not. But for the government, the medium *is* the message and that message is that the terrorist is a violent criminal. The criminalization of the terrorist functions, in turn, to depoliticize his or her actions: This is an ordinary criminal, a kidnapper or a murderer, not a politically motivated one. This, in turn, contributes ultimately to the terrorist's delegitimation.

As long as the media play up the violence and the victimization of innocents at the expense of explaining the political goals of the terrorist and the context in which the terrorism first arose, this depoliticization process is enormously facilitated. Media coverage tends, on the whole, to depict terrorists and their actions in such a manner as to contribute to their delegitimation. By contrast, actions of the authorities tend to be legitimated (Crelinsten, 1987; see also Kelly & Mitchell, 1981; Knight & Dean, 1982; Paletz, Fozzard, & Ayanian, 1982, 1983). Furthermore, government spokespersons tend to be favored sources for information about terrorist incidents, and this further reinforces official perceptions (Crelinsten, 1989). Robert G. Picard and Paul D. Adams (1988) have shown, for example, that government sources tend to use judgmental, inflammatory, or sensationalistic terms to describe terrorist actors and acts, while media personnel and witnesses use more neutral vocabulary. The most prevalent characterization of terrorist acts used by government sources was "criminal" (Picard & Adams, 1988, p. 6). By relying on government sources to set the frame of discourse about terrorism, the media facilitate the depoliticization of the terrorist via the criminalization of his or her image. The primary means of achieving this is to focus on victimization.

IMPACT ON VICTIMS AND THEIR FAMILIES

The most obvious and unfortunate impacts of intense media focus on victims and their families are invasion of their privacy, intrusion into their personal tragedies, and exponential increases in their pain and suffering caused by the repulsive voyeurism that drives the worst media excesses. I have referred previously to this as double victimization: once at the hands of the perpetrator of violence, terrorist or otherwise, and a second time at the hands of the media. Here, for example, is one description of the media coverage of the December 1989 massacre of 14 women in Montreal, written by a well-respected editorialist and columnist:

> There was, ad nauseam, the same gruesome clip of a young woman who had bled to death on a cafeteria table, and the stolen glimpse of a corpse visible from the door of a makeshift morgue on campus. There was, during the days after, the savage hunt for gossip from neighbors and friends, and the ravaged faces of mourners. There was the wolf pack in front of the killer's apartment, and that of his mother. She had to go into hiding, and her private life was reported in minute details taken from divorce papers. (Bissonnette, 1989)

Some are able to withstand this "savage hunt" for news about the victims; others are not. In an article that provided brief descriptions of some of the Montreal victims, information on the victims was gleaned from interviews with family, friends, neighbors, and, in one case, a victim's employer. One brief description (three sentences) stated that "her parents . . . did not want to talk with a reporter. Across the street, a neighbor said Anne-Marie was a 'really sweet kid' " (Harris & Heinrich, 1989). In this case, when relatives of the victim refused an interview, the reporters went to a neighbor.

Reading between the lines of some of the media reports of the impending or actual release of American hostages in Lebanon during the spring and summer of 1990, one can glean hints of the same intense scrutiny and its effect on the victims and families. One report on the release of Frank Reed on April 30, 1990, cites his wife shouting, " 'He's out! He's out!' . . . amid a throng of camera crews and reporters who had transformed her mother-in-law's small apartment into a live TV studio" (Stecklow, 1990). In its August 1989 coverage of the supposed murder of American hostage Lieutenant Colonel William Higgins and the threat to execute another hostage, Joseph Cicippio, suspended after three tense days, *Maclean's*, Canada's national newsmagazine, centered one of its cover stories on Cicippio's family. One of his six brothers, Thomas, was the focus of the article, titled "One Family's

Agony: The Cicippio Family Waits and Hopes." In reading the article, we find that "more than 100 journalists and television technicians from U.S. and foreign news organizations waited outside" his home in Norristown, Pennsylvania, and that "the drama attracted reporters from across the United States and from Canada and Germany." Cicippio is quoted as saying that these reporters "were all trying to interview me at the same time." In reporting its own interview, the magazine duly notes that Cicippio "tearfully told *Maclean's* that he looked up to Joseph," indicating in a rather offhand way how emotional such interviews can be for family members ("One Family's Agony," 1989, p. 24). It is interesting to note that, when Lieutenant Colonel Higgins was first abducted, the media were frantically looking for pictures of his wife, who worked in the Office of Public Affairs in the Pentagon. Knowing that it could not prevent the media from taking her picture, the Pentagon arranged for a photo opportunity, notifying the media when she would be leaving her home. Approximately 10 camera crews arrived at the designated time, took her picture, and refrained from asking questions (Martin & Draznin, 1988, p. 14).

In her survey of victim attitudes toward media coverage of terrorism, Montgomery (1988) lists pushiness and failure to respect the privacy of families as examples of unprofessional conduct. Sensationalism, "being more interested in tears and grief than in the substance of the story," and posing as family members to get into the home were other examples. While local newspaper and radio reporters were singled out for being unprepared and not knowing the stories they were reporting, television reporters were singled out for their obtrusiveness. Some respondents complained that reporters arrived with preconceived notions of what the interviewee would say and did not listen to the answers actually given. Two respondents actually reported being punished by reporters because the victim refused to be interviewed: "In one case, the reporter refused to give the family copies of a picture, and in another, the reporter refused to provide a copy of the newspaper story, explaining that she would have if the victim had cooperated by being interviewed" (p. 4).

Not all media personnel are comfortable with the intrusive aspect of reporting on victimization, terrorist or otherwise. One story editor who was involved in covering the 1989 Montreal massacre for CTV, the only privately owned national television network in Canada, told me in a telephone interview that "you really begin to hate yourself" for prying into people's personal tragedies (I. Colabresi, personal communication, April 23, 1990). While she was ordered to get interviews with people who knew the victims, she decided simply to pass out notes to victims' friends, leaving a number where she could be reached if anyone wanted to speak with her. In this way, she felt she fulfilled her assignment to get information while respecting the rights of potential interviewees. She did get several interviews in this way. In another case, a Canadian woman and her child were killed during a skyjacking in Malta in November 1985. When the husband returned to Canada, he was met at the airport by a "milling crowd of reporters, photographers and TV cameramen," and he told them that they were not invited to the funeral. "He prompted soul-searching in the newsrooms as editors weighed the news value of the event . . . against the human grief and pain involved" ("Media Split," 1985).

The Canadian Press (CP) conducted an informal survey of news organizations and found that most decided not to cover the funeral. CP and its subsidiary, Broadcast News, which serves radio, television, and cable TV outlets across Canada, both decided not to cover the funeral, although CP decided to distribute reports provided by two local newspapers that decided to cover the event. One of those papers decided to cover the funeral because it was to be attended by a high government official, the minister of external affairs. The paper's editor claimed in an interview that the focus of coverage would be the minister's attendance, not the family's grief. The other paper decided to cover the event because, according to the associate editor, it showed how "terrorism has come home to us in a real way" ("Media Split," 1985). The editor also insisted that the family would not be involved. Here we see how a focus on victimization is justified by what Johan Galtung and Mari Ruge (1965) call "cultural proximity," that which is familiar or culturally similar (it *can* happen here), rather than what they call "personification," whereby the news report focuses on specific persons. One local television station decided not to cover the funeral because of the number of letters and phone calls it received criticizing the station for publicizing the family's grief and asking it "to lay off" ("Media Split," 1985).

While the intense scrutiny of media coverage can seem intrusive, invasive, and offensive to some people, it can also be perceived in a more positive light, sometimes even by the same people who resent it. As we saw with the victims and family members surveyed by Montgomery (1988), the same people who complained that the media never left them alone also said they would be interviewed again if a new incident occurred, and some had praise for specific journalists with whom they had interacted (p. 1). Among the positive behaviors described by Montgomery's respondents were sensitivity to families' anxieties and willingness to provide information that the families could not obtain from other sources, particularly the government. In the United States, at least, media coverage and direct contact from media personnel have constituted a primary source of information about victimized relatives. Thomas Cicippio first heard of the death threat against his brother Joseph when a reporter telephoned him ("One Family's Agony," 1989, p. 24). Mrs. Kelly Cullins, wife of one of the TWA hostages, testified before a congressional committee that "it was terrifying to see my husband on television, but it allowed me to know that he was alive, and it allowed him the opportunity to show his family that he was alive" (U.S. House of Representatives, 1985, p. 68). Referring to the press conference in Lebanon that the Shi'ite militia gave with some of the TWA hostages, where reporters pushed and shoved to get a better view, Jerry Levin, whose captivity never received much coverage, stated:

> Margaret Thatcher, Ed Meese, Henry Kissinger and some men and women in the street notwithstanding, I'd rather take my chances with a little pushing and shoving at a news conference staged by my captors than have no coverage at all. I would have given anything to have had that kind of contact, as manipulative as it was, with my wife and family; and I know that most of the other families would have settled for that kind of visual assurance that their loved ones were relatively okay. (U.S. House of Representatives, 1985, p. 65)

This is exactly what Bill Barnett felt when he and his wife saw their 15-year-old son, Alan, among the British children shown on Iraqi television with President Saddam Hussein about a week after the Iraqi invasion of Kuwait in August 1990. The younger Barnett had been among the hundreds of Britons taken off a British Airways flight when it made a scheduled stop in Kuwait on the night of the invasion.

> "We had no news for a week—and there he was in front of us," said Mr. Barnett. "We were just so happy to see him looking so well and fit. For us it was good to see him there."
> "We are obviously still very concerned and anxious, but nevertheless it was a relief in many ways to see him." (Boseley, 1990, p. 1)

As manipulative as the television appearance was from Saddam Hussein's point of view, and as revolting as it was for the Western world to see children used in this way, for the parents of one child at least, and no doubt the others as well, there was some measure of relief at seeing their child alive—the visual assurance that Levin spoke of five years earlier.

This is what makes the tactic of disappearances so terrible for the relatives and friends of the victims. Much as it would be wonderful to have visual assurance that their loved ones are alive and "relatively okay," it would also be some measure of relief if they could at least have some visual assurance that they are dead. Because such assurance is never received, the relatives and friends of such victims never know for sure one way or the other, sometimes holding out hope even in the face of almost certain knowledge ("almost" because of the lack of visual assurance) that the victim is dead.

Perceptions that the media and not the government were the ones that took the time to inform relatives of the fate of their loved ones was particularly strong in the early years of the Lebanese hostage situation, around 1985. Peggy Say, sister of Terry Anderson and a central figure in the hostage family network that has developed in the United States since then, received a call at four in the morning from her brother's employer, the Associated Press, informing her of his kidnapping. During her congressional testimony in 1985, she criticized the government, particularly the State Department, for not being there and leaving a gap that the media filled: "Immediately the media was there. It was a chance to talk about what was happening, and a friendliness and feeling that somebody was there to reach out and touch. There was nobody else there for us" (U.S. House of Representatives, 1985, p. 66). One of the TWA hostages later described how his brother got no information from the State Department but constantly received phone calls from CBS informing him of any new developments, particularly about his brother (Martin & Walcott, 1988, p. 191).

In her congressional testimony, Mrs. Cullins, another relative of a TWA hostage, called this attention from the media "handholding":

> When your Government isolates you as a family victim of terrorism, when they do not give you timely and accurate information for whatever reasons, it leaves a vacuum that does get filled by someone else. In this country, it ends up being the media. They were handholding us. We had various people who called from various networks and said we can help you out this way. They gave us information. They even made arrangements for us to fly to Germany [when the TWA hostages were released]. Our Government did not do those kinds of things. (U.S. House of Representatives, 1985, p. 67)

What Mrs. Cullins does not say, of course, is that the media had their own reasons for providing such help. By offering to fly family members to Germany, the networks could then stage reunion scenes for their audiences. In some cases, such scenes were reenacted for successive networks and presented as spontaneous events (Martin & Walcott, 1988, pp. 190-191; Schmid, 1989, p. 550). Martin and Walcott (1988) capture the trade-off of interests well:

The public wanted to know where the hostages were and how their families were bearing up, and the networks told them. Sometimes, however, news of the hostages was manufactured. . . . But mostly television dispensed information to all the different parties to the hijacking. (pp. 190-191)

Clearly, for relatives and friends of victims of terrorism and other forms of violence, information about their loved ones and about what their governments are doing about them is paramount. For the media, interviews with family and friends at a time when personal tragedy takes on the dimensions of public crisis can be highly valued, a prized commodity to be shared. The passing on of interviewees to successive networks appears to be a rather common way of obtaining interviews: In the wake of the massacre of 14 women in Montreal in December 1989, one friend of several of the victims was first interviewed by a Canadian network, CTV, for its morning show, *Canada AM*. Other media personnel were watching and, impressed by the young man's performance, a major American network interviewed him immediately after he completed the first interview (I. Colabresi, personal communication, April 23, 1990).

Calvin Frederick (1987), a psychiatric expert in treating psychic trauma, underscores the importance of ventilating feelings for victims of terrorism and violent crime. He also points out that family members of hostages are often covictims, experiencing similar reactions to stress, threats, and rumors as the hostages themselves, as well as comparable cycles of denial, bargaining, anger, and depression that are typical of victims of violence. It is clear that, despite some of the worst excesses of media intrusion into personal tragedies, media attention, even in its most manipulative form, can perform a therapeutic function for individuals undergoing psychic shock and trauma. It should therefore not be surprising that many distraught relatives will cooperate with reporters who camp out on their doorsteps and ply them with favors, even to the point of divulging information that could prove harmful to their victimized kin if their captors were ever to learn of it. In his interview with *Maclean's*, Thomas Cicippio stated that the intense media attention during the week in which a death threat hung over his brother helped distract him from the horror of the terrorists' intentions. This is why the network of ex-hostages and family members has stressed the importance of government involvement with family members, so as to preclude the need of relatives to turn to the media for such psychological support.

On the other side of the coin, however, media coverage of events in which people are being victimized can create intense shock and trauma in relatives and friends of the victims who helplessly watch as their loved ones suffer and die. A recent court case in England awarded damages to relatives of people who were crushed to death during a soccer match because of the psychological suffering they experienced while watching television coverage of the event (Alex Schmid, personal communication).

## The Birth, Rise, and Co-optation
## of a Hostage Family Network

The perception among the relatives of the forgotten American hostages in Lebanon that it was the media and not the government that were providing them information about their loved ones was exacerbated by the continued refusal of high government officials and politicians to meet with the hostage families. This refusal was a reflection of the administration's desire to downplay the hostages in Lebanon to prevent what happened to President Carter during the Iran hostage crisis. Individual families would pressure individual officials, but no concerted, organized effort was made throughout most of 1985.

In his testimony to a congressional committee looking into media coverage of the TWA crisis, Jerry Levin, who was the first American kidnapped in Lebanon, recounted how his wife went public about his kidnapping after official silence prevailed for seven months:

> The network [of hostage families and friends] did not exist until Sis [Levin's wife] broke with the Government, press and family advisers and went public 7 hard months after my capture. She found a home on Today, Good Morning America, CBS Morning News, USA Today, the New York Times, the Detroit Free Press, and the Birmingham News. That was about it. But once hearing, seeing or reading Sis' appeals, the families quickly made contact and found that they had more than hostages in common. For one thing, they had been discouraged by the Government from contacting each other. The families had also been advised by the Government not to seek each other out and not to speak out, and it failed to even give periodic updates on the situation to hostage families. (U.S. House of Representatives, 1985, p. 52)

Levin's wife even flew to Damascus in November 1984 to make a public appeal for "peaceful, unthreatening dialog and negotiations" (U.S. House of Representatives, 1985, p. 54) that was carried in the Arab and American press, resulting in a response from the Syrian foreign minister and, Levin claims, better treatment from his captors.

This official silence on the part of the U.S. government led to the development by hostages' friends and relatives of networks and lobbies that would often turn to the media, or threaten to do so, if the government was perceived to be holding back on information or not doing enough to gain their loved ones' release. But in those early years, the threat of a press conference was not always sufficient to trigger a meeting with government officials. Nevertheless, there were occasional successes. For example, the wife of one hostage, Benjamin Weir (since released), organized a press conference in March of 1985 to call publicly for negotiations with the Shi'ites in Lebanon. Only then did Secretary of State George Shultz agree to meet with her. The meeting did not go well, however. Mrs. Weir suggested that the government negotiate, while Mr. Shultz reiterated the administration's no-concessions policy (Martin & Walcott, 1988, p. 221). Despite the standoff, the successful use of the media and its attendant publicity in putting pressure on the government at least to pay attention foreshadowed the development of a formidable lobbying tactic.

This period can be characterized as a power struggle between hostage family interests and government and diplomatic interests, during which the media became the vehicle for increasing pressure on government. As the hostage families began to contact one another and share their experiences, they began to demand to be heard by government officials in the White House and in Congress. When rebuffed, they often turned to the media, calling press conferences to air their grievances. According to Levin, the relatives of Father Martin Jenco (since released) organized a congressional blitz to get attention. At first, the government refused to corroborate what the hostage families were telling the media, and so the impact of the families' revelations was fleeting (U.S. House of Representatives, 1985, p. 52).

The TWA crisis changed everything. The media devoted intense coverage to the TWA victims and their families, and the president even met with some of the families. By contrast, according to Jerry Levin's congressional testimony, "both the wife and son of the Reverend Benjamin Weir, and Mrs. Anderson have been rebuffed up to this day [July 30, 1985] in their attempts to see him" (U.S. House of Representatives, 1985, p. 59). When the family of Father Jenco learned that President Reagan was planning to meet with relatives of the TWA hostages living in their area (Chicago), they insisted on a meeting of their own and finally got one with the help of their congressman. This was the very first time that the president had met with any relatives of the forgotten hostages (Martin & Walcott, 1988, p. 197). The meeting was traumatic for the president and may have been instrumental in the later insistence of his administration that the seven be included in the final release of the TWA hostages, short-lived as that demand turned out to be.

For Peggy Say, sister of Terry Anderson, the contrast between the official treatment of the TWA hostages and their families and the Lebanon hostages and their families was striking. Until then, she had followed the State Department's guidelines concerning "quiet diplomacy," whereby relatives of hostages were advised that the government was doing everything it could and that media attention would jeopardize such activity. She even received a call on the second day of the hijacking and was told not to link her brother and the other six hostages with the TWA hostages.

> My immediate reaction was panic, and to run then to the media and say do you people realize what is happening, they are holding 47 American hostages and they are not even going to ask for the seven back. The direct media attention and pressure that followed that, I directly attribute the change of heart of the administration to request the return of the seven was due to that entirely [*sic*]. It was certainly not something that they had intended to do. They made that very clear to us by saying do not ask; we are not asking.
>
> To watch the opposite of quiet diplomacy bring 39 men home in 17 days and to be left behind and again be told quiet diplomacy is the answer. We cannot, seven families . . . , we can no longer believe that. We have seven men, the longest of which has been held 500 days. (U.S. House of Representatives, 1985, p. 66)

While the U.S. government did finally link the forgotten seven with the TWA hostages late in the negotiations, the demand was quickly forgotten when the latter were released.

Government officials began to take the plight of the "forgotten hostages" seriously. For one thing, the State Department assigned the liaison officer who was responsible for the families of the TWA hostages to the families of the other hostages in Lebanon. Yet this officer continued to advise the families not to link their loved ones to the TWA hostages, even while the president and the secretary of state were, at least temporarily, doing just that (U.S. House of Representatives, 1985, p. 59). In July of 1985, after the TWA crisis was over, Peggy Say was invited to testify before a congressional committee—along with Jerry Levin, Bruce Laingen (a hostage in Iran), and Mrs. Cullins, the wife of a TWA hostage—to give the perspective of the hostages and their families. We have seen how Ms. Say took the opportunity to recount her frustration at being told to keep quiet and not to go to the media and how she finally went public when she saw the saturation coverage devoted to the TWA hostages, not to mention the Iran hostages five years earlier. Clearly, there was tension between the government and the hostage families during that period. While government wished to downplay the hostages to avoid another "hostage crisis," the families were convinced that publicity would save their loved ones. The same concern on the part of the government about triggering a "hostage crisis" surfaced again, five years later, in the early phase of the Iraqi invasion and annexation of Kuwait, when the U.S. government avoided using the word *hostage* to describe the thousands of Westerners detained in Kuwait and Iraq.

Throughout the fall of 1985, pressure built from an increasingly insistent and unified hostage family lobby. Peggy Say had quit her job to lobby full-time, to meet government officials.

> Slowly, persistently, they worked their way through the bureaucracy from the Lebanon desk and the Consular Affairs Bureau, to Assistant Secretary of State Richard Murphy, to [Secretary of State] George Shultz, to [National Security Adviser] Robert McFarlane, to Vice President Bush. By the end of 1985, there was no one left to hear their pleas but Ronald Reagan. (Martin & Walcott, 1988, p. 329)

It was in October that they finally met the president. According to Martin and Walcott, "the President was shaken by the encounter" (p. 330). Throughout 1986, as the secret arms deals with Iran continued, the threat of a press conference by one or another of the hostage families was a constant source of pressure on the U.S. administration. We have already seen how this relentless pressure was an important factor fueling the Iran arms-for-hostages deal. The irony is that, by the end of 1986, the number of American hostages in Lebanon had returned to the same level it had been before the secret arms deliveries to Iran began, thanks to three new kidnappings in the fall of 1986. But by then the hostage family lobby was a recognized fact of political life that had to be reckoned with by government officials and politicians. Whenever there was a new development in the status of the hostages in Lebanon, the media would turn to the relatives of the hostages as a matter of course. Now officials and spokespersons from the various hostage family lobbies constitute standard sources for comments and quotable quotes. Lobbying tactics vary widely. For example, the son of one hostage, Frank Reed, who was kidnapped in September of 1986 and released in May of 1990, persuaded his third-grade classmates to write President Bush, asking him to help get his father released (Stecklow, 1990).

Hostage family lobbies exist in other countries as well. For example, the relatives and friends of British television reporter John McCarthy, held hostage in Lebanon since his abduction in April 1986, lobbied the British government intensely and paid for advertisements in newspapers and on television, even in the United States, under the name the Friends of John McCarthy. They formed the group early in 1988 with the express purpose of keeping his name in the news, staging demonstrations as well as placing messages to him in Beirut newspapers ("I Want to Do Everything," 1991). When Brian Keenan, a Protestant from Belfast with dual British and Irish citizenship, was released on August 25, 1990, the Friends of John McCarthy expressed bitterness that quiet diplomacy by the Irish government had paid off while "the British government is now the only government that has not been able to get a hostage out" (Mitchison, 1990). Keenan was kidnapped six days before McCarthy, and the two were held together for their entire captivity, until Keenan's release. Keenan's two sisters had worked intensively to gain their brother's release, organizing rallies, raising funds, and lobbying the foreign ministry in Dublin. McCarthy himself was finally released almost exactly one year later, on August 9, 1991, the first Western hostage to be freed since the end of the Gulf War.

Since the more troubled period of the mid-1980s, the U.S. government has taken steps to help the hostage family network cope with their trauma. In 1989, for example, it designated Terry Anderson's birthday, October 27, as National Hostage Awareness Day in recognition of Anderson's symbolic status as the longest-held hostage. Kidnapped on March 16, 1985, Terry Anderson has finally been released. Indeed by the end of September 1991, it was widely rumored and believed that all Western hostages would be freed by January 1992. On the fifth anniversary of Anderson's abduction a special ceremony was held in Washington, on the grounds of the White House, that was attended by several dozen relatives of hostages as well as representatives from the U.S. Congress, the State Department, the U.S. armed services, and the media. Just before the ceremony, Peggy Say had a private meeting with President George Bush to discuss the current round of rumors concerning the imminent release of hostages. During that same period, the State Department kept in regular contact with relatives to discuss the many reports and rumors that were circulating (Ayres, 1990).

A flurry of media coverage surrounding the White House ceremony included an interview in the *New York Times* with Thomas Cicippio, who was the focus of so much media attention some seven months previously. The opening line of the article read: "Thomas Cicippio feels like a hostage, too" (Ayres, 1990). Here we see how certain hostage relatives can become media personalities in their own right. From the media's perspective, they probably constitute reliable sources who provide the necessary human interest and personification. From the relatives' perspective, cooperating with the media provides them with an outlet for ventilating their feelings and sharing their trauma with a sympathetic audience (both reporter and the wider consumer audience).

Several days before the Terry Anderson ceremony, another hostage relative also sought out the media, this time to complain that her husband, Lieutenant Colonel William Higgins, was the forgotten "ninth man"—in March 1990, eight Americans were then held hostage in Lebanon—since his death, announced seven months before, had never been officially confirmed. Like relatives of the disappeared, Mrs. Higgins very likely still held out hope because she had never received convincing visual confirmation of his murder. The video purported to be of her husband swinging from a rope that was released by his captors in July 1989 was of such poor quality that a desperately hopeful spouse could understandably wish for more reliable confirmation before giving up completely and accepting the worst, despite the fact that it was widely acknowledged in official circles that he had indeed been murdered. The same person who had been protected from media questioning when her husband was first kidnapped now sought out an interview to vent her feelings of loss and despair: "It's discouraging to see that the media and the American people have, perhaps, given up on Rich [her husband's nickname]" (Sisk, 1990). However, she expressly refused to criticize the government. Here is yet another example of the media serving as a vehicle for ventilating emotions and seeking the kind of hand-holding and moral support that was lacking to the families of the Lebanon hostages before the TWA hijacking and the development of the hostage family network. By 1990, for that network of families at least, if not Mrs. Higgins, government and victim goals had coalesced and media coverage became a vehicle for the public ritualization of private grief.

The contrast between 1985 and 1990 is striking. By 1990, the hostility and tension between hostage families and government officials was ostensibly gone, as evidenced by the White House ceremony that commemorated Terry Anderson's fifth anniversary of captivity with the participation of hostage families, government officials, and the media. What is more, there was no sign of complaints by hostage families about government indifference or insensitivity. At the ceremony, Peggy Say reported on her private meeting with the president:

She said that the President was doing everything possible to speed freedom for the captives, but that he could offer little more at this point than "faith" that he would achieve his goal. The families clapped loudly when Ms. Say finished her report, apparently satisfied that all was being done that could be done. (Ayres, 1990)

It would appear that the hostage family lobby had finally been co-opted into the government policy of quiet diplomacy and not making any waves, whether because they had exhausted all alternatives, playing the media card to its logical conclusion, or because the media had begun to lose interest in playing the hostage family angle to the hilt, or for some other reason. Having received adequate hand-holding and feeling that the government now cared, the hostage families could allow events to take their course, riding the roller coaster of their emotions and sharing the peaks and valleys with the larger public through television, magazine, and newspaper coverage. Public officials could express their concern, meet with family members, attend the public rituals, and, through photo opportunities and media coverage, show their constituents that they cared and were doing all they could. For the media, the absence of visuals engendered by the kind of kidnappings involved in the Lebanese hostage takings was compensated for by the creation of public events that provided their own visuals and by the dramatic playing out over time of rumors about impending releases and letdowns of repeated disappointments.

Of course, when hostages finally began to be released several months later, the focus of coverage immediately narrowed to the released hostages themselves, beginning with the release of Robert Polhill on April 22, 1990. Predictably, Polhill himself became a favored source when, in August 1991, Briton John McCarthy and American Edward Tracy were freed. Like former hostage Jerry Levin, who was asked in 1990 to comment on Polhill's release, Polhill, cast by the media as former hostage in August 1991, was asked to comment on the newly released hostages. Like Levin, Polhill emphasized how dealing with the media would be a major concern. Indeed, when McCarthy was released, London, in particular, went wild:

In Britain, word of Mr. McCarthy's release thrilled friends and family—even strangers. Church bells rang out across London to celebrate the release and passengers on the London subway cheered when the news came over loudspeakers. ("I Want to Do Everything," 1991)

With his release, the hostage story was again front-page news and cover story in magazines (e.g., "A Game of Chances," 1991). One television interview with members of McCarthy's family revealed that correspondence from well-wishers around the world had quite overwhelmed them. After a heady trip to the United Nations to deliver a message from his captors to Secretary-General Javier Pérez de Cuéllar, McCarthy disappeared from the media limelight, apparently by choice.

The next hostage to be released, Edward Tracy, posed special problems for the media. Described by Syrian officials as "sick, disoriented and confused" when he was released on August 11 (Hedges, 1991), Tracy was a loner who had left his home in Vermont in 1958, had divorced his wife in 1974, and had not seen his mother in more than 20 years. This last fact about Tracy was revealed by his mother, now 83 years old, in a television interview shortly after his release, when she was asked if he would be coming home to see her. She replied that she had no idea if he would even want to see her, given such a prolonged absence. Nevertheless, a small article in the *New York Times* coverage of Tracy's release was headed "Mother Is Delighted" (1991) and reported that President George Bush had called Mrs. Tracy to say, in her words, that "he was very happy Ed had been released and a lot of other stuff I can't remember." While the hostage's mother was sought out by both media and the president, underscoring the importance of family members both to the media and to the government, the media could not easily frame this particular hostage release as a happy reunion of a close-knit family torn asunder by an act of terrorism.

During the buildup to Jack Mann's release at the end of September, speculation about who would be next was rampant. When McCarthy emerged from Lebanon with the news that Briton Terry Waite was still alive, attention immediately focused upon him and American Terry Anderson, the longest-held hostage. *Time* referred to them as "the best known hostages," suggesting that "because of their high profile," they might be the last to be freed ("A Game of Chances," 1991, p. 12). One television anchor even used the phrase "one of the important hostages" while speculating about whether Anderson or Waite would be the next released. When it turned out to be Mann, a frail 77-year-old Briton who many had thought was dead, the coverage was restrained, focusing primarily on his brief news conference in Syria, his reunion with his wife, Sunnie, who had come to Syria upon news of his impending release, and rejoicing by his family back in England. What followed was continuing speculation on imminent releases and perhaps an end to the entire hostage saga. Eventually, as could have been predicted, the releases of Waite (particularly in Britain) and Anderson (particularly in the

United States) were treated as major news indeed. *Time*'s prediction proved correct and those hostages with the highest profiles were freed last, an ironic twist that only served to highlight the double-edged nature of media coverage of terrorist victims, as well as efforts by friends and family to raise their public profiles.

## The Victim as Active Participant

In reviewing the nature of media coverage of terrorist victimization and its impact on victim goals, we have seen how the interests of the victims themselves and their families interact with those of the other parties, clashing with some while coinciding in some way with others. In the case of hostage taking, for example, government officials and crisis managers consider the hostage to be a totally passive agent in the potential resolution of the incident, and this often runs counter to the goals of the hostage or family and friends. This official attitude is consistent with the nature of terrorist victimization, whereby the direct victim is a mere pawn in a larger game, a conduit for messages. In a very real sense, the target of violence is a *secondary* victim, while the target of demands is the primary victim (see Crelinsten & Szabo, 1979, pp. 5-6, for a more detailed discussion of this terminology). But the hostage *can* play an active role in the resolution of an incident, escaping (as Jerry Levin did in Lebanon in 1985) or sometimes taking the side of the hostage taker, as in the so-called Stockholm syndrome. This term derives from an incident that occurred in Stockholm in 1973. A bank robbery turned into a barricaded hostage situation when police responded to a call for help. During the resulting siege, which lasted several weeks, one of the female hostages purportedly had sexual relations with the man holding them hostage. After the siege was over and the bank robber had been arrested, convicted, and imprisoned, this woman continued to visit him in prison and eventually married him.

It is not untypical for such identification with hostage takers to persist once an incident is resolved, and this can be manifested either by continued expressions of support for the hostage taker's cause or by continuing hostility toward the authorities. As an example of the latter, Gerard Vaders, a newspaper editor who was among the hostages held by South Moluccans on a train in the Netherlands in 1975, exhibited persistent mistrust of the authorities following the incident's resolution. He even wrote a few articles critical of the government and received threatening phone calls and letters as a result.

The government claimed that he was sick, and some colleagues spread rumors that he had collaborated with the Moluccans to save his life: Vaders had been selected for execution but had been spared after he had made a kind of personal confession to another hostage while the terrorists listened (Ochberg, 1977).

In a similar vein, Jerry Levin has continued to criticize the U.S. government's no-negotiation policy and its hard-line refusal to pressure Kuwait to release the prisoners that the Lebanese hostage takers consistently demanded. During his 1985 testimony before Congress, he called at several points for the release of the Kuwaiti prisoners (U.S. House of Representatives, 1985). As recently as his CTV interview in April 1990, he was maintaining his critical attitude toward the U.S. government. This is not to say that Levin necessarily identifies with his captors, but that such a critical attitude toward the government is consistent with a persisting identification. As for the Kuwaiti prisoners, since one of the first things that Iraq did after invading Kuwait in August 1990 was to transfer the Shi'ite prisoners held in Kuwaiti jails to Baghdad, they ceased to be the object of Shi'ite demands in renewed negotiations after the Gulf War. Instead, the focus of demands shifted to Israel and Shi'ite and Palestinian detainees in Israel and Southern Lebanon. One hostage, Irishman Brian Keenan, was released after the invasion, but before the onset of the Gulf War. Since the end of the war, there were occasional rumors of impending releases throughout the spring and early summer of 1991, until the release of McCarthy and Tracy in early August. Recurrent rumors of impending releases were drowned out by the attempted Soviet coup and subsequent events within the Soviet Union. They resurfaced only in mid-September, culminating then in the Revolutionary Justice Organization's release of Jack Mann on September 24.

   The families and friends of hostages or other victims of terrorism can also play an active role that may not always be anticipated by government officials or crisis managers. Because their primary interest is the fate of their loved ones, they are understandably not too sympathetic to no-concessions policies or to the larger political picture. Like hostages, they can take the side of the terrorist in the name of saving their loved ones. When sought out for comments by the media, their public statements criticizing the government or calling for negotiations can come across as legitimating the terrorist cause. In similar fashion, TWA hostage Allyn Conwell's opening statement at the infamous press conference in Beirut that produced a shoving match made a moral equivalent between the holding of the TWA hostages and Israel's detention of hundreds of Shi'ites (Martin & Walcott, 1988, p. 190). Transmitted unedited and uncommented upon by the media, Conwell's statement also came across as legitimating the terrorists' cause. The hostage is interested in survival. Anything the media do that jeopardizes this can cause added stress or danger. Media coverage can sometimes reveal information about hostages that could be used against them by their captors. In the TWA case, for example, a relative of a passenger revealed that he was Jewish during a local interview that was held at just about the time the hijackers were separating passengers with Jewish-sounding names. The interview was picked up by a national paper and several wire services, but luckily never reached the hijackers (Elliott, 1988, p. 71).

If media coverage or the behavior of reporters at the scene antagonizes a hostage taker, this could also endanger the hostages. For example, during the Hanafi Muslim siege in Washington, D.C., in 1977, where members of a little-known sect took a large number of hostages in several locations, one reporter called the Hanafi leader a Black Muslim. Since the leader's family had been murdered by Black Muslims, this unfortunate remark triggered an angry tirade and a threat to kill a hostage. A subsequent apology by the reporter mollified the terrorist leader (The Media and Terrorism, 1977). In the Turkish embassy siege in Ottawa in 1985, a reporter asked the Armenians occupying the embassy if they had any demands other than the vague ones announced to the media. In another incident, a hostage taker was asked if he had a deadline, when no time limit had been imposed. In these examples, a thoughtless question by a reporter had the potential to make the situation of the hostages worse. Elsewhere, I have argued that only training and education can help media personnel avoid the most egregious kinds of errors that have the potential to endanger victims' lives, but that the competitive nature of news gathering plus the high turnover rate in personnel make it inevitable that such incidents will occur during spectacular incidents (Crelinsten, 1989, pp. 331-332).

Another tricky area that pertains specifically to the role of the hostage is that of media speculation about coded messages in communiqués that their captors force them to compose. In 1970, some journalists wondered if the British diplomat, James Cross, was sending coded messages, since he had worked previously for British military intelligence. When finally released after several months of captivity, Cross reported that his treatment deteriorated significantly at about the same time, until he could convince his captors that the speculations were false. Ironically, the other hostage in that crisis apparently did attempt to send hidden messages to the authorities, misdating a letter to his wife (the 12th instead of the 11th) and referring to "a dozen persons" in his family in a letter to the Quebec premier. The double use of the number 12 was commented upon in one tabloid paper several days later. That same evening, the hostage tried unsuccessfully to escape. Because he was killed the next day, it can never be confirmed whether the supposed code was intentional or not or whether his escape attempt was triggered by the media speculation. However, it was later discovered that a large number 12 was written on the roof of a nearby airplane hangar that could have been visible from the room in which the hostage had been held.

When Father Jenco was released from his captivity in Lebanon at the end of July 1986, the other hostages held with him were forced to make video-tapes that were delivered with Jenco. In his, David Jacobsen expressed his condolences to the wife and children of William Buckley, who had died in captivity, not knowing that Buckley was a bachelor. A Lebanese television report speculated that this error represented a coded message, and Jacobsen was threatened by his guards. Another time, he was forced to write a letter as dictated by one of his guards, grammatical errors and all, since he was suspected of previously sending codes. Again the media speculated, this time about the grammar, and he was beaten and placed in solitary confinement, since the guard who originally dictated the letter remained silent (Martin & Walcott, 1988, p. 353). Interpretations of hostage behavior in the media can feed back to their captors just as easily as speculations about what the terrorists will do next or what the government is up to. Imagery and symbolism are very important in the communication process underlying terrorism, and we have seen how depictions of the victim in the media can have a significant impact on the goals of those involved.

Anything that the media do to reduce the hostage's stress or danger is appreciated by hostages and their families. For example, the opportunity to talk to the media, even if such coverage is viewed negatively by government, allows family and friends to see hostages and to know they are all right. It also gives them an opportunity to plead for negotiations, to argue against an assault, or even to send coded messages. Victims of other kinds of attacks may also wish to use the media to convey certain messages. One of the survivors of the Montreal massacre of 14 women underwent surgery for her wounds and, while still in her hospital bed, agreed to meet reporters because she wished to convey a message to her fellow students (Aubin, 1989). Many hostages believe, like Jerry Levin, that media attention keeps them alive. This is true of their families as well. Yet some hostages feel that the media would prefer dead hostages, so as to have bigger headlines and more sensational stories. This was the case with victims of the Hanafi siege, as we shall see shortly, although this is probably because of some of the aggravating things the media did to provoke the terrorist leader and because the hostages were treated in a very violent and abusive manner throughout the siege.

Finally, it should not be forgotten that journalists can be victims of terrorism too—not just indirect victims, but direct victims (Picard, 1988). They have been targets of assassination, kidnapping, and disappearances in many Latin American countries, kneecapping by the Red Brigades in Italy, and intimidation by both governments and insurgents in the exercise of their profession. Gerard Vaders, one of the hostages in the first South Moluccan incident, was a journalist. Jerry Levin, Terry Anderson, John McCarthy, and Charles Glass, all journalists, were held captive in Lebanon. Charles Fenyvesi, who was one of the hostages held by the Hanafi Muslims in Washington in 1977, was also a journalist. When the journalist becomes a victim of terrorism, two different perspectives collide. Fenyvesi's testimony at a Chicago media seminar is particularly interesting in this regard. When the hostages were finally freed, the buses transporting them to the hospital for a checkup were besieged by reporters, and Fenyvesi was recognized by a colleague. When he stuck his head out the window to start a conversation, several of his fellow ex-hostages yelled at him not to talk to the press:

> "They are poison," shouted one young man. "They don't care about us. They would be happier if we were dead because that would make a much bigger story." There was a loud murmur of assent. I caved in to the pressure and pulled my head back from the window. (The Media and Terrorism, 1977, p. 27)

In this case, the group pressure from the victims overpowered the professional ties of the reporter.

## Conclusion

When we speak of the problem of terrorism and the media, we tend to think of it in bipolar terms, either as the media aiding and abetting terrorists in their fight against legitimate government or as the media promulgating and reinforcing government perceptions of the terrorist problem. Elsewhere, I have tried to argue that the situation is more complex, involving many audiences and many constituents of the three major players: the terrorist, the government, and the media (Crelinsten, 1989). In this chapter, we have seen that there is another major player in the equation that, typically, is usually forgotten by every other player: the victim and those who are close to the victim because of personal ties of love, friendship, or close association in daily life. Victims have a central stake in the struggle between terrorist and counterterrorist and in the media portrayals of this struggle. Because they are but message generators from one party to the next, it is all too easy to ignore them and to focus on the other players. But because they are the vehicles by which messages are transmitted from one party to the next, their behavior and their concerns affect the communication network that underlies terrorism and terrorist victimization. That they and their loved ones should have their own messages to convey should come as no surprise.

# References

Aubin, B. (1989, December 9). Don't have feelings of guilt, woman hurt in massacre urges her fellow students. *Globe and Mail*, pp. A1-A2.
Ayres, B. D., Jr. (1990, March 17). Families of hostages tell of living a seesaw life of hope and despair. *New York Times*, p. 5.
Bissonnette, L. (1989, December 16). The self-centred hype of Montreal massacre. *Globe and Mail*, p. D2.
Boseley, S. (1990, August 25). Parents' joy as Iraq frees boy, 15. *Guardian* (International), p. 1.
Crelinsten, R. D. (1987). La couverture de presse et ses fonctions légitimantes. *Criminologie*, *20*, 35-57.
Crelinsten, R. D. (1989). Terrorism and the media: Problems, solutions and counterproblems. *Political Communication and Persuasion*, *6*, 311-339.
Crelinsten, R. D., & Szabo, D. (1979). *Hostage-taking*. Lexington, MA: Lexington.
Elliott, D. (1988). Family ties: A case study of coverage of families and friends during the hijacking of TWA flight 847. *Political Communication and Persuasion*, *5*, 67-75.
Frederick, C. J. (1987). Psychic trauma in victims of crime and terrorism. In G. R. VandenBos & B. K. Bryant (Eds.), *Cataclysm, crises, and catastrophes: Psychology in action* (Master Lecture Series). Washington, DC: American Psychological Association.
Galtung, J., & Ruge, M. H. (1965). The structure of foreign news: The presentation of the Congo, Cuba and Cyprus crises in four foreign newspapers. *Journal of Peace Research*, *1*, 64-90.
A game of chances. (1991, August 19). *Time*, p. 8.
Harris, L., & Heinrich, J. (1989, December 9). Young lives cut short: Talented, ambitious Quebec women fall to killer's bullets. *Ottawa Citizen*, p. B7.
Hedges, C. (1991, August 12). Freed U.S. hostage emerges a frail and disoriented man. *New York Times*, pp. A1, A8.
"I want to do everything," Briton says as captivity ends. (1991, August 9). *Globe and Mail*, p. A7.
Kelly, M. J., & Mitchell, T. H. (1981). Transnational terrorism and the Western elite press. *Political Communication and Persuasion*, *1*, 269-296.
Knight, G., & Dean, T. (1982). Myth and the structure of news. *Journal of Communication*, *32*(2), 144-161.

Lule, J. (1987). *The myth of my widow: A dramatistic analysis of news portrayals of a terrorist victim.* Boston: Emerson College, Terrorism and the News Media Research Project.

Lule, J. (1988). *Sacrifice, scapegoat, and the body on the tarmac: A terrorist victim in the New York Times.* Paper presented at the Terrorism and the News Media Research Project Conference, Communication in Terrorist Events: Functions, Themes and Consequences, Boston.

Martin, D. C., & Walcott, J. (1988). *Best laid plans: The inside story of America's war against terrorism.* New York: Harper & Row.

Martin, J. L., & Draznin, J. (1988). *Broadcast gatekeepers and terrorism.* Paper presented at the Terrorism and the News Media Research Project Conference, Communication in Terrorist Events: Functions, Themes and Consequences, Boston.

*The media and terrorism.* (1977). Seminar sponsored by the *Chicago Sun-Times* and *Chicago Daily News.* Chicago: Field Enterprises.

Media split on whether or not to provide coverage of hijack victims' funeral. (1985, November 30). *Ottawa Citizen,* p. A16.

Mitchison, A. (1990, August 26). A triumph for Ireland and for two sisters. *Sunday Correspondent,* p. 7.

Montgomery, L. F. (1988). *Media victims: Reactions to coverage of incidents of international terrorism involving Americans* (Paper No. 12). Boston: Emerson College, Terrorism and the News Media Research Project.

Mother is delighted. (1991, August 12). *New York Times,* p. A8.

Ochberg, F. (1977). The victim of terrorism: Psychiatric considerations. In R. D. Crelinsten (Ed.), *Dimensions of victimization in the context of terroristic acts* (pp. 13-35). Montreal: International Centre for Comparative Criminology, Université de Montréal.

One family's agony: The Cicippio family waits and hopes. (1989, August 14). *Maclean's.*

Paletz, D. L., Fozzard, P. A., & Ayanian, J. Z. (1982). The I.R.A., the Red Brigades, and the F.A.L.N. in the "New York Times." *Journal of Communication, 32*(2), 162-171.

Paletz, D. L., Fozzard, P. A., & Ayanian, J. Z. (1983). Terrorism on TV news: The IRA, the FALN, and the Red Brigades. In W. C. Adams (Ed.), *Television coverage of international affairs* (pp. 143-165). Norwood, NJ: Ablex.

Picard, R. G. (1988). *Journalists as targets and victims of terrorism.* Paper presented at the Terrorism and the News Media Research Project Conference, Communication in Terrorist Events: Functions, Themes and Consequences, Boston.

Picard, R. G., & Adams, P. D. (1988). *Characterizations of acts and perpetrators of political violence in three elite U.S. daily newspapers* (Paper No. 5). Boston: Emerson College and California State University, Fresno, Terrorism and the News Media Research Project.

Pinder, J. (1989, December 16). Soviet tears flow for Sakharov. *Ottawa Citizen,* p. 8.

Rapoport, D. C. (1977). The politics of atrocity. In Y. Alexander & S. Finger (Eds.), *Terrorism: Interdisciplinary perspectives* (pp. 45-61). New York: John Jay.

Schmid, A. P. (1989). Terrorism and the media: The ethics of publicity. *Journal of Terrorism and Political Violence, 1,* 539-565.

Schmid, A. P., & De Graaf, J. (1982). *Violence as communication: Insurgent terrorism and the Western news media.* Beverly Hills, CA: Sage.

Schmid, A. P., Jongman, A. J., et al. (1988). *Political terrorism: A new guide to actors, authors, concepts, data bases, theories, and literature.* New Brunswick, NJ: Transaction.

Sisk, R. (1990, March 18). The invisible hostage: Higgins' wife insists on ghost of a chance. *New York Daily News,* p. 32.

Stecklow, S. (1990, May 1). Call ends 3½ years of hell. *Ottawa Citizen*, p. G1.

Stoler, P. (1986). *The war against the press: Politics, pressure and intimidation in the 80s*. New York: Dodd, Mead.

U.S. House of Representatives (1985). *The media, diplomacy, and terrorism in the Middle East* (Hearings before the Subcommittee on Europe and the Middle East, Committee on Foreign Affairs). Washington, DC: Government Printing Office.

# Index

# About the Authors

**Mark Blaisse**, Editor in Chief of *European Affairs*, is an internationally known television and print journalist who publishes regularly in *NRC-Handelsblad, Die Zeit, Weltwoche, Liberation, Expresso, Der Spiegel*, and *Rolling Stone*. He is the author of *Abu Nidal bestaat niet* (Arbeiderspers/Singel, 1989) and *Sadat, the Last Hundred Days* (Molden, Viking Press, Thames & Hudson, 1981).

**John Boiney** is a Ph.D. candidate in political science at Duke University. He specializes in electoral politics, political communication, and political psychology. The coauthor of several publications, he is currently writing his doctoral dissertation on deception in televised political advertising.

**Ronald D. Crelinsten** is Associate Professor in the Department of Criminology of the University of Ottawa. He is the coauthor of *Hostage-Taking* and the author of *Terrorism and Criminal Justice* and numerous other publications on terrorism and counterterrorism.

**Robin P. J. M. Gerrits**, Editor of *Het Parool*, is a social history graduate from Erasmus University, Rotterdam, the Netherlands, and the author of *Shiver and Listen: An Exploratory, Qualitative Inquiry into the Uses of Publicity by Terrorists in Europe, 1875-1975*.

**Christopher Hewitt**, Associate Professor, Department of Sociology and Anthropology at the University of Maryland, is the author of *The Effectiveness of Anti-Terrorist Policies* (University Press of America, 1984) and of articles in the *British Journal of Sociology, British Journal of Political Science, American Sociological Review, Journal of Conflict Resolution*, and other journals.

**Jennifer Jane Hocking** is Lecturer in the Department of Political Science at the University of Melbourne. Her book *Australia's Counter-Terrorism Strategy 1972-1988* is to be published by Allen and Unwin, and her work has appeared in *Crime and Social Justice, Politics, Australian Quarterly*, and other journals and in the edited volume, *Australia Towards 2000* (Macmillan, 1990).

**Cynthia L. Irvin** is a graduate student in the Political Science Department at Duke University. She is completing her dissertation, which examines shifts in strategies and internal political structures by insurgent organizations that have adopted electoral politics as a tactic while continuing to engage in armed struggle. She is a U.S. Institute of Peace, 1991-1992, Jennings Randolph Peace Scholar.

**David L. Paletz** is Professor of Political Science at Duke University and Chairperson of the Political Communication Research Section of the International Association for Mass Communication Research. In addition to his numerous other publications, he is the editor of *Political Communication Research* (Ablex, 1987) and coauthor of *Media Power Politics* (Free Press/Macmillan, 1983) and *Politics in Public Service Advertising on Television* (Praeger, 1977).

**Alex P. Schmid** is Professor of Political Science and Senior Research Fellow at the Center for the Study of Social Conflicts at the University of Leiden and Director of the Interdisciplinary Research Projects on Root Causes of Human Rights Violations. Dr. Schmid is also Extraordinary Professor at the Erasmus University, Rotterdam, where he teaches in the field of social conflicts and conflict resolution. He is the author of *Political Terrorism: A New Guide to Actors, Authors, Concepts, Data Bases, Theories, and Literature* (North-Holland, 1988), *Violence as Communication: Insurgent Terrorism and the Western News Media* (Sage, 1982), and numerous other publications.

**Laura L. Tawney** worked on the "Guidelines" project as an undergraduate at Duke University, where she received her B.A. in 1991 in economics and political science and her certificate in film and video studies. She is currently working in advertising and journalism at the *Daily Times* of Salisbury, Maryland.

**C. Danielle Vinson** is a graduate student in the Department of Political Science at Duke University. She specializes in political and international communication.

3 5282 00526 4992

Printed in the United States
6012